PHENOMENAL
BLACKNESS

THINKING LITERATURE
A series edited by Nan Z. Da and Anahid Nersessian

Phenomenal Blackness

BLACK POWER, PHILOSOPHY, AND THEORY

Mark Christian Thompson

The University of Chicago Press
Chicago and London

The University of Chicago Press, Chicago 60637
The University of Chicago Press, Ltd., London
© 2022 by The University of Chicago
Published 2022
Printed in the United States of America

31 30 29 28 27 26 25 24 23 22   1 2 3 4 5

ISBN-13: 978-0-226-81641-8 (cloth)
ISBN-13: 978-0-226-81642-5 (paper)
ISBN-13: 978-0-226-81643-2 (e-book)
DOI: https://doi.org/10.7208/chicago/9780226816432.001.0001

Library of Congress Cataloging-in-Publication Data

Names: Thompson, Mark Christian, 1970– author.
Title: Phenomenal Blackness : Black power, philosophy, and
   theory / Mark Christian Thompson.
Other titles: Black power, philosophy, and theory | Thinking
   literature.
Description: Chicago ; London : The University of Chicago Press,
   2022. | Series: Thinking literature | Includes bibliographical
   references and index.
Identifiers: LCCN 2021035773 | ISBN 9780226816418 (cloth) |
   ISBN 9780226816425 (paperback) | ISBN 9780226816432
   (ebook)
Subjects: LCSH: African Americans—Intellectual life—20th
   century. | African American philosophy. | Philosophy, German. |
   Critical Theory—History. | African American aesthetics. |
   Criticism—United States—History. | American literature—
   African American authors—German influences.
Classification: LCC E185.89.I56 T47 2022 | DDC 973/.0496073—
   dc23
LC record available at https://lccn.loc.gov/2021035773

♾ This paper meets the requirements of ANSI/NISO Z39.48-1992
(Permanence of Paper).

FOR MY DAUGHTER,
GERALDINE GIOVANNA

Contents

The Essence
of the Matter

In 1926, W. E. B. Du Bois famously asserted, "All art is propaganda and ever must be, despite the wailing of the purists" (295). This statement, while open to challenge in its day, was mostly rejected by the generation of African American writers that came to prominence during, and directly following, World War II. Richard Wright would agree in principle with Du Bois's assessment, yet not unconditionally. For Wright, literature made more than ideological claims; it also participated in a history of apolitical aesthetic practices.[1] In disagreeing with Wright, and later in his exchanges with Irving Howe, Ralph Ellison would take this point further, insisting that literature's aesthetic dimension existed independently of propagandistic ends.[2] Like Du Bois and Wright, Ellison was influenced by historical and sociological thought, to which he added a deep investment in anthropological discourse that led him to reach different conclusions than those arrived at by his older colleagues. Reflecting on art in social ritual, Ellison saw literature as sacrificial, finding the aesthetic truth of human relations in their psychologically ritualized, and racialized, social contexts.

As used by Ellison and Zora Neale Hurston, anthropological theory exercised a strong influence on mid-twentieth-century African American literary thought.[3] Along with sociology and Marxism, anthropological discourse provided a basis for African American cultural criticism. While Du Bois, Alain Locke, and others clearly incorporated philosophy in their work, it generally did not become the main mode of cultural criticism and social critique among African American literary theorists until the 1960s. *Phenomenal Blackness* examines the ideas that lead to this change in analytical method. To be clear: this book does not claim that, before the 1960s, African American cultural critics avoided, or were unfamiliar with, philosophical criticism. Instead, this book maintains that a shift in methodological focus occurred in the early sixties, from sociology and anthropology to philosophy and critical theory. This shift is announced by Amiri Baraka (LeRoi Jones) in his jazz essays of the period and in his 1963 study *Blues People: Negro Music in White America*, in which he insisted on philosophy as the critical means by which to grasp African American expressive culture.

Baraka insists on this in order to posit an African essence that goes beyond any previous conception of Blackness, to present an ontology of Black being. While more sociologically oriented thought, such as Du Bois's, understood Blackness as a singular set of sociohistorical characteristics, and possibly as a biological singularity, it did not subscribe to the idea that "Black being" could survive all sociohistorical influence unaltered. Du Bois believed that equitable social assimilation and cultural amalgamation of the races was possible, whereas Baraka did not. To be sure, Baraka relies on social, political, and historical analyses to assert this essential Blackness; yet his work also includes a metaphysics of Black being that requires ontology in addition to sociology, political science, and history. Again, while Du Bois, for example, was deeply influenced by Hegel's dialectical method, phenomenology of mind, and philosophy of history, he did not introduce an ontologically singular, independent, atemporal Black being into sociological thought and cultural criticism. Du Bois's intervention was not in metaphysics or ontology. Ralph Ellison did verge on doing this in his blues writings, most notably in the Prologue to *Invisible Man* (1952). Yet he stopped short of suggesting that an unchangeable Black essence ultimately determined the historical nature of African American blues culture. "After LeRoi Jones," as Don L. Lee (Haki Madhubuti) might put it, when "thinking literature," African American literary theory is always to some extent "thinking Blackness."

Ten years Baraka's senior, and ten years younger than Ellison, James Baldwin bridges the literary timeline between the two writers.[4] While Irving Howe openly associated Baldwin's literary production with Ellison's modernist, anthropological aesthetic, Baldwin's later view, consonant with the younger generation of African American cultural theorists coming to prominence in the midsixties, actually reflected a strong interest in philosophy. This is not to say that Ellison undervalues, misunderstands, or refuses to use philosophy in his work, but rather that, unlike Baldwin's, Ellison's criticism displays a much stronger preference for sociology and anthropology. *Phenomenal Blackness* shows that, when placed in their philosophical contexts, Baldwin's literary-critical essays, and those of Black Power writers in the sixties, use a "Black hermeneutic" to interpret "phenomenal Blackness"—the "nexus of meaning" defining Black being-in-the-world.[5] In identifying phenomenal Blackness as at the center of African American expressivity, these works require an ontological argument and a mode of hermeneutical interpretation appropriate to it. While their initial reliance on Western aesthetic ontology speaks to the unprecedented occasion of this criticism, it still forces early Black Power critics to use the categories and terms of critical theory in order to begin to think against them. Baldwin, Baraka, and others attempt to articulate Black aesthetic ontology beyond Western conceptual and lexical limits, and with these shifts, new, non-Western critical paradigms emerge. Until the late 1960s, however, Black being is explored in Western philosophical terms derived mostly from contemporary German thought.

When seen in relation to Western philosophy, mid-twentieth-century African American philosophy has often been associated with French existentialism.[6] Indeed, works by Richard Wright and Ralph Ellison are often read as examples of "Black existentialism," which has its roots in French thought and American pragmatism.[7] On the whole, Black existentialism is believed to be derived from white American cultural theorists in direct dialogue with African American artists and critics and from experiences abroad, primarily in Spain, France, and francophone lands, where African Americans spoke directly to their continental peers. While this was certainly the case until the immediate post–World War II period, the situation had changed by the mid-1960s. The popular influence of German émigré intellectuals in the United States after the war was difficult to ignore.[8] Superstar philosophers such as Herbert Marcuse and Hannah Arendt captured the attention of the American postwar intelligentsia and mainstream commentators, and German intellectual thought remained current in political theory and practice. While French existentialism had carried great weight in the American cultural scene of the forties and fifties, Sartre was not living, teaching, and writing in New York, Chicago, or Los Angeles. Important contemporary German philosophers such as Hans Morgenthau, Leo Strauss, Max Horkheimer, Theodor Adorno, and Franz Neumann were, and each underwent some degree of integration into American society while in the United States.

Added to this, French existentialism traced its roots to the same source as did the thought of many German intellectuals in the United States: Heidegger. Many of the star émigré philosophers had been Heidegger's students, including Hannah Arendt, Herbert Marcuse, Paul Tillich, Hans Jonas, and Eric Voegelin.[9] Because of this, Heidegger's more phenomenological existentialism, and the "new hermeneutic" of another famous former student of his, Hans-Georg Gadamer, struck a familiar chord with African American philosophers in the 1960s, even from a distance. This occurred for many African American theorists in opposition to the cultural criticism of the immediate postwar period, which was dominated by the aesthetic concerns of the generation formed intellectually in the 1930s. Including writers such as Wright, Ellison, and to some extent Baldwin, this generation's thought was shaped by the Black existentialism developed before the war and by the Marxism of the same period. More materialist methodologies than those of Heideggerian hermeneutic phenomenology frame their concerns and characterize their thought, as do theoretical positions based in sociology, anthropology, and political science.

More attuned to the mid-1960s moment than Ellison, Baldwin begins to feature philosophy in his cultural criticism as a major mode of analysis, and a strong engagement with German thought is evident. This shift occurs in his work because the current explanatory model for African American culture undergoes a significant change in focus. Anthropological criticism—assuming a single human race divided culturally and by material inequality—no longer suffices for a younger generation of African American cultural theorists who accept neither the premises of white supremacy nor the idea that all races are created equal. Against the intellectual profile of the civil rights movement, this book shows, many African American intellectuals begin to formulate a theory of Blackness that claims spiritual superiority to whiteness.

In order to claim this advantage, it was necessary to define Black being as a heritable quality which is historically separate, and inherently different, from white being. The task was not to emphasize a shared Americanness between blacks and whites, but rather to articulate an essential racial foreignness between the two. Without wanting to reduce their arguments to examples of the scientific racism they denounced, theorists turned to philosophy to reimagine racial hierarchy and Black singularity. This led to a phenomenological understanding of Blackness as a racial nexus of cultural meaning, as opposed to the previous sociological and materialist view of Blackness that dominated cultural criticism and theory. That said, African American theorists showed no inclination at this time to abandon materialist concerns for Idealism's abstraction, an existentialism that rejected the primacy of essence, or a purely speculative metaphysics. Instead, they incorporated two modes of philosophical thought that developed out of philosophical traditions that already existed in African American thought: Marxism and biblical hermeneutics.

Critical theory allowed for continued cultural-materialist social intervention while accommodating the more hermeneutical aspects of African American religious thought.[10] The art of biblical interpretation and exegesis has been a part of the African American literary imagination from the start and has been integral to African American culture since its inception.[11] African American political and cultural criticism's theological investments made hermeneutics attractive as a means of both reading and theorizing Black racial singularity and spiritual superiority. Black Power in the 1960s gave rise to Black liberation theology, which formalized this religious tradition as a social movement. The result was a critical theory of the African American lifeworld that was particularly attentive to the interaction of capital, culture, and race.[12] Because of the new hermeneutic's focus on language—and in particular literary language—the object and occasion of critical reflection is aesthetic in nature. The recognition of African American "being-in-the-world" as aesthetic leads to the theorization of what Amiri Baraka has called "Literary Negro-ness," or the phenomenal mode of Blackness.

Adapted from German philosophy and critical theory, phenomenal Blackness is a mediating field of representation, or a "Black aesthetic dimension"—a creative space in which, modifying Herbert Marcuse's thought, utopian social configurations may be presented as aspirational models for Black liberation. Aesthetic theory in particular provided Black writers with the communicative basis for traversing segregated boundaries—and for foreclosing on knowledge capable of being equally exchanged in communicative acts. For thinkers as different as James Baldwin and Eldridge Cleaver, a monolingual conception of power and aesthetic representation was essential to equal participation in the public sphere. It formed the basis for their insistence on Black cultural translation over Black cultural assimilation. Fraught with interpretive inequality, the question of literary-critical authority became one of racially determined linguistic and cultural recognition. A common concern, then, for the writers considered in *Phenomenal Blackness* was the role German thought played in philosophizing segregated lifeworlds.

To make these claims, *Phenomenal Blackness* takes three methodological approaches. The first is to show direct influence between German and African American philosophy. In some cases, this is easy enough. Angela Y. Davis studied with Marcuse in the United States and with Adorno, Habermas, Haag, Schmidt, and Negt in Frankfurt, and Cleaver responded directly to Marcuse's mix of Marx and Freud. The second methodological strategy is inferential. The themes explored—such as aesthetic autonomy, capitalist exploitation, linguistic community, civil disobedience, freedom, and equality—are the same. These conversations take place at the same time and place and involve highly visible participants. They use the same terms and concepts and refer to the same institutions and events. The third critical method is speculative and has to do with the work of those twentieth-century German philosophers whose writings are important for this time period yet who did not emigrate to the United States. In such cases, representative work by the relevant German philosopher was already available in translation.

This intellectually rich, creatively productive dialogue between African American and German philosophy does not mean that it was free of racism. Indeed, aspects of it were explicitly racist. This is a simple fact that need not have prevented, and indeed did not prevent, African American philosophers from engaging positively with their German counterparts; likewise, it need not detract from how we read, respect, and practice Black Power philosophies today. The stature and complexity of Baldwin's and Baraka's or Davis's and Cleaver's works are not so fragile that an acknowledgment of obvious influence from a potentially racist source diminishes its power. Indeed, the goal is to relate the brilliance of their thought in full awareness of its flaws.

In telling this story, *Phenomenal Blackness* does not retell the stories of Black Power figures' lives. Nor is this study an intellectual biography of any African American leader or artist of the 1960s and early 1970s. Rather, it is a contribution to the understanding of African American philosophy and literary theory that takes a wider view of philosophical and literary activity centered on questions of freedom, equality, recognition, civil disobedience, and violence in the United States of the postwar era. While this book does not offer a narrative of Black Power lives in America, it does present a fuller picture of their common philosophical and literary concerns and influences.

Indeed, in the 1960s no strong distinction would have been made between African American philosophy and African American critical theory. While their interaction does not develop along a thematically limited, chronologically linear trajectory, a basic outline of their common positions can be sketched. As early as the 1950s, Baldwin begins to produce a Black hermeneutic that looks to Black English for the defining characteristics of African American social being. Although this in itself is not new, and his account remains indebted to a sociologically inflected existentialism, nevertheless his interpretive model implies essential features of literature and Black linguistic expression generally.

By the mid-1960s, Malcolm X excludes essentialist elements from his view of language, focusing instead on its practical application in community construction and the exercise of will to power in any social or political transaction. For Malcolm, language signifies Black history as Black essence, rather than as any specific racial characteristic to be exhibited and manipulated by the individual. For him, self-fashioning in language and literature is always racially representative. His genealogy of language reveals the truth of Black history as teleologically oriented and leading toward the material instantiation of Black separatism. In Malcolm, language does not reveal the truth of race in its expression: it elaborates the truth of Black history beyond its ideological obfuscation. Language provides the site for the genealogical recovery of Black truth.

At this time, Baraka explicitly calls for the application of philosophical "truth and method" to the analysis of race in America, including to any language-based, ontological definition of American Blackness. He would merge hermeneutics and discourse theory to suggest that language is both historical and essential. Relating linguistic phenomenality to music, Baraka then posits an ontological, aesthetic dimension to language that conveys Black essence as expressive form. This aesthetic dimension is supplemented by compositional and lyrical content that provides the historical-material field for genealogical recovery. In other words, Baraka hears in music the combination of Baldwin's literariness with Malcolm's genealogical critique of ideology and synthesizes the two by positing the linguistic character of aesthetic production. As production, African American expressive culture is subject to commodification and exchange by the culture industry yet avoids its totalizing reification through the aesthetic autonomy of racial essence.

Taking autonomous racial essence for granted and accepting Baraka's Marxist critique of culture, Cleaver, in the latter half of the 1960s, jettisons all the rest, including an aesthetic theory of Blackness. Instead, he distinguishes his critique of culture by appropriating Herbert Marcuse's utopian understanding of libido and original, sociosexual unity. Any "aesthetic dimension," for Cleaver, serves either to liberate or adulterate the racial truth of libidinal originality and freedom. To support this idea, his thought recalls Malcolm's reflections on history, locates them in the penitentiary, and posits the African American inmate as the revolutionary subject of history. The result is Cleaver's partial rejection of Marxist-Leninist critical histories and New Left "third-world" ideology, in favor of a dialectical history of the Black Absolute.

While Davis may have agreed with the revolutionary potential Cleaver assigns to the prisoner, her critical-theoretical approach, in the late 1960s and early 1970s, would be very different, despite having had Marcuse as her mentor and friend. Davis's critical theory is shaped by her time spent at the Frankfurt School itself, with Adorno, Habermas, Negt, Schmidt, and Haag. Her philosophy of history is dialectically attentive to unresolvable negation and racism as the response to the negative. Her work contains all previous positions, articulating them in a single, coherent, critical theory of racial alienation, containment, and domination. Her work on Frederick Douglass in particular establishes the Black subject of history not as the return of some racial repressed but rather as the assertion of racial realism characterized by racist ideology and historiographic falsification. While racial essence remains real as "nature" for Davis at this time, "second nature" determines its historical and social expression so thoroughly as to make this point inconsequential. For Davis, while language maintains its ability to convey aestheticized race forms, these constellations are social and historical, yielding no metaphysical insight into racial essence. Despite being, if not antiessentialist, then descriptively realist in systematic critical method and philosophical conclusion, Davis's work was taken piecemeal rather than as the grand system it is, leading to a split in African American philosophy and literary theory from the 1970s onward, between sociologically and anthropologically oriented analytic philosophy and more ontologically oriented aesthetic theory. For a time in the 1960s and early 1970s, there was no separation between these approaches.

Chapter 1 identifies the type of philosophy most often used in the theorization of Black art in the 1960s. The "new hermeneutic" being introduced in the United States from Germany in the mid-1960s spoke well to the theological underpinnings of race-based literary sensibilities. After a detailed discussion of Gadamer's philosophy of language, the chapter examines some of James Baldwin's writings on language, collectivity, and literary self-fashioning. Baldwin theorizes a Black hermeneutic for the critical analysis of African American literature in relation to social formation, racial self-determination, and power. While Baldwin categorically rejects natural racial hierarchy and essentialized inequality, he believes in race as a neutral cultural fact shaped by, yet ultimately independent of, historical contingency. Baldwin's hermeneutic interpretation of culture avoids sifting through historical layers to arrive at an indelible racial essence and instead describes and evaluates race itself as a strictly historical phenomenon. In this respect, Baldwin advances a form of existentialism, whereby an unreachable race-form unfolds its essence as the historicity of social reality. In other words, existence precedes essence, without vitiating it. For Baldwin, then, racial essence is content without value, thereby making all races equal, yet different. The history of race, however, debases this fundamental aspect of racial difference. Black hermeneutic analysis clarifies the specificity of Blackness while critiquing the racist ascription of value to race. Baldwin's position, then, is a type of sociological existentialism modulated by a Heideggerian sense of being. His thought stands between the younger generation's preference for philosophy and critical theory and the previous one's faith in sociology and anthropology.

Chapter 2 discusses Malcolm X's philosophically engaged understanding of language and power. For reasons similar to those that led Habermas to reject Gadamer's hermeneutics as the conservative valorization of Eurocentric cultural tradition, Malcolm questions the naturalization of linguistic convention and the unity of the literary canon. Informed by his prison readings of Western philosophy, Malcolm rejects literature as coercive, conceiving instead a theory of literacy, language use, and power that posits literary self-fashioning in the absence of literature. For Malcolm, the subject is created in the act of reading and therefore must choose reading matter wisely. This mode of self-fashioning provides training and insight into social convention, language use, and the dynamics of political force. The subject formed in this way can cultivate the will and exercise power in literary language without the constriction of tradition-based literature.

Malcolm X would agree that language reflects racial situatedness and can be used to alter sociopolitical circumstances, although he did not theorize the Black lifeworld in this way. This is not to say Malcolm X posited a Black essence but rather that he saw the strength of racism's hold on social reality as impervious to deconstructive reason. It made little difference to him whether race was an essence or a social construct; the result would be the same, as would be the type of resistance he might employ. As part of that resistance, linguistic analysis that deconstructs racist relations of power defined his hermeneutic practice. He assumed race was real without bothering with the philosophical complexities of that assumption, because for him philosophical questions were themselves derived from racist propositions. Western philosophy had value only insofar as it provided another field of racist linguistic practices to be exposed and undermined. In this respect, Malcolm X cares little for anthropology, sociology, ontology, and *Existenzphilosophie*. He is interested in analytics of power in language, which hermeneutic interpretation reveals.

Chapter 3 looks more closely at African American theory's move away from sociology and anthropology as the dominant interpretive models and toward hermeneutics. It begins with Ellison's anxiety over the descent into racial essentialism in criticism occasioned by legislated assimilation. He fears that African America's cultural integrity will be compromised by legislated integration with no social mechanism in place to mitigate decades of Jim Crow racism, leading to Black militancy. To meet this challenge, he posits literature as able to act as this necessary social mechanism. Literary representation reveals the hidden equality between all members of society. Ellison's critique of Baraka's *Blues People* expresses anxiety over the growing Black militancy in African American art. Arising in response to the unfulfilled social promises of civil rights legislation, Black militancy in art threatens the recognition of equality literature provides. The bulk of the chapter then looks at how Amiri Baraka, in *Blues People*, posits the primacy of race for the development of autonomous Black art that posits Blackness as superior to whiteness, represented by the culture industry. In *Blues People*, Baraka relies heavily on Adorno's aesthetic theory and critique of the culture industry for his argument. Baraka disregards Adorno's jazz writings, appropriating instead his theorization of "new music" in order to posit an autonomous, avant-garde African American art form, "Black art." Baraka's "Literary Negro-ness" is the formal aesthetic frame for Black art's expressivity, in any aesthetic form.

Baraka thus maintains the critical-theoretical focus of the Baldwin's hermeneutic while largely jettisoning any deference toward sociology and anthropology and amplifying race's platonic character. In Baraka, racial essence does not stand outside of history to be elaborated historically as contingent social expression. Rather, it is history, insofar as racial character decides the historicity of social relations. Any social expression of racial character, or being, is mediated only by the form it takes, and not by history itself. In this respect, all racial expression is to some extent aesthetic, as any social form must accommodate racial being in its historicity as a form. This means expressive culture represents racial being, and all representation is to some extent determined by aesthetic form. For Baraka, this is "Black art," which is any social expression of African American existence, as defined formally by Black essence. In this respect, the Black hermeneutic does not describe or interpret; it reflects Blackness as a mode of Blackness's aesthetic presentation. In this respect, philosophy, literary theory, literary production, and any other form of social representation that practices Black art are one.

In chapter 4, this concern for power, and in particular for Black power preconditioned by hermeneutic knowledge, foregrounds Eldridge Cleaver's work in the 1960s and early 1970s, in prison and as a Black Panther. Eschewing more metaphysical approaches to hermeneutic interpretation, Cleaver follows Malcolm X's lead to focus on Marx, Lenin, and ideology critique. Positing race as an ideological construction obscuring the "primal unity" of human being, Cleaver attempts to uncover pathways leading back to oneness using the critical theory of the New Left mixed with racial metaphysics. For Cleaver, race is an authentic aspect of reproductive primal unity, in which difference obtains reproductively yet without use value. In this respect, race is purely decorative, with its attributes relating essentially only to modes of sexual union. Ideology exploits racial traits meant originally as sexual attributes for the exploitative purposes of capitalist domination. The Black hermeneutic here offers a mode of anti-ideological reading to bring race back to its authenticity in sexual reproduction.

Displaying a preference for hermeneutical explanation through autobiographical literary production, Eldridge Cleaver interrogates the "Marxist-Leninist" orientation of radical Black political thought through literary self-fashioning. Chapter 4 examines Cleaver's rejection of Marxist-Leninist universalism as inadequate, and his preference instead for a race-based understanding of the lumpenproletariat, the model for which he derives from African American cultural phenomena. Relying on a literary-critical mode of hermeneutical analysis, Cleaver presents a Black nationalist theory of racial particularity and Black superiority based largely on autobiographical presentation. Consciously following Herbert Marcuse's *Eros and Civilization* (1955), Cleaver relies on the literary testimony of eroticized self-fashioning—his own and that of other Black Panther leaders—to identify the essential racial characteristics that indicate Black transcendence as the revolutionary subject of history.

Finally, in chapter 5, Angela Y. Davis provides the most complete vision of Black hermeneutic reading as she fuses it with critical theory. Davis in the 1960s sees race as real and, along with Cleaver, ideologically elaborated in history. While Cleaver appropriates and expands Marcuse's New Left theory to posit racialized sexuality as the origin of libidinal human being, Davis sets aside the sexualized aspects of her mentor Marcuse's philosophy to concentrate on dialectical history as the engine of oppression. In this sense, Davis's negative dialectics of Black liberation owe a great deal to her advisor in Frankfurt, Theodor W. Adorno. In her hands, the Black hermeneutic becomes a philosophy of history revealed in Black literary texts, the blues, and all other forms of African American expressive culture. Unlike Baraka, however, Davis does not suggest that all social activity is representational Black art. The aesthetic domain is a unique space in which to encounter Blackness hermeneutically as liberation rather than racial content. For Davis, to "think" Black literature is to think Black liberation.

Davis sees Black subjectivity as the active, redeeming subject of universal history and human freedom. Her study at the Frankfurt School, with the institute's most prominent philosophers and with Adorno as her advisor, as well as her long relationship with Marcuse, trained her in critical theory and Hegelian philosophy. Grounded in the struggle for Black liberation, her critical-theoretical work also focuses on autobiography as the textual record of phenomena for hermeneutic investigation. Articulating the Black lifeworld by literary theoretical means, Davis then posits its primary role in the recuperative project of human freedom in the recognition of Black dignity.

The book concludes with a glance at Black aesthetic criticism in relation to theory and philosophy. This discussion then shifts to the context of Davis's later work, including her use of Marcuse's "aesthetic dimension" as a way of understanding blues production and Black intimacy. Then, following a short presentation of Baraka's poem, "Revolutionary Love," *Phenomenal Blackness* concludes with a brief look at African American theory and how it "thinks literature."

The Politics of Black Friendship

CHAPTER ONE

Gadamer, Baldwin, and
the Black Hermeneutic

I. Gadamer and Friends

The idea of "culture and word" as socially constitutive is represented in 1960s America in Gadamer's "new hermeneutics," which had a strong impact on theological discussions of the time.[1] While *Wahrheit und Methode: Grundzüge einer philosophischen Hermeneutik* (1965) was not translated into English until 1975, Gadamer's work was nevertheless well known in the United States by the mid-1960s. His emphasis on tradition, linguistic expression, and cultural translation provided a model for understanding language and culture. It also raised the ire of more radical critics like Jürgen Habermas, who famously accused Gadamer of advancing a repressive, authoritarian sense of tradition in his work.[2] However, in addition to an English summary of the debate between Gadamer and Habermas in 1970, Gadamer's thought was also well known in Christian hermeneutical discourse in the 1960s.[3] His work on Schleiermacher in particular was of great interest to American theologians.[4] This is not to say that *Truth and Method* was unknown until its translation.[5] The year of German publication, E. D. Hirsch provided a scathing evaluation of it for the *Review of Metaphysics*.[6] Yet nowhere in the review does Hirsch deny the stature and importance of the work for continental and Anglo-American philosophy.[7] In 1966, Gadamer published "Notes on Planning for the Future" (in English translation), an article very much indebted to Husserl's reflections on the crisis of the European sciences:

> The concept of world order necessarily assumes a substantive differentiation corresponding to the guidelines of the kind of order that is proposed. This is manifest methodologically by taking such a concept and contrasting it with the possible forms of its negation. For it lies in the nature of things that our ideas of right and good are less exact and definite than our notions of wrong and bad. Consequently, the concept of disorder, with

whose elimination we are concerned, is always more easily defined; it facilitates the understanding of different meanings of order. (573)

Expanding the sciences to mean "order" more generally, Gadamer rumi-
nates on the problem of international relations as one of instituting a form
of interaction that, based on no existing practice, requires legitimacy before the fact of its foundation. He questions whether it is justified to abandon tradition in favor of a new configuration of sociopolitical relations
based on a purely theoretical knowledge. His answer falls firmly on the
side of tradition, in effect undercutting the validity of any revolutionary
movement and condemning the type of critical practice that would call
into question the legitimacy of tradition for deciding matters of state and
international relations.

In hoping to establish the viability of an untested, imagined state of affairs, Gadamer suggests the use of the dialectical method of positing order's negation in each specific instance.[8] The problem with this method is
that it always begins with disorder, which the state achieved by the overturning of order, at least until such time as, in Hegelian dialectics, the synthesis or negation of the negation has been achieved. Gadamer takes a not
unpredictable Hegelian approach to the question of the new world order.
However, Gadamer does not adhere to this method. Indeed, with regard
to politics he accepts its premises as axiomatic, only then to call them into
question. Is it right, he asks, to understand politics as inherently mutable,
and if so, would not one need to search for a form of politics that does not
invite or allow its own negation? In this respect, and in light of the nuclear threat Gadamer perceives as absolute negation without hope of synthesis, there must also exist an absolute positive state of political affairs.
While never absent from the Gadamer reception, the focus on language
philosophy accompanied the reception of his work as it moved from biblical hermeneutics into the disciplinary American philosophy of the late
1960s and early 1970s.[9] Gadamer's "On the Scope and Function of Hermeneutical Reflection" appeared in English in 1967. In it, Gadamer writes:
"Thus it was that the many-layered problem of translation became for me
the model for the linguisticality of all human behavior in the world, and
from the structure of translation was indicated the general problem of
making what is alien our own. Yet further reflection on the universality
of hermeneutics eventually made clear that the model of translation does
not, as such, fully come to grips with the manifoldness of what language
means in man's existence" (278). Shortly after this essay appeared in English, Verhaar wrote of "language and theological method." As Verhaar
indicates, Gadamer's philosophy of language was so well known by this
point that it required little more than shorthand description (13). Within

a few years, but before the English translation of *Truth and Method*, Gadamer had become passé in American Christian hermeneutics (Stevenson 1971, 856). Nevertheless, the high estimation and profound influence of Gadamer's work only increased in philosophical discourse in the United States through the decade, and after the 1975 translation of *Truth and Method*, his place was effectively canonized in American histories of hermeneutics.[10]

In *Truth and Method*, Gadamer champions the concept of *Bildung*, citing it as the most important cultural idea to emerge from the eighteenth century. Tracing the meaning of the word from its medieval and baroque uses in mysticism to its "naturalization" in Herder as "rising up to humanity through culture," Gadamer sees in *Bildung* the enduring hermeneutic by which all cultural achievement is evaluated. This is so because, following Herder, *Bildung* is the natural introduction of spirit and intelligence into the universal community of the ideal human being. In this respect, Habermas is not entirely wrong to point out the extent to which Gadamer accepts tradition and authority as natural and definitively right, as his conception of *Bildung* depends on these conceits. The "natural" order Gadamer sees as underlying Habermas's own philosophical program exists in *Truth and Method* on the surface of the hermeneutical text.

That said, *Bildung* is not *Erziehung*, and as late as 2001, in "Education is Self-Education," Gadamer still pushes back against Habermas:

> Now we have reached the central point of what, in my own philosophical world, I regard as a decisive perspective; namely that only in conversation does language fulfill itself. To be able to realize this in practice is a limited possibility, even for the teacher. It is of course quite clear that certain uniform units of study must be followed, but the decisive point is this: that one ultimately develops in teenagers the capability to overcome their lack of knowledge through their own initiative. Self-education must above all consist in this, that where one perceives one's shortcomings, one strengthens one's own resources (*Kräfte*) and that one does not relinquish this responsibility to the school, or rely on school grades, or on school reports or on whatever is given a premium by parents. (535)

Here Gadamer distinguishes between self-education and self-cultivation, indicating that the primary educative experience teaches the child first and foremost to communicate effectively. This does not mean simply to express desires; rather, it names the ability to engage in conversation with others as a means of knowing and experiencing the world. The linguistic techniques taught during one's education enable self-cultivation within the common realm of culture by the means and modes of communication made available through institutional and individual learning. To cultivate oneself means, for Gadamer, to recognize one's shortcomings and strengths within the learned field of shared communicative expression and to compensate for or enhance them according to linguistic means. One's education occurs in the acquisition of the means to recognize and articulate these shortcomings and strengths as given in the field of language into which one is traduced. Education is not discovering how to speak; it is learning to communicate effectively within the conventions of a particular linguistic community. In essence, Gadamer has suggested that any communicative action is a priori conventional and will accept a certain degree of traditional authority as necessary, if not natural.

This would be, of course, greatly at odds with Habermas's understanding of communicative action, in particular with the role it plays in the public sphere. Indeed, as Gadamer noted, Habermas found the idea that public language, even when granted to be thoroughly ideological, could still be true, cognitively dissonant, and critically false. The notion that knowledge and human interest were somehow fortuitously aligned or objectively represented at any juncture speaks against Habermas's sense that all communicative action seeks to advance a particular knowledge paradigm in the interest of authority, through means of rhetorical persuasion rather than fact-based reason. Language is always spoken in the interests of authority, and as these interests are not those of the totality, they are ideological even when effectively factual. A truth statement uttered in an ideologically compromised communicative act still carries the expressive force of authority's interests, even when factually correct. Embedded in language, respect for authority is at the origin of culture.

In "Culture and the Word" (1982), Gadamer investigates the origins of culture by turning to the "elemental givens" of word and language: "When a historian with a philosophical talent wants to make a contribution to the investigation of this topic he turns back to the origins of culture, i.e., to elemental givens such as word and language" (13). In those origins he finds the basic substance of a "single conversation" of humanity, in which all words and languages, past, present and future, participate:

> The more we learn of cultures and traditions of the past and present that do not stand in the Christian tradition as we do, the more we see that it is a single conversation, even if it is one in always different, but always human and so learnable, languages.... That human beings "have" language is a proposition in philosophy that is first put forth at the time as the most remarkable creation of the Greeks, "science", in Aristotle's *Politics*. There it is said that man is the being that has "*logos*": With one fell swoop we are at the heart of the matter. (13)

Gadamer does not ignore or elide cultural difference to arrive at a definition of culture true to the phenomenon's origin. Rather, he collapses all
cultures into a single, revelatory medium, that of language, which then
expresses the particularity of each culture in the primary lexical unit. In
this way, within the continuum of word and language, each word and each
language relate to the other authentically by a form of translation that is
not "cultural" but rather is culture. The way in which a people translate
themselves to other peoples in the medium of word and language is their
culture. Cultural expression is thus one culture's expression for another
culture in a neutral language and in words with identifiable meaning for
both peoples.

Following Aristotle in the *Politics*, Gadamer defines "word" as logos,
and therefore as the condition of being human, or a rational animal:

> Of course, logos does not mean "word"; but "discourse," "language," "ac-
> countability"; and ultimately it speaks of everything that is expressed in
> discourse: thought, reason. Thus, the definition of man as animal ratio-
> nale, the being who has reason, lasts for centuries, confirming the latest
> pride in reason. But logos is not "reason"; it is "discourse": words that one
> speaks to another. It is not the mere heaping up of words which, like the
> fragments of words composing the so-called dictionary, are classifiable in
> their fragmentation. It is more appropriate to say that logos is the joining of
> words that forms the unity of sense, the sense of a discourse. (14)

Here Gadamer is not content with the traditional understanding of Aristotle's use of logos as "reason." Indeed, he specifies the word's meaning
in its linguistic context as "discourse," which he expands in signification
to include the entirety of that which can be communicated linguistically,
where this communication is foundational. That is to say that Gadamer,
while avoiding any suggestion of nominalism, nevertheless understands
discourse (logos) as the making-present of the being of culture by means
of its exchange. He suggests that where the word as discourse is not present there is only silence, insofar as silence does not mean lack of sound
but rather the absence of cultural exchange, or the practice of cultural so-
liloquy, and therefore solipsism. Having established logos as cultural exchange in expression, Gadamer returns to the letter of Aristotle's text by
way of first highlighting that Aristotelian thought situates logos in the public sphere as the basis of all politics.

Gadamer emphasizes that Aristotle grounds his presentation of logos
in nature, only to specify the extent to which the hermeneutic understanding of the natural phenomenon specifies intentional communication. In
nature, Gadamer insists, calls among animals give immediate information

pertaining to preexisting natural states. Human communication, however, offers mediated messages that share uncertainty in expectation. The temporal distance between communicative concern and the origin of communication provides the space in which the speaking subject shares her world with the intended target of speech. The temporality of human communication is therefore fundamentally different from that of animals, providing a medium of intention that communicates more than factual information. It transmits the totality of the speaker's concern, as conditioned by her cultural apprehension of the material conditions determining the matter at hand. The speaker communicates her cultural being in the distance between the subject of communication and the form of its expression:

> That is what we recognize in the essence of language, in this distance in which, through the tone of our voice, we can embody and make audible and communicate to others what is really meant and to be found in something fleeting. Obviously it is a distance to ourselves that opens us up to others. Language for us is not merely certain expressive movements, not merely warning cries or mating calls such as animals offer to one another; it is rather a genuine effort to communicate something, to share something. "Communication"—what a lovely word! It says that we share and communicate something with each other that does not become less in the sharing, but perhaps even grows.
>
> In this we have our first access to the topic of culture as the region of all that becomes greater the more we share it. (1990, 15)

In effect, Gadamer describes a system of sharing in which the one who imparts information reveals the entirety of her epistemological understanding of the conditions of sharing. The information shared is that of the objective conditions of sharing information, from the perspective of the one who shares information, for the conditions of information sharing will be those of the world as experienced through the culture of sharing to which the sharer belongs. Culture is the epistemologically construed material conditions of objective knowledge expression, or the circumstances and means by which one person communicates with another. In some situations, these conditions are shared, and therefore the epistemological assumptions underlying the exchange of information are the same and need not be translated. In other instances, these assumptions are different and require a linguistic intermediary to provide a means of cultural understanding through translation. In either case, culture is the sum total of the material conditions mediating the exchange of information between speaking subjects. In this respect, the first word one speaks is not the infant's utterance; it is, rather, the first recognition of the Other in the attempt to provide information about the self. The infant seeks to express herself, to be certain; yet she does not do so discursively, as a means of communication that recognizes the discourse of the Other as objectively valid.

The discourse recognized in and through the word signifies the community brought into being by its elevation from nature to convention. Communal understanding exists in nature for Gadamer only as a linguistic possibility. Language and the articulated word designate the terms of culture as tools that decide the product conceived and achieved. While language may be natural, the community it produces and the culture it expresses are not natural: they are conventional. Be that as it may, the community and culture created by natural language is a natural result of language and therefore not without an element of necessity in its form and content. This language achieves this community and culture, as opposed to that language which produces that community and culture. That said, community and culture are still conventions that facilitate the expression of the linguistic nature of their speakers as something essential and unique. The human being revealed phenomenologically in the critical investigation of communal structure and substance, and the words and phrases used to articulate these properties, lead to epistemologically valid knowledge of the authentic being of a people. Word and culture signify specific objects and ideas, and they reveal the essence of the people to whom they belong "naturally."

Gadamer, however, speaks of "second nature" as a property of the Greek *ethos*, or that which through force of habit comes to appear as natural to the subject:

> To name this, Aristotle found the word from which the word "ethics" is derived: ethos. "*Ethos*" initially names nothing more than the habits that have become second nature. But then we also speak this way about the habits of animals. On the other hand, when we speak of ethos and of the possibilities of ethics, we are concerned with more than mere "established customs": We are concerned with a self-relatedness and a comportment that is able to discourse about itself, a comportment capable of being responsible for itself. That is the enormous distinction and, at the same time, the enormous danger of human beings: that we are the ones who choose to the extent that we "have before us" the whole of our lives. (1990, 17)

Suggesting that ethos belongs to animals as well as human beings, Gadamer then insists that the ability to examine one's ethos ethically distinguishes human beings from animals. The ability to survey the totality of a life lived and yet to be experienced, and to evaluate it ethically, characterizes human being as such. This distinction is possible only in language, as it is there that a life and the ethical choices qualifying it are made visible to the subject. The totalizing expression in which life is presented linguistically conveys ethical propositions based on the ethos of the speaker, or the combined habits of second nature that determine the speaker's lifeworld and her position within it. The entire process is in turn embedded in nature, as the medium for "human orders and forms." The characterization of nature as ground for human order and forms indicates that there is a natural, or naturally embedded and so placed, order to human orders, and that these orders are determined by human forms. In other words, human forms are ordered in nature and are therefore hierarchical.

Because of its hierarchical nature, the "authentic human task" according to Gadamer is "to practice mastery and to honor service." The delineation of this authentic human task implies that there are, among human beings, masters and servants, for it is not without contradiction that one both masters and serves nature. Therefore, Gadamer intends to suggest that among human beings there are those who follow humanity's authentic task and those who do not. Deriving his notion of authentic human purpose from the Greek concept of *paideia*, which he understands as the attainment of culture through education as cultivation, Gadamer reads Plato's presentation of "pig city" as an indication that communities that do not fulfill humanity's authentic task are not human. These "pigs" instead exist in an abject state, seeking to use power to gain more power. Only the cultivated community understands that power's purpose is the achievement of harmony between masters and servants. This means that education teaches who is an authentic master and who an authentic servant.

The cultivation of culture in education teaches the pupil how to be a master over those who are servants. Paideia in this sense teaches the naturally select to be human beings. Those who are naturally servants cannot be taught to be human beings in this highest sense. Indeed, the purpose of culture with regard to servants is not the use of free time in the pursuit of cultivating the highest spiritual degree of humanity but rather learning how to serve in the sense of agricultural cultivation. Following the etymology of the word "culture" down its second major pathway in Roman thought, agriculture and land cultivation form the basis of servitude necessary in order to build a successful agrarian society. Paideia in its Roman variation thus adds to its fundamental task the cultivation of servitude in lower-order human beings to the refinement of the human spirit in the highest human type. For Gadamer, the order paideia endows provides society with the ordered reason of human being that prevents it from committing atrocities worse than would any animal.

Gadamer grants that there are other means by which to differentiate human beings from animals; however, he privileges language and in particular the word because linguistic expression transmits cultural tradition:

> The mystery of the tradition and transmission of human culture rests upon the word. The very expression "tradition" already closely connects itself with words, and with good reason. With the notion of "tradition" we mean above all the body of knowledge that comes down to us through writing and copying and reproduction. Of course, there is such a thing as an oral tradition, and today, we are no longer so convinced as we were fifty years ago of the priority of writing in poetic forms. (1990, 19)

For Gadamer, human being is defined by cultural continuity based not on instinctual experience but rather on a learned conformity to a written record of being particular to a people. Because of this, all forms of writing—and in this respect the oral transmission of a historical record would be considered a form of writing—share the basic property of communicating cultural tradition, and each form can be analyzed critically for cultural knowledge, translation, and poetic linguistic exchange.[11] While the content of a literary work may be foreign to its extracultural target audience, its literary procedures as writing transmissive of cultural tradition will be the same as those in the culture in which it seeks to intervene. Literary content is limited; yet aesthetic articulation, as recognized and determined critically by philosophical hermeneutics, provides a universal basis for cultural exchange.[12]

Gadamer describes this poetic exchange as esoteric terms borrowed from a general Christian framework yet transformed so as to become almost unrecognizable as such. He claims that the word (already resonant with biblical religions) is questioning, leading to the word as wisdom, which is followed by the word as forgiveness (1990, 20). Having seemingly departed the discursive realm of lived culture, Gadamer in fact reinscribes it as the exchange of knowledge through the materiality of language.[13] Each word draws on the cultural resources of its language, as realized existentially in its speaking subjects, in order to ask "scientific" questions about the physical world of which being is a part. However, questioning also articulates the problem of knowledge's expressive form as the epistemological horizon of various forms of worldly human being. Each scientific question posed is also one of cultural translation and communicative knowledge of the other. Any language must learn to express what is given first in another language, unless the discovery to be communicated is an indigenous matter to the speaker's linguistic world picture.

The communicative word questions its speaker and in so doing elaborates the possibility for the representation of both the speaker and her culture in the language of the Other. This "language" is discursive, signifying any mode of communication that does not belong by nature and is made historically relevant by the culture to be shared. Put another way, the word shares, if not the immediacy, then the totality of the speaker's culture, as experienced by the speaking subject, to the discursive Other. The Other is separate from the speaking subject both by nature and by cultural inheritance. The word transcends these differences in the mediated form of linguistic translation, considered here as any act of interpretive mediation that naturalizes and acculturates to culture that which is foreign to it. In this way, the speaker comes to be known to the Other as the representative of a culture that seeks reconciliation and atonement. To be reconciled is difference itself, and to be forgiven is its hierarchical nature. In other words, the speaker seeks to reconcile her cultural difference from the Other in the open act of communication. Then, as a way of bridging the natural hierarchical division between them, the speaker asks the Other for forgiveness in understanding.

That is to say that Gadamer freely admits, and indeed accounts for structurally, the natural inequality of speakers. This does not mean that he understands this inequality within a culture, insofar as a culture can be considered synonymous with a class, gender, or nation. Rather, an antagonism exists between cultures understood within broad linguistic categories, in which speakers who are native to the same language can be said also to be native to the same culture, whatever that culture's internal conflicts and differences may be. Gadamer's distinction between cultures rests on the assumption that language, as the vessel of culture, arises naturally and spontaneously from within an already unified subset of the population. The natural unity of peoples is expressed authentically in language and is elaborated historically by the materiality of formally articulated linguistic use. Part of this history is the teleological definition of a people's place in the hierarchy of the human family, in which all members are ranked according to their natural gifts, as evidenced by their language. To prevent the willful domination of the superior population over all other groups, linguistic exchange must take place in humility and forgiveness. In this way, no one group can claim moral authority to domination, despite having the natural right to do so. Friendship and solidarity mediate relations of power between constituents' interests.

Gadamer feels a powerful tension in the relation of friendship and solidarity, in which friendship forms the subject of a continuous philosophical discussion reaching back to ancient Greece, yet solidarity enters discursive consideration mainly with Kant and modern philosophy.[14] Indeed, in "Friendship and Solidarity" ([1999] 2009) Gadamer understands solidarity in association with a term introduced by his predecessor and friend, Karl Jaspers:

> Karl Jaspers, my predecessor in the teaching chair that I held in Heidelberg, had already in 1930 called our age the age of anonymous responsibility. A term ahead of its time, it is becoming ever more true. It has become so direfully true that nowadays there are clinics where the patient no longer has a name, but instead receives a number. Indeed the question that we must in all earnestness ask ourselves is how those things that support human happiness can be developed and preserved in the new forms of life that arise from the industrial revolution and its consequences. I do not presume to proclaim any great wisdom about this. I would like, however, to reflect on just these changes in things and perhaps present some illustrations that can help our reflections. That the theme of friendship and solidarity contains a tension filled truth is something that one immediately hears. ([1999] 2009, 3–4)[15]

"Anonymous responsibility" describes the current civic expectation to perform the tasks and exercise the behaviors necessary for the proper working of society without any sense of filiation. For Gadamer, this both arises from and leads to a sense of "interrelated foreignness" among citizens. In other words, anonymous responsibility is felt by those who depend on each other for survival and yet are strangers to one another in terms of that which binds a society in its essence as the ontological continuum of a demonstrable, shared cultural identity.

Using the ancient Greek understanding of friendship as a guideline for his investigation into the meaning of the term, Gadamer offers multiple definitions, with each fulfilling certain characteristics of the phenomenon without being able to provide a complete picture of its truth. However, Gadamer limits his examples of friendship to boys and men, presumably of cultural circumstances similar to his own, taking the basic social conditions of the term for granted:

> So it is probably no wonder that the first Socratic question asks if friendship is based on like finding like. That idea should be clear to the boys, but also that it cannot hold up. They see right away that that cannot hold up. Perhaps instead the opposite is true: the choice of friends is formed by those differences worthy of admiration and love that one discovers in another. Or perhaps, above all, it is the search for the model in a world where children are so often pulled back and forth between good and bad, hideous and beautiful. To find a model—perhaps that is what one sees in a friend

and is all that one likes in a friend and so draws friends to one another. ([1999] 2009, 5)

In focusing on juvenile, male friendships, Gadamer leaves the universal conditions of friendship unaccounted for, until he arrives at his account of true friendship. Here Gadamer posits that the search for the friend begins, either instinctively or unconsciously, with the recognition of "home" and "homeland" in the Other. He writes: "Then, however, there is the true, the complete friendship. The actual friendship. What is that, what does it mean that it is supposed to be called the *Oikeion*? The at-home, that whereof one cannot speak, is what it is. We hear it all through a more melodious and mysterious concept when we speak of home and homeland" ([1999] 2009, 7). This would, then, not be the Other in cultural, social, or political terms but rather strictly in a philosophical sense of the subject's self-constitution as such, from a purely existential perspective. The Other in self-constitution is the self as compatriot: "The bold thesis is: friendship must exist first and foremost with oneself. That is required so that one can actually be bound to the Other and with the Other" ([1999] 2009, 8).

For Gadamer, then, friendship begins when one is the friend to oneself. Indeed, for friendship to exist, one must be complete in oneself in order to see the character of the Other as something other than a reflection of oneself. In this respect, friendship can acknowledge the Other as other because the self is selfish and does not need the Other to complete itself. Solidarity, however, calls on the self to renounce aspects of itself for the purposes of living with the Other, who has been acknowledged as other than the self. This compromise can only take place properly subsequent to the establishment of true friendship. This means the grounds for and terms of self-love must be set forth for friendship to exist. Furthermore, friendship is prior to and prerequisite of solidarity. Without this order of love's operations, solidarity would be based on a false assumption of needs, both of the self and of the Other. In such a case, true solidarity would not be possible, and the organizational relations and political associations supported by solidarity would be constitutively corrupt.

Gadamer's sense of solidarity depends on his understanding of *Bildung* and self-cultivation. *Bildung* cultivates the subject within spirit and intelligence. The subject's self-cultivation occurs linguistically through culture and word.[16] Manifest in language, culture provides the medium in which subjects recognize each other as a community. This cultural identification in word distinguishes human beings from animals, despite both being capable of communal existence. "Human" is defined according to communication, where cultural being and community are transmitted in language. Culture and community express human being's linguistic nature, and this understanding is hierarchical, with the most culturally cultivated community possessing the greatest insight into human nature. The traditions of hierarchically superior cultures reflect a greater conformity to nature and are therefore more "authentic." In this respect, not all speakers and cultures are equal, reflecting the truth and method of their *Bildung*. Inequality among speakers and cultures makes friendship impossible for those of unequal linguistic-cultural capacity. Equality among speakers is possible only at the highest level of community and is therefore monocultural. Lower-order cultural understanding creates the possibility of fluctuations in cultural competence and linguistic capacity. Only those who have attained, or in their being have the possibility to attain, the highest level of culture are equals and thus capable of crafting enduring, authentic friendship. All others are in solidarity with one another, agreeing politically to support each other without being equal. Solidarity can exist among races, classes, genders, groups, and individuals; it cannot exist among equals. Any race, class, gender, group, or individual excluded from the possibility for the highest attainment of normative culture through the self-cultivation of tradition is incapable of the highest friendship. Conditioned on equality, the highest friendship is private. Those individuals and cultures excluded from the highest medium for self-cultivation form only political bonds of solidarity.

II. The Language of Black Solidarity

From Gadamer's perspective, James Baldwin could only have shown solidarity with, not friendship to, Angela Y. Davis in a now-famous open letter to her while she was in prison.[17] In "solidarity," he unapologetically refers in the letter to her plight as similar to that of "the Jewish housewife on her way to Dachau" and insists that "you do not honor Sarah by denying Hagar, and the anguish of her children" (1970, 4). Even had Baldwin confined his comments to Davis herself and the specificity of her situation, his letter could only be political rather than aesthetic or personal. For Gadamer, all African American *Bildung*, self-cultivation, and art would be solidarity-based propaganda, including and especially the published personal letter. The rest of this chapter will discuss the extent to which Baldwin might agree with that assertion.

While his Holocaust analogy is highly problematic, Baldwin makes it to draw attention to Black despair and the protracted history of African American genocide he sees taking place, in which mass incarceration is yet another method of mass murder. The comments, however, were not received without the suspicion of anti-Semitism. Whether true or not, with regard to religious practice Baldwin was generally atheistic. As a writer, he often used the biblical imagery of his childhood, as the son of a pastor, and Christian themes to explore aspects of rigorously secular life. Because of his homiletic, rhetorical style and fluency with Christian beliefs and ideas, Baldwin was associated with related discourses.[18] This occurred to such an extent that the World Council of Churches invited him to speak at their annual meeting in 1968. Here Baldwin delivered the speech, "White Racism or World Community?" A good portion of the short speech is devoted to Stokely Carmichael, who plays a pivotal role in Baldwin's critique of the church at the conference. After reminding his audience that Carmichael "began his life as a Christian," Baldwin says:

> And a day came, inevitably, when this young man grew weary of petitioning a heedless population and said in effect, what all revolutionaries have always said, I petitioned you and petitioned you, and you can petition for a long, long time, but the moment comes when the petitioner is no longer a petitioner but has become a beggar. And at that moment one concludes, you will not do it, you cannot do it, it is not in you to do it, and therefore I must do it. When Stokely talks about Black power, he is simply translating into the Black idiom what the English said hundreds of years ago and have always proclaimed as their guiding principle, Black power translated means the self-determination of people. It means that, nothing more and nothing less. But it is astounding, and it says a great deal about Christendom, that whereas Black power, the conjunction of the word "Black" with the word "power," frightens everybody, no one in Christendom appears seriously to be frightened by the operation and the nature of white power. (1968, 373)[19]

In order to be as clear as he can about Black Power, Baldwin focuses on translation and Black idiom. Carmichael begins as a Christian yet is unable to translate Christian ideals into the Black idiom. Christian social praxis translated into the Black idiom is Black Power, which the Council of Churches would recognize in Carmichael (who Baldwin admits terrifies him) if not for the racially hegemonic nature of their discursive practice. The "conjunction of the words 'Black' and 'power' are too frightening for the Church, whereas that of 'white' and 'power' passes without notice" (1968, 373). Voicing these concerns, Baldwin articulates the basic tenet of insurgent Black liberation theology that formed a part of the Black Power movement.[20]

Both Black Power figures, Davis and Carmichael (Hagar and a type of Ezekiel), are understood biblically. Baldwin had no such rhetoric for Eldridge Cleaver. When belatedly addressing Cleaver's attack on his sexuality, Baldwin leaves room for a construction of the Black male revolutionary subject that is as aggressively masculine as Cleaver suggests yet whose manner of sexual expression remains fluid.[21] That said, Baldwin does that at the expense of an inclusive definition of Black male homosexuality, chastising any appearance of effeminate affect. In other words, Baldwin takes Cleaver to want to determine the limits of Black male sexuality's cultural rather than physical expression, understanding a separation between the two.[22] Baldwin sees quite plainly that Cleaver wants to police Black culture rather than Black bodies. Accepting a hermeneutic interpretation of "word and culture," he also understands that to do this, attention must be paid to linguistic expression as the basic substance of any culture. Racialized linguistic culture thus demands a historical account of a language as it is used by different races.

For this reason, Baldwin begins his discussion of Black English with a history lesson, citing a few milestone events in the long record of race relations in America and qualifying his highly attenuated account as atemporal, insofar as there is no distance between the auction block, then and now. In "Black English: A Dishonest Argument" (1980), Baldwin writes:

> I want to suggest that history is not the past. It is the present. We carry our history with us. We are our history. If we pretend otherwise, to put it very brutally, we literally are criminals. We just saw our history, just heard it, not five minutes ago [referring to the Tennessee Baptist Choir's rendition of Black history in song]. I have been to a place which the Western world pretends has not happened. I'm talking about the auction block. We are also talking about the automobile assembly line. I want to make this clear, sitting in your town, talking in your town. One of the architects of this peculiar town is a man named Henry Ford, who is probably responsible for building it—paying workers, Black and white; clubbing down workers, Black and white—who was a friend of Hitler's; who was no friend of the Jews. (He hadn't yet heard about us.) I challenge anyone alive to challenge me on that. (154–55)

Like Gadamer, Baldwin suggests that, because history dwells linguistically in each individual, everyone continues to have a stake in the past, even if oblivious to its events and the attitudes of those who shaped them. In this respect, the auction block persists in the lives and lifeworlds of African Americans and whites alike, determining relations between the two spheres and forging the individual subject within the realm of each racial-social regime of political and cultural practices.[23]

Because of this history and the continuing practice of cultural determination and appropriation, Baldwin can write:

We, in this country, on this continent, in the most despairing terms, created an identity which had never been seen before in the history of the world. We created that music. Nobody else did, and the world lives from it, though it doesn't pay us for it. In the storm which has got to overtake the Western world, we are the only bridge between their history which is the past and their history which is the present. We are the only Black Westerners. We are the only people under heaven, the Black Americans, who have paid so much for their father's father's father's father's father and mother. (1980, 158)

He then personalizes the process, transitioning from the "we" to the "I" when speaking about language acquisition. In "Why I Stopped Hating Shakespeare" (1964), Baldwin suggests, "the language was not my own because I had never attempted to use it, had only learned to imitate it" (67). Using language means to change it, as a writer. In "On Language, Race, and the Black Writer" (1979), Baldwin writes: "Writers are obliged, at some point, to realize that they are involved in a language which they must change. And for a Black writer in this country to be born into the English language is to realize that the assumptions on which the language operates are his enemy" (140).

At this point, Baldwin focuses on himself as a representative individual, while reintroducing the stated topic of his talk, the existence of Black English as a tool of literary self-fashioning.[24] He understands this topic through his own life experiences, which he takes to be consonantly paradigmatic for all native speakers defined by and embedded phenomenologically in this racial lifeworld of the writer. The philosophical implication is that the fundamental ontology of race as revealed in literary language is the true expression of social experience as racial essence. Indeed, in a line that could have come out of Gadamer, Baldwin writes, "it is experience which shapes a language; and it is language which controls an experience" (1964, 68). The Black experience shapes Black English. In turn, the literary use of Black English controls the Black experience. Baldwin thus wishes to assign ownership to experience and history in the form of literary originality and creativity, where the Black community controls its sociopolitical representations and self-understanding through its intentional utterances in a language that belongs to it historically and ontologically, as a product of racial being and the cultural response to oppression.

In other words, Baldwin, like Gadamer, concentrates on how beings, objects, and events are called and described as a means of ascribing belonging and assigning ownership to them. For each such fact describes the totality of the world, yet the language in which the case is expressed alters it to suit the needs of the dominant racial group. In this sense, Baldwin wishes to establish, first, that language as *Bildung* is the articulation of racial essence in its contingent expression as reaction formation to the historicity of social being, and that second, any given historical language represents the exercise of power in whatever limited or unrestricted material sense. In this instance, the concretion of historical events and the ontological facticity of racial being merge and manifest in the social totality of all political economic relations. For Baldwin, language is racial will to power.

To claim this power, Baldwin must first clearly establish the field of its intervention and formative influence. He does this by insisting emphatically that Black English is not only a language apart from the English spoken by whites but that, as the language of African Americans, it is the only one native to the United States. He bases this claim on an understanding of language and history that sees the two locked in a reciprocal relationship of mutual constitution whereby the living embodiment of their union— the individual as a contained psychical entity and as a political animal mediated socially—clarifies its cultural being through the refined articulation of the collective experience.[25] Baldwin at times performs this collectivizing process in his text by referring to himself in the third person as "we" and as "us." The easy shift from singular to plural and back allows Baldwin to demonstrate the collective nature of the Black subject even while speaking so-called white English. In this way, the distinction of race and history can be said to exist outside of language as a psychical and ontological fact derived historically and expressed through culturally contingent linguistic performance. Black English claims priority and indeed exclusive provenance over the linguistic scene in North America because its history alone begins there and is shaped by the unique historical forces pertaining to the formation of the United States as a nation.

Turning to *Erziehung* and self-cultivation, Baldwin then introduces the hypothetical of a child who goes to school for the first time. This child has to describe her surroundings, both to herself and to others. In order to do this, the child obviously requires a language. This language will not be necessary merely to ask for things and to get along socially in the new environment; it is requisite for the child to gain power over her new setting and indeed over her world. For Baldwin, the act of describing an object, setting, or event is the means by which to master it, thus making of such description a survival mechanism that facilitates the subject's encounter with the world in terms of dominance and submission as epistemological categories illuminating the methods and means of procuring necessities and satisfying needs. In this sense, language informs the subject who she is as a survivor, negotiating what is assumed to be an a priori hostile environment, by constituting through linguistic mediation the cultural expression of a lifeworld. The recognition of the self in language is, then, completed through the acquisition of a collective identity in traditional strategies for meeting and surviving recurrent existential challenges. The language of the schoolhouse is that of the self as mediated by the expressive totality of the racial-political collective.

In this respect, Baldwin locates the originary linguistic center of Black American *Bildung* in the home and sees it fostered in the education system, where schools are segregated precisely so that the descriptions African Americans form of their white counterparts need not be heard or under-stood in the language of their dominance. Baldwin thus claims that edu-cation in the United States remains segregated despite the Supreme Court ruling some thirty years previous to his speech because Black English as the only authentically Western American language in existence is too so-cially genuine and politically honest for white America to allow their chil-dren to hear it. It is a priori obscene to white ears. Baldwin posits no split between the American public and private spheres, where Black America suffers from an inverted sociopolitical space as determined by language.[26] The speech of the private realm is the only mode of linguistic communi-cation available to the African American speaker. Conversely, the linguis-tic mode of communicative action appropriate to public discourse belongs exclusively to whites as the sole manner of expression they possess in the public and private domains of social interaction. As Baldwin explains:

> Actually, we all know something very important that has brought me here. Let me try to spell it out for you, again. And let me suggest that the argu-ment concerning Black English is one of the most dishonest arguments in the history of a spectacularly dishonest nation. I kid you not. I grew up in Harlem. I was a shoeshine boy. I scrubbed toilets. And I can still cook. I was dealing with cops before I was seven years old and sleeping in base-ments before I was ten, watching my mother and my father, my brothers and my sisters, in the land of the free and the home of the brave, living as though every day was going to be our last. Now, how exactly do you expect me to explain that, to describe that to Greer Garson when she comes to teach me English? There is an irreducible gap between my teacher and my experience, between my teacher and my education. I would not have said it when I was ten, could not have said it when I was thirteen, but I can say it now: I don't want anyone I love, including my nieces, my nephews, my great-nieces, my great-nephews, to grow up to be like Jimmy Carter, Ron-ald Reagan, and all those people. (1980, 126)

For Baldwin, African Americans are prevented from deliberating consen-sus in the public sphere by coercive social conditions rather than legal norms. They are therefore excluded from democratic political participation, including the vote, regardless of what the Supreme Court may decide. Any African American contribution to the public sphere must take place "in translation" and is therefore a priori politically representative of the race. Conversely, white Americans (Greer Garson, Jimmy Carter, Ronald Reagan) possess no private sphere and operate only in public discursive modes of sociality and self-understanding. Everything white Americans do and decide is political, carrying the weight of law, even in the sphere of culture.[27] White Americans can have deliberative difference among them, whereas African Americans only ever occupy one political position: that of the minority.

This self-conception of white America as a psychological process by which the West in its entirety comes to fashion a positive identity through the negation and destruction of the Other is realized first linguistically. While interpreting this fact follows Gadamer's hermeneutics of translation, Baldwin's conception of linguistic situatedness differs strongly from Gadamer's "linguisticism." Unlike Gadamer, Baldwin sees linguistic appropriation, or being-in-translation, as the only form of linguistic situatedness possible, for all, thus emphasizing the language's own constitutive character over any essentialist understanding of linguistic production. For Baldwin, language is the historical accretion of power as the ability and right to name the world in terms of psychological cost or, as Baldwin puts it, the "price of the ticket." In this respect, his assertion that Black Americans are the only nonwhite Westerners takes on a potentially troubling aspect, as the West is here defined as a psychological disposition leading to the sociopolitical practice of naming others in order to fix their being as inferior to that of the dominant linguistic group. Baldwin states explicitly that whiteness itself does not exist and is merely a construct of this linguistically exercised, culturally manifested will to power. He states: "I attest to this: the world is not white; it never was white, cannot be white. White is a metaphor for power, and that is simply a way of describing Chase Manhattan Bank. That is all it means, and the people who tried to rob us of identity have lost their own. And when you lose that, when a people lose that, they've lost everything on which they depended, which is the bottom of their moral authority, and their moral authority is the power to persuade me that I should be like them" (1980, 158–59).

This would therefore also mean that Blackness does not signify outside of a given semiotic system in which it is conceived as a point of reference for calling into existence and defining one mode of that will to power, that of the "racial" collective, as the means by which to exploit another such group so constituted, for the purposes of economic gain. The mention of Chase Manhattan Bank as the most pervasive and powerful signs of collectivist sociopolitical power designates deficiency, debt, and default as the current material expressions of a, structurally speaking, linguistic mode of rapacious control. Linguistic identity is thus a commodified form of exchange yielding profit to a single collectivity defined by its place in the grammar of the West. It is a position that demands the commodifying dehumanization of the Other, regardless of the identity occupying it. In this sense, Black Americans have the potential to become or function grammatically like their white counterparts, depending on the nature of the language they speak. The specificity and authenticity of Black English protects African Americans from the possibility of structurally becoming the oppressor and from tacitly agreeing to their oppression by being part of the grammar of the West.

That said, the African American writer does not have the luxury of this separation, intervening in the master's tongue, so to speak, without recourse to the racial resources of Black English. Baldwin, then, does not recognize vernacular writing as essentially outside the purview and definition of white English. Indeed, he sees it as a pronounced yet simulated departure from standard usage deployed in order to achieve the effect of counterinsurgency within the text while accomplishing a type of cooptation and appropriation of Black speech that "naturalizes" it to the racially identified master discourse. It is the task of the African American writer to alter or pervert this discursive mastery through subversive linguistic acts within its identifiable domain and under the aegis of its highest expression. Baldwin quotes *Othello* in order to establish his point that standard English in its most basic assumptions vilifies Blackness as an inferior quality separate from its interpolated white speaker. In this way, he also indicates the level at which this insurrectionary act of sabotage must be performed in order to create a useful and authentic, or noncorrosive, Black literature. Baldwin will seek to undermine a normative conception of *Bildung* and tradition by using Shakespeare as the case study in how to approach literary production as an African American author. He confesses: "But I feared him, too, feared him because, in his hands, the English language became the mightiest of instruments. No one would ever write that way again. No one would ever be able to match, much less surpass, him."

For Baldwin, Shakespeare represents the highest expression of the English language, in which English has been fashioned into its most powerful form as a weapon.

Indeed, Shakespeare weaponized the language to such a degree and with such great success as to make it unavoidably offensive to any non-English speaker who did not participate by birth or self-disfigurement in the "chauvinism" of Shakespeare's nationalism. The challenge this chauvinism presents to the non-English writer producing literature in English, and especially to the nonnative English speaker creating in the language, is formidable to nigh insurmountable when faced with the irresistible linguistic power of Shakespeare's texts. The situation becomes nearly untenable for the African American author writing in Shakespeare's English, in that her linguistic situation is utterly unique, as she is a native speaker of a form of English that is not Shakespeare's, much in the way a white American is, yet which has no historical connection to the positive aspects of the English chauvinism that is the ideological source of the poet's vast, indeed definitive, linguistic power. Inextricably entwined, language and ideology reach the height of expressive, racially exclusionary force in Shakespeare's indomitable oeuvre.

Baldwin therefore wishes to assert that because his work is held up as the unassailable paradigmatic and authoritative articulation of the English language, Shakespeare becomes the locus for all signifying practices within this linguistic order, indicating that deviation therefrom can only be recognized and measured by reference to his achievement, even and perhaps especially with regard to the chauvinism exhibited therein. This would extend to the man himself as identified as interchangeable with his works, where Shakespeare also presents the archetypical human type associated with the highest expression of the English language. Instead of subscribing to this idea, Baldwin puts forth a notion of the plurality of the English language that nevertheless coalesces into a unified concretion of English language groups and their domains of use in the work of a more representative author figure, one reflective of the various worlds of English and who therefore betrays no sense of chauvinism of any kind. For this manifestation of English, Baldwin looks to its more inclusive, democratic American variant, which nevertheless is plagued by race chauvinism as an adapted form of Shakespeare's English. The multifarious and brilliantly evocative figurative configurations and breathtakingly beautiful associations Shakespeare creates in his work punctuate a standardization of trope, image, and lexical precision that become the bedrock of the English language's essential chauvinism, no matter the subject of its valorization or demonization. As Baldwin sees it, the

> structure of the French language told me something of the French experience, and also something of the French expectations—which were certainly not the American expectations, since the French daily and hourly said things which the Americans could not say at all. (Not even in French.) Similarly, the language with which I had grown up had certainly not been the King's English. An immense experience had forged this language; it had been (and remains) one of the tools of a people's survival, and it revealed expectations which no white American could easily entertain. The

authority of this language was in its candor, its irony, its density, and its beat: this was the authority of the language which produced me, and it was also the authority of Shakespeare. (1964, 68)

Baldwin then goes on to relate the experience of living in France and learning to speak French. It is at this time and through this specific linguistic experience that Baldwin comes to appreciate Shakespeare, whose works to this point he had never liked, and to read the Bible again, presumably the King James Version. This newfound love of the Bard and the Bible belays the realization that language shapes experience, and that experience in turn symbiotically transforms the linguistic lifeworld of its subject. In other words, Baldwin has made a linguistic-structural gesture in which he affirms the diachronic and synchronic characters of language while assigning each a subjective value. Here the historical duration of the specific linguistic medium in question produces its speakers, who must conform to its basic rules of being and expression. Each individual speaker has in the immediacy and synchronicity of her linguistic experience the ability to improvise the various rhythms and harmonies language entails. In this sense, Baldwin understands jazz experience as reflective of Black English's historicity in the synchronic sense. This is revealed and punctuated by the syncopated background of the "King's English," meant as a synonym for Shakespeare.

In this sense, Baldwin is tacitly linking Shakespeare and the Bible as purely linguistic entities derived from a specific historical time and place, under certain conditions of political ontology and sovereign control. In this shared historical space, a racially specific epistemological legitimacy is being both assumed and created for the purposes of ideological cultural and religious indoctrination through the communicative means of social actors and actions. Baldwin can appreciate the beauty of the Bible's early modern aesthetic demonstrated in the King James translation as standing shoulder-to-shoulder with that of its contemporary, Shakespeare, as the two poetic artifacts continue to shape the intensity and distributive structure of political power in Baldwin's twentieth century and beyond.[28] For Baldwin comes to appreciate the fact that the unmatchable splendor of these poetic works is made possible by political assumptions both about the culture that produced them and about the nature of language itself as the means by which to shape the reality it describes while being dialectically responsive to the willful materiality of the world of which it is the case. Language as history is the embedded material truth of race. It is that which determines human difference as both cultural and physical facts. For Baldwin, race is a physical reality not due to biological difference but rather due to the material concretion of history achieved in linguistic performance, as given in all social exchange yet raised to axiomatic human truth in literature as the highest example of language use.[29] The task of the racially representative writer is to be aware of the responsibility her work carries in being responsive to the racial history present in language and shaping her reality.[30]

This task becomes all the more urgent when taken in conjunction not with Shakespeare but with the Bible, which Baldwin has practically smuggled into this occasional piece as a cognate for Shakespeare's poetic achievement, yet which signifies on a register far removed from the literary giant's works. For while the political designs centered on the chauvinistic Shakespearean oeuvre and those of the King James translation may have similar aspects, and their respective poetic achievements may reach the same dizzying heights, the Bible ultimately speaks with a vastly different universal authority than does the Shakespearean text. While this is abundantly clear in itself, the fact remains unspoken and elusive in Baldwin's essay, as he essentially relativizes the Bible to the Bard as two poetic interventions, each speaking to the resilient beauty of the human spirit as it survives the assault of history and ideological appropriation to inhuman ends. For Baldwin's exclusionary understanding of the King's English makes it evident that he views the chauvinistic exercise of power as obviously and imminently ostracizing and demonizing, and that language as the material basis of world-building subjectivity posits the self, over and against the Other, rather than as in a cooperative relationship of being-with, in equality. The antidemocratic, indeed monarchical nature of the King's English as imposed on discursive Christian morality as religion is transformed poetically into an ideological tool of the state.

This means that for Baldwin the Bible is a tool for the racial state to control nonnative speaking minorities within its borders and under its sovereign control and that nevertheless uses prophetic language predicting that state's destruction.[31] This prophetic language shapes the subjective nature of the individual and the historical character of the minority population in question. The Bible, far more than Shakespeare, acts as a direct delivery mechanism with which to disseminate all the racist ideological assumptions the state wishes to inculcate in each of its subjects.[32] In other words, Shakespeare, for all of his glory and horror, does not transcend racial distinction in order to qualify and establish his works' historical life as the formative element of each citizen subject. While Shakespeare may be the concern of the Black writer, his work filters through to that of the minority population largely through allusion and the cultural assumptions of the majority race. The Bible, however, is part of the fabric of the nation as a whole, offering unity of moral teaching while qualifying this message racially, where good and evil carry specific countenances as expressed ideologically through poeticized racist presumption.

The ideology inconspicuously embedded in the King's English and continuing to determine subjective disposition vis-à-vis the racial life-worlds of majority and minority communities with the single social total-ity are intransigent and insurmountable from within the parameters of the language set by its politically and culturally dominant speakers. However, there are two fields of linguistic operation and intervention where the ideo-logical assumptions of the racially dominant majority can be challenged, and they are in poetry itself, which is that linguistic regime whereby the ideological precepts for racial domination through the creation of the psy-chical subject through language was first established and authorized, and in translation, a linguistic event to which Baldwin has ostensibly little to add in direct conversation with the hegemonic quality of English literature as it determines all aspects of sociopolitical life. Yet Baldwin prefaces his discussion of Shakespeare with a strong qualification in the form of a nar-rative in which he moves from an almost natural antipathy for and aver-sion to the King's English as exemplified and indeed created by Shake-speare's works and the King James Bible to an acceptance and even love of these texts won through learning a foreign language. In effect Baldwin could only circumvent and indeed assault the racist structures of white supremacy and national chauvinism in the King's English by approaching it from the perspective of translation. Black American writing and transla-tion have an essential common feature.

Baldwin felt alienated by the English language because it reflects none of his experiences. He notes that he did not feel like a native son to his mother tongue until he began speaking French. The experience of "be-ing in translation" awakened him to the nature of all experience as medi-ated by language. In other words, on a basic level, Baldwin's experience of French is every speaker's encounter with her native language in its ob-jectivity and historicity. Translation thus alerts Baldwin to the mediat-ing objective state of all language, encountered by all native speakers at the preliminary stage of linguistic acquisition and that while not mirrored in secondary, tertiary, etc., linguistic "naturalization" is nevertheless re-vealed as formatively paradigmatic in its objective character by the act of translation that learning a foreign language and using foreign words in na-tive speech entails. The implications for Baldwin's ability to find his ex-periences through adequate expression in English relate directly to Black English's status as a language, in that, negatively associated, if the King's English was a translation for him, Black English must be a language unto itself because it allows Baldwin to comprehend and articulate his subjec-tive experience naturally.

Baldwin suggests that, as his own test subject, the individual can be taken as representative of the group. Therefore, the writer's own experiences are paradigmatic for the race, where the collectivity the writer represents is qualified racially. In this sense, literary representation is always racially defined through the linguistic ability to authentically articulate existential experience that is poetically specific to a biologically identified population the lifeworld of which is reflected in turn by its language. The mediating character of the linguistic continuum to which the literary producer belongs, and which presents the racial character of the political collective into which the writer is born, passes unnoticed by the intellect and is imperceptible to the body as the determinative condition of the racial subject's existence in the linguistically expressible world. Here the author forms one more object among those construed ontologically in their existence in a particular language. The nature of this existence is revealed as objective only when the subject leaves her native linguistic lifeworld and is forced to acquire a foreign language within an alien social totality. At this point the objectivity of all language as the definitive medium of sociopolitical existence can be perceived through the experience of both acclimating to and remaining alienated from the targeted sphere of linguistic assimilation.

Baldwin understands race as productive of language, where race is both an inherent ontological condition and a cultural complex contingent on historical elaboration, as given in educative modes determined by sociopolitical situations and the particularities of place. In this respect, Baldwin's conception of language is nativist and objective, in that language as the transcendental elaboration of social being determines certain subjective characteristics through which a series of generally defined experiences are determined in advance and, as it were, a priori, providing a form of racial belonging that moves beyond mere biological attribute and comes to include the articulable as the case itself. That is to say, linguistic limitations and possibilities form patterns of the self through which all experience, no matter how divergent, will be perceived in common fashion by those to whom the linguistic lifeworld pertains, in effect providing a common experience in racial terms to an otherwise unfamiliar political collective, even when encountering incommensurate existential circumstances. Language, then, creates the racial lifeworld of a people predetermined as a race by the cognitive, linguistic-transcendental property qualifying the nativist lifeworld into which each subject is born.

In this respect, Baldwin predicates racial being as a historical reality on linguistic expression, whereby the individual subject is determined in her being by the social totality reflected by the language into which she is born.[33] This nativist understanding of linguistic subjectivity decides the speaker's fate at the moment she is introduced into the order of language "native" to her sociopolitical collective. For only through language does the speaking subject comprehend the totality of social experiences as the extension of the self in time and space. All social experience is thus assimilated to the ego through the self's ability to make linguistic sense of events as relating exclusively to its being. In this respect, Baldwin advances a notion of linguistic solipsism through which the speaker's social existence is created entirely in the linguistic encounter between self and world, where the world is an extension of the self's ability to express it. Those others who share the same language are then unconsciously assumed by the speaking subject to experience the same things in the same way, because the two, self and other, speak the same language. This recognition is, for Baldwin, an acknowledgment of the essential racial bond between speaking subjects, as given in language and perceived as a common history and culture. Baldwin's idea of objective history in language is in fact the personal account of a single subject's encounter with the world as the collection of utterable facts, where a fact is alone that which can be uttered.[34]

Therefore, Baldwin presents an understanding of unlimited subjectivity as the basis of social belonging in which the individual determines the social bonds between members of the same race by establishing the existential fact and terms of the race in question through the linguistically mediated specificity of the individual's experiences. The tacit assumption animating Baldwin's conception of the interdependency of race and language in elaborating the political collective's identity as that of the individual is the idea that for an experience to exist at all it must do so world-historically. If the individual is able to communicate her experience to another individual and be understood, then the two individuals are of the same social substance, the binding structure of which is that of sociality as reflection of inscribed universal racial being. The political collective is the conglomerate identity of subjects, with each determined by the same social structure as given naturally by innate racial blueprint. The evidence of this is the fact of communication itself between racial agents who, if not for this common element, would not be able to reach each other discursively, not in a purely informational sense, but rather in terms of sympathetic intuitive understanding. Language activates intuition and unspoken, reflective identification between speakers of the same racial lifeworld. For Baldwin, language then provides the phenomenology of race.

The ground of racial-phenomenological investigation is language as used in monolingual public and private discursive spaces. For Baldwin, these are the locations of segregated linguistic publics in which language disappears as a conscious factor for the subject's appropriation of her world as the linguistically expressible collection of social facts and norms.[35] In other words, linguistic spaces in which language goes uncontested and therefore untranslated offer the sites in which the phenomenology of race discloses the objective nature of racial-linguistic world-building through the subjectively articulated, isolated experiences of the individual as they are recognized in the Other. Because of a shared language group, the racial subject comprehends herself and her world in the same way as the other racial subject encountered. Members of the same race are thus native speakers of the same language who as such share the same experiences, as each language contains a limited number of expressible facts as the world. For Baldwin, then, the limits of racial objectivity are bound to that of language, as the two codetermine the experiential being of the individual subject in and as the world. The world is the collection of racial affairs expressed through the facts disclosed by the objective field of social possibility given to a race in its language.

Baldwin feels himself to be giving legal testimony to this fact:

> I am a witness to and a survivor of the latest slave rebellion, or what American newspapers erroneously term the civil rights movement. I put it that way because Malcolm X and I met many years ago when Malcolm was debating a very young sit-in student on a radio station which had asked me to moderate the discussion. Malcolm asked the student a question which I now present to you: "If you are a citizen, why do you have to fight for your civil rights? If you are fighting for your civil rights, then that means you are not a citizen." Indeed, the "legalisms" of this country have never had anything to do with its former slaves. We are still governed by the slave codes. (1979, 141)

Baldwin presents a complex phenomenology of race in which the individual subject projects her experience onto the Other in search of racial matches that would evince the same mode of experiential accumulation. That is to say that the common racial bond among a population is the mechanism and manner by which its individual members experience the world, which will in turn decide the range and indeed specificity of the experiences available for particular subjects to encounter. This also means that, taken out of her racial context, the racial subject must translate both the language of the event and the event itself as produced linguistically, meaning that the individual's lifeworld is constructed of language as the sum total of the possible experience for native speakers. This measures the aggregate total of experiences available to the nonnative speaker's cognition, as translated into the semiotic system of her own social totality. For Baldwin, there is no difference between social and racial identification, as the phenomenological experience open to the racial subject in her native lifeworld is not available to a nonnative subject in the same setting. Translation thus reveals the objective setting of race and the indelible, permanent, and indeed essential character of its historical being. Race, then, is not a biological fact but rather an objective historical necessity structuring a socially delimited collective's idiosyncratic, expressive forms of communication. In this respect, race is not a biological fact; it is an existential one.

By this definition, Baldwin avoids the physically hierarchical attribution of racial character and worth yet is still able to maintain a sense of natural superiority among races. This ascription of worth is decided by history rather than biology, with priority given to the historical authenticity of a particular race, as revealed in its language.[36] Determined in its character by the range and legitimacy of the historical events it describes, the language best suited to translating the objective experience of a people within a particular environment while living under unique material circumstances indicates the value of the race itself. Its language is the dominant expression of the race's inner imperatives and drives. This means that, for Baldwin, African Americans are the preferable, superior race in the United States because only Black English can say that it is an indigenous incarnation of English in the Americas, and among Americans.[37] While all other forms of English spoken in the United States are derivative of the King's English and thus have their racial essence elsewhere, among alien sociopolitical circumstances, Black English is entirely of the United States. It thus linguistically and objectively reflects the racial character of the American public sphere, as deduced by the new hermeneutic interpretation of culture. It does not, however, reproduce a Black racial essence, or anything essential at all.

Baldwin thus arrives at a hermeneutical model of language similar to Gadamer's. Like Gadamer, Baldwin accepts that language mediates the expression of cultural character and historical lifeworld of a "people." He agrees with the situatedness of race in language and the historical elaboration of race in language-based cultural expression. Yet, unlike Gadamer, Baldwin insists that the overdetermined political character of this expression can be subverted by minority discourse found in "minor literatures." For Baldwin, literature becomes the means by which disenfranchised minority populations participate in a public sphere otherwise closed off to their deliberations. The knowledge and subversion of the hegemonic racial majority's "authoritative" literary tradition creates a space within the public sphere for the contribution of a counterpublic to the formation of public opinion and the public sphere.

The Aardvark of History   [CHAPTER TWO]
Malcom X, Language, and Power

I. The Gadamer-Habermas-Malcolm X Debate

By 1970, Gadamer's debate with Habermas had received extensive attention as a discussion over the role of language in hermeneutic philosophy and
the public sphere. Writing in a 1970 English-language journal, the number
of which had been specifically planned as an introduction for Americans
to current social thought in Germany, Habermas sets out his case against
Gadamer. Habermas condemns Gadamer's hermeneutic as delusional, in
that it does not question the basis of its own linguistic foundation. The
truth of Gadamer's method does not take into account the "conditions of
plausibility" under which it claims legitimacy, instead relying on tradition
for authorization and in effect ontologizing language. Habermas insists instead that "truth" is a matter of consensus over an acknowledged ideal-
ized social state, established by "unlimited and control-free communication." In other words, through communication between ideally free and
equal members of a deliberative society, "truth" is not universally given
but rather universally agreed upon. Critique evaluates those instances
where these conditions are not met, with particular attention to the linguistic distortions that attempt to present them as operative and in force.

The aforementioned "debate" between Habermas and Gadamer hinges
on the meaning of interpretation as it relates to "authoritative" cultural
tradition. Specifically, it focuses on Gadamer's broad definition of translation, in which he insists that language is the reflection or mirror of being in which both objects and relations are reflected. For Gadamer, these
reflections may or may not be ideological, that is, in support of authority
and thus predetermined and potentially false. Ultimately, language will
reflect the truth of its situation, as hermeneutic method is applied to distinguish between actual and ideological relations between subjects and
objects. For Habermas, language is far more insistent on its ideological position, demanding an interpretive method that does not seek a truth that

may not be given in linguistic expression. Rather, interpretation must focus on the deliberative goals of ideology or its praxis within the lifeworld. Translation may signify, then, irreducible acts of hegemonic power, defying hermeneutic interpretation, which, because of its certainty of truth in its method, may actually contribute to oppression.

This aspect of *Truth and Method* is not immediately obvious because Gadamer assumes these relations of power, even in something as perspicuous as casual conversation. For Gadamer, "We say that we 'conduct' a conversation, but the more genuine a conversation is, the less its conduct lies within the will of either partner. Thus, a genuine conversation is never the one that we wanted to conduct. Rather, it is generally more correct to say that we fall into conversation, or even that we become involved in it" ([1960] 1993, 383).

Gadamer insists the most "genuine" conversation is conducted not by its participants but rather by language itself.[1] He ascribes to language an agency that shapes the speakers' intention through the play of all available linguistic means of expression. The language of genuine conversation mediates a genuine human relation in which the being of each participant is revealed in its historical contingency. Conversation of this sort establishes the shared cultural identity of each speaker. The conversation between partners reaches a genuine level of discursive understanding made possible in advance by the genuine social bond shared between culturally related beings. For Gadamer, the discursive encounter between subjects reflexively sharing a genuine social relation is registered only when a divergence of intention occurs in genuine conversation. Conversational *authenticity* appears when the immanent needs of linguistic expression come into conflict with their social setting, cultural commitment, and historical situation.

Any disagreement in genuine conversation is made possible by the autonomy of the language itself rather than an imperfection in the speakers' cultural competency. The speakers are formed as subjects in language before they encounter each other in a linguistically constructed social space. Language thus has two spheres of social existence. One is existential-phenomenal, in which its practical attributes fashion individual subjects dialogically within a preexisting social grammar. Prior to this, however, social mediation is individual and proceeds from the idea of language as a categorical imperative for the construction of reality. This reality must

> establish its validity within it in a new way. Thus every translation is at the same time an interpretation. We can even say that the translation is the culmination of the interpretation that the translator has made of the words given him.

The example of translation, then, makes us aware that language as the medium of understanding must be consciously created by an explicit mediation. This kind of explicit process is undoubtedly not the norm in a conversation. Nor is translation the norm in the way we approach a foreign language. Rather, having to rely on translation is tantamount to two people giving up their independent authority. Where a translation is necessary, the gap between the spirit of the original words and that of their reproduction must be taken into account. It is a gap that can never be completely closed. (Gadamer [1960] 1993, 402)

The conditions of understanding are revealed in their frustration. Where the communicative process breaks down, the rules by which discursive understanding occurs become the subject of investigation as a recuperative means. This investigation can take many forms. The form it takes will by necessity conform to the nature of both the rupture and the realm of its medium. In this respect, while dysfunctional communication may withhold its truth, the method of its analysis can be known. The analysis of this method can yield objective data leading to epistemologically valid, hermeneutically derived knowledge. However, the objective knowledge acquired is not of the object itself but rather of the method by which it is best approached in philosophical inquiry. For this method is provoked directly by the object for hermeneutic interpretation.

Hermeneutics, then, observes the methods and procedures by which the interpretive act functions and has value for the interpreter. For this reason, "only that translator can truly re-create who brings into language the subject matter that the text points to; but this means finding a language that is not only his but is also proportionate to the original. The situation of the translator and that of the interpreter are fundamentally the same" (Gadamer [1960] 1993, 405). While the subject of language exists prior to speaking, only linguistic articulation allows the subject to enter into historical relation with itself and with others. Thought that is not historical is pre- or extralinguistic and cannot be communicated to the self or to others. There are states of knowing that do not rely on language; however, they become historical only once they become known to the self as linguistically articulated knowledge. The subject can only be considered social as a form of self-consciousness that is constituted and mediated in the historicity of linguistic expression. Historical being and social being are two manifestations of the same linguistic ground of thought. Interpretation translates one world into another while measuring the irreconcilable, unbridgeable distance between them. The linguistic relations Gadamer presents are ontologically constitutive of individual subjects within a sociolinguistic totality. As such, they are fraught with relations of power and inequality. To overcome this inequality, Gadamer, in "Aesthetics and Hermeneutics" (1964), suggests aesthetic experience overwhelms the specificity of the work's historical-cultural character, communicating instead universal attributes shared by all. This hermeneutical perspective on the work of art includes all traditions on level ground of the public sphere.

Habermas's critique of *Truth and Method* concentrates on the public sphere as tradition "in translation," seeing "translation" as the use of other words to say what cannot otherwise be said in a language. Where "exact translation" is not possible, translation as interpretation is required. Exact translation presumes that the primary and target languages each have the ability to say the same thing, according to the same rules. Interpretive translation acknowledges that one of the languages cannot accommodate the communicative content in question without supplementary material chosen by a process of interpretation. This interpretation is guided by the grammatical rules of the language in need of supplement along with consideration of its tradition in solving similar problems.

In this sense, as Gadamer points out, "Hermeneutic experience is the corrective by means of which thinking reason escapes the prison of language, and it is itself constituted linguistically" ([1960] 1993, 363). The "foreign" content to be assimilated to the target language, or uttered in the primary, occasions revision in the use of supplementary forms of expression deduced from grammatical rules and semantic tradition. As Habermas notes, "translation is the medium in which these revisions take place and language is continuously developed further" (1988, 148). That is to say, translation both interprets and alters the language in question. Grammatical rule and tradition are respected while uttering what previously had not been thought in the language they constitute and govern. Habermas thus concludes, "Hermeneutic understanding, which is only articulated in situations of disturbed consensus, is as fundamental to the understanding of language as is primary consensus" (148). For hermeneutic understanding forces consensus where disagreement prevailed. It does not have the ability to negotiate or mediate consensus; it dissolves disagreement in the illusion of dialectical resolution, in which interpretative translation is taken for exact.

In this way, Habermas suggests, the "unity of language, which disappeared in the pluralism of language games, is dialectically restored in the context of tradition. Language exists only as something traditional, for tradition mirrors on a large scale the life-long socialization of individuals in their language" (149). As Habermas insists, "Hermeneutic understanding begins at the points of interruption; it compensates for the discontinuous quality of intersubjectivity" (150). This compensation is not without loss. Indeed, the obfuscation of intersubjective discontinuity assumes consensus where there may be none. In this case, tradition takes on an authoritative role, deciding disagreement in favor of social and institutional norms. Deviation from this normative structure becomes impossible from without, without its consent. Habermas thus accuses Gadamer of positing "that the applicative understanding of eminent traditions bearing authoritative claims provides the model for hermeneutic understanding as such" (162). The authoritative nature of the "model for hermeneutic understanding" is authoritarian, relying on tradition to resolve all contested issues, according to a clearly rigid normative structure. Within this structure of knowledge, improvisation is impossible.

Habermas's critique of Gadamer signaled a turn in his thought "from the theory of knowledge to the theory of communication [that] makes it possible to give substantive answers to questions that, from a metatheoretical vantage point, could only be elucidated as questions and clarified in respect to their presuppositions" (1988, xiv). In other words, Habermas seeks an action-oriented interpretative model legitimately capable of social intervention rather than being confined to description. As Habermas admits, "By its very structure, hermeneutic understanding aims at gaining from traditions a possible action-oriented self-understanding for social groups and clarifying it. It makes possible a form of consensus on which communicative action depends" (164). In this respect, Habermas does not reject the tradition from which Gadamer derives his hermeneutical method, "this experience of reflection [that] is the permanent legacy bequeathed to us by German Idealism from the spirit of the eighteenth century" (170). Rather, Habermas objects to its authoritarian articulation of a consensus-based model for action-oriented interpretation. He does not dislike the traces of Idealism in Gadamer's thought; he abhors its Heideggerian aspects. Habermas sees clearly that the authoritarian elements of Gadamer's hermeneutics rely on oppressive, coercive power in resolving dialectical tension and dissensus in communicative action. Minority discourses are not excluded from the public sphere; they are silenced in it and then ventriloquized.

In "Language and Understanding" ([1970] 2006), Gadamer responds to Habermas by insisting that the notion that radical dissensus positions are a priori eliminated from the public sphere would be either too naive or too intentionally misrepresentative of his hermeneutics (17). Indeed, as Gadamer understands him, Habermas accuses hermeneutic interpretation of validating authority by leaving ideology intact and unexamined. Gadamer retorts that hermeneutic criticism evaluates all that is given in language, a process that may or may not leave the assumptions of its textual object in a place of authority (1970b, 86). In other words, Habermas believes that any text is a priori ideological, given the historical conditions of its production.

II. The Transformation of the Black Public Sphere

For Habermas, the public sphere is a realm or discursive space for the democratic formation of public opinion. The public sphere is not a space for voicing unreconcilable opinions. Instead, the public sphere allows for the articulation of a consensus public opinion. Because all citizens must have equal access to the same public sphere, Habermas must assume a preexisting, common culture that enables participants to recognize themselves in dissenting opinions. Habermas thus premises the public sphere on universal enlightenment, and, to a certain extent, multiculturalism mediated by ideal forms of communication common to all. The public sphere's reliance on forms of communicative reason and action instead of cultural recognition and social tradition ensures, at least theoretically, the democratic legitimacy of public opinion. In order to produce inclusive, deliberative debate in the formation of democratically adduced public opinion, no physical characteristics or marginal social condition qualifies for the public sphere. For Habermas, there could be no Black public sphere, as the public sphere reflects the universal values of the entire society.

Because it has no definitional place in Habermas's theory of the public sphere, the Black public sphere is often defined negatively, or by what it does rather than what it is. For example, in their brief introduction to the now-famous issue of *Public Culture*, editors Appadurai, Berlant, Breckenridge, and Diawara write: "The Black public sphere is thus not always a resistance aesthetic which defies modernity and finds comfort in the politics of identity and difference. To think the Black public sphere, we have to be willing to rethink the relationship between markets and freedom, commodity and identity, property and pleasure. The Black public sphere puts engagement, competition and exchange in the place of resistance, and uses performativity to capture audiences, Black and White, for things fashioned through Black experience" (1994, xii). As one reviewer of the volume noted, "little attention is given to lucidly conceptualizing the public sphere, apart from stating the inadequacy of Habermas's notion of the bourgeois public sphere for African Americans" (Harvey 1996, 817–18). Without this clear conceptualization, the exact definition of a Black public sphere changes from writer to writer.[2] Michael C. Dawson solves the problem by stating: "A Black public sphere does not exist in contemporary America, if by that we mean a set of institutions, communication networks and practices which facilitate debate of causes and remedies to the current combination of political setbacks and economic devastation facing major segments of the Black community, and which facilitate the creation of oppositional formations and sites. I argue that such a public sphere did exist within the Black community as recently as the early 1970s. More precisely what no longer exists is a Black counterpublic" (Dawson 1994, 197). Dawson diagnoses here not insufficiencies in Habermas's account of publicity—although his essay does that as well—but rather several deficiencies "within the Black community." These can be summarized as institutional networks for public debate on how to solve problems the Black community faces. For Dawson, Fraser, Eley, and others, Habermas's "romanticized version of Western European history" did little to address the concerns of multiculturalism and minority discourse in the public sphere's formation of political consensus. Fraser writes, "too credulous of the bourgeois public's claim to be the public, Habermas had overlooked women's and workers' counterpublics, which housed more robust, contestatory modes of public participation" (Fraser 2017, 248). Fraser extends this analysis to include all subaltern positions within the public sphere, generally understood, to posit counterpublics that propose "revisionist historiographies of public life" (Fraser 2017, 248). She suggests "counterpublics contested the exclusionary norms of the 'official' bourgeois public sphere, elaborating alternative styles of political behavior and alternative norms of public speech" (Fraser 1993, 4). Following Fraser, Dawson suggests the Black community formed a counterpublic, which, first, "is not a bourgeois sphere in the sense that Habermas describes; Black institutions and publics have been largely multi-class, at least up to 1970, due to the long regime of enforced segregation. Secondly ... its leadership has been male and patriarchal, due in no small part to the importance of male religious leaders in the Black community" (1994, 197). According to Dawson, the consolidation of the political right's power over the public sphere in the 1970s, along with the economic deprivation of Black America and dissent within the Black community, dismantled the Black counterpublic.

Regardless of which sphere is chosen, a Black public sphere or a Black counterpublic sphere, most writers agree with Habermas that a transformation in publicity has occurred. Whether or not it is the one Dawson describes remains debatable, as many writers tend to place the transformation earlier, as an effect of 1950s desegregation legislation and a coterminous "crisis of Black politics" (Hanchard 1996, 101). There is also general agreement that the transformation of the Black public sphere entailed a shift from debates among Black public intellectuals such as Du Bois, Baldwin, and Ellison, to athletes, entertainers, and other practitioners of more publicly performative intervention. As Diawara writes, "the most obvious difference between the Black public sphere in the 1920s

and the 1940s involves the decreased influence of writers and political figures such as W. E. B. Du Bois, Langston Hughes, Marcus Garvey and Alain
Locke and the increased popularity of entertainers such as Duke Elling-
ton, Dizzy Gillespie, Billy Eckstine, Billie Holiday, Ella Fitzgerald and Diana Washington" (Diawara 1994, 47). Houston Baker continues the history, writing "By the mid-1960s in the United States such a convergence
had come to fullness in the North with the organization of the Black Mus-
lims and the charismatic leadership of Malcolm X. Moreover, the necessity for a new agenda beyond nonviolent, direct action protest in the South
had been made clear by the suddenness and ferocity of the Los Angeles
Watts Riot of 1965. Suddenly visible to national and international publicity was the Black urban ghetto, where migration had brought so many
former Black southerners in quest of a promised industrial land" (Baker
1994, 26). For Baker, the Black public sphere experiences "convergence"
in the "Black urban ghetto" of the 1960s, represented most forcefully not
by Martin Luther King Jr. but rather by Malcolm X.[3]

A number of famous "debates" in twentieth-century philosophy inter-
sect in this "convergence." Foucault's and Derrida's critiques of Habermas
reflect Malcolm's strong concern for counterdiscursive incursion and the
refutation of Enlightenment as the ideological justification of race and racial hegemony. In other words, Derrida and Foucault see more similarity
than difference in Habermas's and Gadamer's positions. Although Foucault did not "debate" with Gadamer, strong differences in defining diversity and the conceptualization to inclusion make any surface similarities in
their work moot. Gadamer, Habermas, and Foucault would all run afoul
of Derrida, whose deconstructive approach was too reductive to allow for
strong practical readings of politics, law, and ethics. For his part, Derrida
challenged the premises of all three on the basis of inconsistencies in logic
and irrational textual construction, leaving little doubt that the center of
hermeneutic, discursive, and genealogical critique did not hold. While
these debates offer great interest and insight, they remain blind to the letter of experience of those it collapses under the heading of "Other."

In each instance, the Other is something that can be constructed out
of categories derived from the philosophical tradition that denies its existence or voice. Here, even Derrida is not deconstructive enough. For, despite all description to the contrary, all philosophical positions engaged in
these debates are complicit in constructing the Other, even when only as a
transcendental or purely negative category. That is to say, Derrida's Other
is *Derrida's* Other as much as Gadamer's tradition belongs to anyone who
infiltrates, either by invitation, stealth, or force. "Reverse discourse" at
least has the value of acknowledging the Other's speech without romanti-
cizing it, positively or negatively, as outside "culture and word." For Fou-

cault, reverse discourse occurs when an aberrant, atypical, or nonnormative subject position begins "to speak in its own behalf, to demand that its legitimacy or 'naturality' be acknowledged, often in the same vocabulary, using the same categories by which it was medically disqualified" (Foucault 1990, 101). From the reversed discursive perspective, Malcolm X would have viewed all sides of each debate as ultimately one more powerplay among people who did not realize that reality had already defeated them. In this sense, his philosophy is a purposeful mix of Machiavelli and Mephistopheles.

III. Malcolm X and the Public Sphere

Like Habermas, Malcolm understands the public sphere as both monolingual and monocultural. Because of this, he does not recognize a Black public sphere, yet he does posit the possibility of Black intervention in the public sphere as Foucauldian "reverse discourse" rather than counterpublic. Because for Malcolm the public sphere is mediated by a single, categorical language of power, the social relations it determines can be exploited on the basis of linguistic performance within the dominant language. Malcolm posits that extreme fluency of expression within the dominant idiom of the public sphere requires literary self-fashioning guided by a philosophy of Black communication. The rhetoric of "by any means necessary" is above all else a communicative act of this sort. This is not to say that Malcolm would stop short of violence; rather, it means that the frontline of revolutionary struggle was the language of public opinion.[4]

In "The Ballot or the Bullet" (1964a), Malcolm is quick to point out the limitation placed on discussion by the choice of terms used to describe the goal of Black activism:

> And now you're facing a situation where the young Negro's coming up. They don't want to hear that "turn-the-other-cheek" stuff, no. In Jacksonville, those were teenagers, they were throwing Molotov cocktails. Negroes have never done that before. But it shows you there's a new deal coming in. There's new thinking coming in. There's new strategy coming in. It'll be Molotov cocktails this month, hand grenades next month, and something else next month. It'll be ballots, or it'll be bullets. It'll be liberty, or it will be death. The only difference about this kind of death—it'll be reciprocal. You know what is meant by "reciprocal"? That's one of Brother Lomax's words, I stole it from him. I don't usually deal with those big words because I don't usually deal with big people. I deal with small people. I find you can get a whole lot of small people and whip hell out of a whole lot of big people. They haven't got anything to lose, and they've got everything to gain. (319)

To be forced to debate the matter within the narrow limits of segregation or integration fails to introduce the sense of the matter as all factions of the African American struggle for freedom experience it. The selection of these words also determines the conceptual field in which any conversation can take place. Understanding the power this linguistic determination possesses, Malcolm does not condemn its mechanism or structure but rather its result. To rectify what he sees as an error and to shift the balance of power in the discussion, Malcolm rejects the terms that have been insisted on in advance and the imposition of an either/or and elects to address the matter conjunctively, as recognition and respect. For Malcolm, all African American political intervention demands recognition and respect as that of human beings.

Because of this, Malcolm mocks his interlocutor, Louis Lomax, for his hypocritical use of the word "reciprocal," which he calls one of "those big words" that he says he does not care to use. The reason why Malcolm refrains from their use is not because they indicate a racial status that he does not care to reflect, as if somehow "reciprocal" fell outside the usable vocabulary of Baldwin's "Black English." Rather, he avoids using big words because they do not help him in reaching "small" people. Here Malcolm borders on ascribing a racial essence to language yet pulls back from so doing, inferentially insisting instead on language as a product of class. The "big people" use big words, and they can be influenced by anyone who also uses these words. That said, Malcolm prefers to influence small people, as enough small people under one influence can defeat big people. Therefore, he usually only uses small words.

The reason for this is, following the progression of his speech, that the small people who use small words have a legal right to that which made the big people big and which is being criminally withheld from them. Again, the dichotomy of big and small is here an economic distinction and not yet a racial one. Malcolm suggests that the small people to whom he speaks built the country with their forced labor and that because it exists by their toil, the wealth of the country is theirs:

> I might stop right here to point out one thing. Whenever you're going after something that belongs to you, anyone who's depriving you of the right to have it is a criminal. Understand that. Whenever you are going after something that is yours, you are within your legal rights to lay claim to it. And anyone who puts forth any effort to deprive you of that which is yours, is breaking the law, is a criminal. And this was pointed out by the Supreme Court decision. It outlawed segregation. Which means segregation is against the law. Which means a segregationist is breaking the law. A segregationist is a criminal. You can't label him as anything other than

that. And when you demonstrate against segregation, the law is on your side. The Supreme Court is on your side. (1964a, 321)

While not a racial distinction, it is a categorical definition of the division of labor made identifiable by race. The small people are the descendants of New World African slaves. They have a natural legal right to the wealth produced by their labor, indicating that, for Malcolm, by natural law one owns what one produces. The Supreme Court, for instance, upholds or strikes down laws that are a priori illegal and any entity thus acting illegally is outside the boundary of natural law. For Malcolm, by law of nature, African Americans own the wealth of the United States.

For Malcolm, not all African Americans wish or deserve to share in this wealth. Discussing racial nationalism in terms of revolutionary love, after a brief account of revolutionary motives in recent centuries, Malcolm, in "Message to the Grassroots" (1963), insists that all revolutionary endeavor derives from love of the revolutionaries' race and the desire to build it a racialized nation, for "if you love revolution, you love Black nationalism" (265–66). Black revolution is Black nationalism, which is a celebration of the independence of the race. Malcolm then cites his famous analogy of the house and field slaves, elaborating that the African American who does not love revolution does not love the race, preferring that of the master. The field slave embraces her racial identity and hates that of the master. The analogy of the revolutionary field slave and the accommodating house slave hinges, then, on both race and class. Indeed, it is not even an analogy; it is a genealogy of Black revolution and counterrevolution in America, in which the Black bourgeoisie plays the role of assimilationist race traitor to the line of the heroic race- and revolution-loving Black nationalist field slave/lumpenproletariat.

In order to establish his credentials as part of the lumpenproletariat while simultaneously explaining how he came to speak so well without a "white" education, Malcolm begins his "Saved" chapter with the scene of language acquisition through writing. He describes his attempts to write for the first time to Elijah Muhammad from prison and how he struggled with two things while composing the letter: he feels he does not possess the appropriate language skills to record his thoughts on paper in a fully coherent and eloquent manner, and his penmanship is so poor that his text cannot be deciphered, at times even by himself. He writes in *The Autobiography of Malcolm X* (1965): "I was trying to make it both legible and understandable … and I apologized for my poor letter" ([1965] 1992, 195). Indeed, Malcolm writes over twenty drafts, attempting to make at least his text legible to the prophet, which he apparently does, as he receives a typed response that "had an all but electrical effect upon me to see the signature of the 'Messenger of Allah'" (195).

The contrast between the two letters is for Malcolm literally illuminating, for it contains both the great admiration and the disdain that would characterize Malcolm's relationship with the Imam in the future. For as unsophisticated as Malcolm's letter may have been, it was still organically authentic. Elijah Muhammad's calculated rejoinder, while not cold, is canned and could have been sent to almost anyone writing from prison, which Malcolm suggests by the response's rote scorn for white institutional criminalization and most notably by the typed missive's lack of personal touch, even in the sense of the letter's material production. Malcolm indicates this also by recording that the prophet's letter almost had an electrical effect on him. Playing with artificial notions of enlightenment (artificially produced electricity instead of natural enlightenment), the prophet leaves Malcolm in the dark, no matter how stimulated he may be by the Imam's real interest in him.

Malcolm signals this by recounting that Elijah Muhammad promised him "true knowledge," which Malcolm places in quotes as if to disown the very idea of such a thing issuing from this source. He goes on to relate that the prophet included five dollars in that first envelope, something he does for prisoners to whom he writes. Malcolm relates that the prophet "told me to have courage. He even enclosed some money for me, a five-dollar bill. Mr. Muhammad sends money all over the country to prison inmates who write to him, probably to this day" (195). By including this information, it could be said that Malcolm laces his description of his conversion with pointed criticism for the man who purportedly inspired it, suggesting that the Imam was buying loyalty with five dollars and a form letter. In this respect, there is something casually demonic about Elijah Muhammad, as Malcolm describes him. It is the same quality Malcolm assigns to himself in his unenlightened past as a thief. This dark period in his life vanishes only when he, after a week of trying, is able to kneel before God. He states that his inability to kneel easily was due to the evil he embodied, meaning that supplication before God is possible only once inner evil is overcome. Malcolm believes that, for "evil to bend its knees, admitting its guilt, to implore the forgiveness of God, is the hardest thing in the world. It's easy for me to see and to say that now. But then, when I was the personification of evil, I was going through it. Again, again, I would force myself back down into the praying-to-Allah posture. When finally I was able to make myself stay down—I didn't know what to say to Allah" (196).

After this event the narrative accelerates temporally as Malcolm's previous life is erased or purified by the light of God, so much so that "I would

be startled to catch myself thinking in a remote way of my earlier self as
another person" (196). To ground himself in his new life, Malcolm relates
that he wrote to Elijah Muhammad every day, yet he does not mention if
the prophet wrote back. He does make clear that, of the scores of letters he
sent to anyone and everyone he could think to write to about the Imam's
teachings, only his family and close friends responded. "Every letter I received from them added something to my knowledge of the teachings of
Mr. Muhammad. I would sit for long periods and study his photographs"
(196). All past associations are mediated by photographs of the prophet, as
Malcolm integrates his lives. Malcolm writes to pimps, pushers, con men,
and other criminals he knew in his previous, impure existence, attempting to spread the word to them, as perhaps Paul once did—to no avail. "I
never got a single reply," he writes. "The average hustler and criminal was
too uneducated to write a letter. I have known many slick, sharp-looking
hustlers, who would have you think they had an interest in Wall Street; pri-
vately, they would get someone else to read a letter if they received one.
Besides, neither would I have replied to anyone writing me something as
wild as 'the white man is the devil'" (197).

Having no specific address for most of these ex-associates, Malcolm
sent his letters in care of bars, halfway houses, and other public and semi-
public spaces, hoping that they would be read communally.[5] As he notes,
most of the people to whom he wrote were illiterate and had to have their
letters read to them. In other words, with his letters Malcolm attempts to
educate all of Harlem much in the way Paul sought to teach all of Chris-
tendom through the epistle form. What Malcolm sought to teach is unclear
through the strict content of his autobiography, as he here does not quote
directly from Elijah Muhammad, writing instead that he spent hours contemplating the prophet's photograph. Malcolm's teaching was his own.[6]

Musing on the fact that his letters detailing how the white man was
the devil always passed prison censorship—including those letters sent
to high-ranking white government officials and even to the president—
Malcolm surmises that his scrawls, as he calls them, were allowed through
because the white man knows that he is the devil and therefore approves
of being so described. Malcolm states plainly: "But at that time, I felt that
the real reason was that the white man knew that he was the devil." Yet
there is an implicit question in this statement, namely: How was Elijah
Muhammad able to trawl the prisons for membership in the face of censorship and surveillance? By introducing this question, even tacitly, Malcolm raises a suspicion and a critique. His praise of Elijah Muhammad in
relating the prophet's role in his conversion is Janus-faced, in that Malcolm's use of language suggests that, unbeknownst to him at the time, the
Imam is a false prophet running a racket. Simply put, Elijah Muhammad is

a conman much like Malcolm himself was. If the prophet's letters, money, and message pass through censorship and flourish in prison, it is because the prophet is in league with the white devil. That said, Malcolm's letters survive censorship and surveillance because he is still using Elijah Muhammad's words, which have already been approved by the white devil, and therefore belong to the white devil. When Malcolm states plainly that the censor recognizes his own acknowledged evil in the letters and general activities of the Nation of Islam, it is because the white devil dictates these seditious activities to him. In order to say something truly dangerous, truly "sacred," Malcolm will need his own words.

Malcolm notes that as a hustler he was hyperarticulate, being the most well-spoken man on the street. Yet this form of linguistic competence was limited to what he refers to as slang.[7] Being unable to speak and write in "proper English" is of course now an issue, as the manner in which Malcolm wishes to engage the matter suggests that the thoughts he wishes to express to Elijah Muhammad and to his own readers can only be related in the standard form of the language. This is why Malcolm "became increasingly frustrated at not being able to express what I wanted to convey in letters that I wrote, especially those to Mr. Elijah Muhammad. In the street, I had been the most articulate hustler out there—I had commanded attention when I said something. But now, trying to write simple English, I not only wasn't articulate, I wasn't even functional. How would I sound writing in slang, the way I would say it, something such as 'Look, daddy, let me pull your coat about a cat, Elijah Muhammad—'" (197). That is to say, slang is both inappropriate to the content of his conversion and to the idea of effective political agitation Malcolm wants to enact. In this respect, Elijah Muhammad has achieved the high linguistic competence necessary to intervene in these matters. However, this does not mean that by having done so his words automatically relate inherent truths that accurately portray the sociopolitical nature of Black life in the United States. Properly used, hyperarticulate English can also lend rhetorical force to a higher sort of conman.

Noting that anyone who would hear him today could never guess that, formally, he had little more than an eighth-grade education, Malcolm informs the reader that his true formal training in language arts came in prison and was inspired by his desire to write effectively to others about his political and religious concerns and to communicate well with Elijah Muhammad.[8] He was also motivated by conversations with Bimbi, who could take over a discussion with references to authors and ideas he was familiar with through his extensive reading. In other words, Malcolm understands that language is literary power. In its acquisition and exercise, he seeks the same influence possessed by Elijah Muhammad, yet with an authenticity of character that Malcolm represents textually in his constant return to handwriting, as opposed to typing. The handwritten letter is as authentic as the voice, indicating the integrity and honesty of the speaker and transforming the high culture hustle into heartfelt concern for the community and the race. Malcolm must therefore enter the master's discourse yet retain the legitimacy of character that will enable him to become master of the fate only language may determine.

The method by which Malcolm learns new words is simple yet ingenious:

> I saw that the best thing I could do was get hold of a dictionary—to study, to learn some words. I was lucky enough to reason also that I should try to improve my penmanship. It was sad. I couldn't even write in a straight line. It was both ideas together that moved me to request a dictionary along with some tablets and pencils from the Norfolk Prison Colony school.
>
> Finally, just to start some kind of action, I began copying. In my slow, painstaking, ragged handwriting, I copied into my tablet everything printed on that first page, down to the punctuation marks. (198)

The comprehensiveness with which he does this is matched only by the industry of his zeal, which is itself underscored by the fact that he performs this work in his "ragged" handwriting, which, previously illegible even to himself, he can now read: "Over and over, aloud, to myself, I read my own handwriting" (198). Indeed, Malcolm writes that while reading and copying the dictionary, with "every succeeding page, I also learned of people and places and events from history. Actually the dictionary is like a miniature encyclopedia" (199). The state of the legibility of Malcolm's handwriting is that of his soul with regard to the level and intensity of encyclopedic knowledge he possesses. He reads his handwriting, sometimes aloud, now capable of expressing himself properly, authentically, and in a way that imparts knowledge to others. The process of learning to speak well as a form of social power comes about in tandem with gaining knowledge of the self through writing. Malcolm's self-insertion into the master's tongue allows him to find his own voice of mastery, indicating that language in itself is race blind, even if its usage is utterly conditioned by race and racism. Speaking and writing well does not amount to speaking and writing white. Quite the opposite: it is a way of harnessing the power inherent in language and using it against the way in which the white power structure perverts the spoken and written word.[9] To do so, however, requires a critical knowledge of linguistic being and expression and the understanding that "white" and "Black" language use are equally ideological, with both favoring white supremacy.

Malcolm is amazed to find that there are words in the world he had never known existed. The fascination with which he explores and digests the dictionary reveals an understanding of words as material objects that can be used as physical weapons with which to conquer and shape reality as the speaking subject sees fit. The material world is therefore constructed out of language, insofar as calling a thing by its name both conveys information properly and acts creatively to bring the thing into existence as a social fact. Malcolm remembers many of the dictionary entries he copies, to a large extent photographically, as the act of writing is also for him that of mnemonic inscription. He recalls in particular the definition of the word "aardvark," which is also accompanied by a picture of the animal:

> I woke up the next morning, thinking about those words—immensely proud to realize that not only had I written so much at one time, but I'd written words that I never knew were in the world. Moreover, with a little effort, I also could remember what many of these words meant. I reviewed the words whose meanings I didn't remember. Funny thing, from the dictionary first page right now, that "aardvark" springs to my mind. The dictionary had a picture of it, a long-tailed, long-eared, burrowing African mammal, which lives off termites caught by sticking out its tongue as an anteater does for ants. (198–99)

Malcolm's aardvark serves as the perfect example of his understanding of language as material-social fact.[10] For it shows the nature of African American consumption in all things, including the acquisition of higher linguistic learning, as the self-directed excavation of a buried or hidden form of sustenance that, in itself, seems of little value yet which can destroy an entire home from the inside if left unchecked. In other words, in Malcolm's seemingly innocent description of one of the words he seems to remember as if almost by happenstance, the termite is just as important as the aardvark. Malcolm gives a clear sense of the aardvark's physical difference, while refusing to describe its main feature, its nose, choosing instead to portray it as an almost physically endearing animal that through the work of its prodigious tongue is able to collect its prey. Malcolm thus omits the snout so as to emphasize the tongue, which can also be read anthropomorphically as linguistic ability. The process of lapping up termites places the dictionary in the analogous position of the wood-consuming termites. Malcolm (who notes the large size of his ears on occasion) seeks to appropriate words as the means by which to rot the edifice of white power from within. He will do this through the acquisition of linguistic skill usually possessed only by whites that will allow him to subvert their words-to-power at their definitional source. The dictionary is the wood in which the big-eared African aardvark roots for both sustenance and weapons.

Observing that the dictionary is actually a type of encyclopedia, Malcolm turns worlds in his mind as he lay atop his bunk letting time pass without notice as he digests book after book, which he can now understand. Reflecting on this experience, he is able to "suppose it was inevitable that as my word-base broadened, I could for the first time pick up a book and read and now begin to understand what the book was saying. Anyone who has read a great deal can imagine the new world that opened" (199). For each word carries within it a world unto itself, unlocked by literature of all sorts. Malcolm appears in his recollection of this period as a type of monk scribe working from dusk till dawn not in a prison but rather in a monastery. Indeed, he states that during his time incarcerated he had never felt so free in his life. Be that as it may, this period of intense study and learning is punctuated by the faith in Elijah Muhammad that started it. Yet it is driven more ferociously by Malcolm's deep desire to dominate those around him, including whites in positions of authority, through the mediating power of language. The monastic image Malcolm presents captures well the zeal and effort with which he approached the task of carceral self-fashioning, yet it serves to obscure the worldliness with which he approaches the desired end of his scribal labor.

Charlestown State Prison had an extensive library, the posthumous gift of a wealthy collector deeply interested in history and religion. Academics from universities throughout New England lectured and taught there, and the incarcerated held debates in the old schoolhouse, where the library was also located, on topical subjects. Malcolm mentions one: Should babies be fed breast milk? That inmates of a men's prison should take up this subject serves Malcolm's rhetorical purpose, to show that the prisoners would debate passionately any socially relevant subject.[11] Yet it also shows the extent to which Malcolm's examples perform several textual tasks at once.

The communal space of the converted schoolhouse, where debates take place, books are kept, and reading tables provided, is literally the schoolhouse Malcolm refers to when he suggests that the education of the general African American community has to be organized by that community and practiced outside of white American society. Malcolm thus suggests a collusion between the white supremacist power structure and the nature of language, which was thought to be objective or inconsequential to that power structure by those it oppresses. Malcolm thus teaches that the language one uses also uses the speaker. To remain oblivious to this fact is to do so at one's peril, and at the peril of the race. That said, Malcolm also presents the acquisition of knowledge as autodidactic and as taking place literally outside of community, by electric light. Malcolm "confesses" that he "preferred reading in the total isolation of my own room," especially after "lights out" (200). Malcolm insists that he reads alone in his cell in the night, setting the stage for him to return to his metaphor of light and enlightenment when he relates how enraged he would become at "lights out" in the evening: "Fortunately, right outside my door was a corridor light that cast a glow into my room. The glow was enough to read by, once my eyes adjusted to it. So when 'lights out' came, I would sit on the floor where I could continue reading in that glow" (200). Playing hide and seek with a guard, Malcolm reads through the night, sleeping only about three to four hours a day, learning alone by his own electric lights.

Indeed, Malcolm claims he read the teachings of Elijah Muhammad the most and that his writings acted as a guide in prison for him and for all incarcerated Black men who were inclined to hear the truth in them. The encounter between prisoner, prophet, and public is the occasion for Malcolm's parrhesiac self-fashioning.[12] For when describing the content of the prophet's works that so struck the inmates, Malcolm does not write of a religious message and instruction of how best to celebrate faith and venerate Allah. Rather, Malcolm concentrates on the history of peoples of African descent that Elijah Muhammad recounts, and this history is what truly enlightens him. Referring back to his elementary school days in the South among all-white classmates, Malcolm recalls learning a version of world history in which Africans were mentioned only once. This "teaching moment" provided the teacher with the occasion to joke that the only thing Africans were good for historically speaking was their oversized feet and the crater-like footprints they leave behind.

Attempting to follow in these footprints for very different reasons than the schoolteacher had in mind, Malcolm begins to trace the African intervention throughout history, tracking it all the way to Toynbee, who claims whites are bleached blacks; that blacks are the source of civilization; and that Europe is merely an extension of Africa and Asia. He writes: "During the last year or so, in the *New York Times*, Arnold Toynbee used the word 'bleached' in describing the white man" (202). As Malcolm's focus in his account of his prison reading becomes world-historical, he relates that he focused on the work of various historians, philosophers, and theologians. He read only one novel. "Of course I read *Uncle Tom's Cabin*. In fact, I believe that's the only novel I have ever read since I started serious reading" (202).

Concentrating almost exclusively on works of history, philosophy, and religion—and *Uncle Tom's Cabin*—Malcolm outlines a plan and process of autodidactic learning that seeks to reshape the world as a textually mediated set of targeted historical phenomena related historiographically by sympathetic scholars. He "read Herodotus, 'the father of History,' or, rather, I read about him. And I read the histories of various nations, which opened my eyes gradually, then wider and wider, to how the whole world's white men had indeed acted like devils, pillaging and raping and bleeding and draining the whole world's non-white people. I remember, for instance, books such as Will Durant's story of Oriental civilization, and Mahatma Gandhi's accounts of the struggle to drive the British out of India" (203). This means that for Malcolm, historiographic writing is always subjective, as the facts presented, while objective, require a narrative in which to be set in order to have meaning to the reader and the lifeworld in which the text intervenes. Malcolm therefore understands that language, not events in themselves, is the site of hermeneutic interpretation and phenomenological understanding. In this respect, he is presenting parrhesiac self-fashioning in terms of transubstantiation, where the event in itself, even if it can be known in itself, is irrelevant in comparison with the manner in which it is introduced into and assimilated to the totality of social relations determining the political and economic conditions of its members.[13] Given his reading in philosophy, he has chosen the terms of his self-fashioning quite consciously: "Schopenhauer, Kant, Nietzsche, naturally, I read all of those. I don't respect them; I am just trying to remember some of those whose theories I soaked up in those years. These three, it's said, laid the groundwork on which the Fascist and Nazi philosophy was built. I don't respect them because it seems to me that most of their time was spent arguing about things that are not really important. They remind me of so many of the Negro 'intellectuals,' so-called, with whom I have come in contact—they are always arguing about something useless" (207).

The gesture toward Kant, Nietzsche, and Schopenhauer is not incidental, as Malcolm states directly that he read these specific philosophers during this time of incarcerated reading.

Malcolm therefore understands his critical engagement with language as one determined by power in its formative relation to the speaking subject as a social agent confined in its representation to a fixed limit of ideologically inflected positions. Here, linguistic performance measures the creativity with which self-fashioning as political submission or resistance takes place. Language is therefore a transcendental structure of social thought and being for Malcolm, conditioned and exploited by the subject's will in usage to decide the particular register of "rhetorical dissent" in any usable word, sentence, or phrase.[14] In this way, lexical attributes are inverted or otherwise exploited to create inner connections to ideas that run counter to the common ideological content and conception of the linguistic construction. Malcolm will thus pierce through the veil of the linguistically disseminated, psychologically invasive ideological attributes that form the basis of sociopolitical self-presentation and power, in order to force language to work against the interests of the master class it overtly serves. Malcolm's understanding of language and ideology thus follows the historical development of idealist philosophical thought beginning with Kant's critical-transcendental intervention in empiricism and concluding with Nietzsche's objectification of the will in rejection of Schopenhauer's subjectivism in the face of raw, world-shaping power. He uses the unfinished project of the Enlightenment as a weapon to wield against those who fashioned it.

These "Nazi philosophers," as Malcolm calls them, hold little of value for the activist, as they wasted their time—and that of their readers—writing about nothing of importance. Indeed, they remind him of the "Negro intellectuals" who expend their energy, and that of the public, debating irrelevant aspects of important issues. Malcolm's rejection of Kant, Schopenhauer, and Nietzsche as much ado about nothing rings false when these philosophers and the traditions of thought they represent appear cryptogrammatically in Malcolm's work. Indeed, Malcolm's understanding of ideology and power is in part derived from these writers. The works, which Malcolm states he read, are directly relevant to his understanding of language and power. However, because he labels these works "proto-Nazi," he cannot avow their contents. Kant is in the contradictory position of being simultaneously the father of Nazi ideology and a blowhard with nothing of interest to say. Indeed, the only philosopher Malcolm has any use for is Spinoza, whom he admires because he was excommunicated and exiled from the Jewish community and also because he was, according to Malcolm, of African ancestry. Malcolm admits:

> Spinoza impressed me for a while when I found out that he was Black. A Black Spanish Jew. The Jews excommunicated him because he advocated a pantheistic doctrine, something like the "allness of God," or "God in everything." The Jews read their burial services for Spinoza, meaning that he was dead as far as they were concerned; his family was run out of Spain, they ended up in Holland, I think. I'll tell you something. The whole stream of western philosophy has now wound up in a cul-de-sac. The white man has perpetrated upon himself, as well as upon the Black man, so gigantic a fraud that he has put himself into a crack. He did it through his elaborate, neurotic necessity to hide the Black man's true role in history. (208)

Malcolm then makes an implied connection between Spinoza's pantheism and African thought, where the idea of God in all things, as revealed in nature, harmonizes well with Malcolm's unspecified notion of an African philosophy that professes just that.

As Malcolm presents it, Spinoza's pantheism is in part produced by his Blackness as a type of innate response to the historical conditions of his life and thought. The excommunication and exile he suffers come as the results of racial difference displayed in Spinoza's deviation from the traditional image of the Western philosopher and by the eventual exclusionary reaction of the Jewish community in which his early, radical work comes to fruition, and which Spinoza's philosophy so grievously offends. Pantheism itself is in Malcolm's *Autobiography* no incidental suggestion but rather an indication of an ideological alternative to the Western philosophical tradition as generated from within it. It is also an attack on the nature and power of philosophical expression considered as a specific, yet highly abstract form of language use that promotes white power by the nonsense of its doublespeak. In some ways, Malcolm is closer here to Wittgenstein than to Nietzsche. Yet in combining a position that derides philosophy as meaningless prattle in relation to practical concerns while simultaneously being the highest expression of the linguistic will to power, Malcolm is able to claim that this discursive form more than any other has helped to perpetrate the biggest con in human history, that of white supremacy. Because it is nonsense, philosophy says nothing in itself. It is philosophy's use of language that gives its practitioner so much power. In this respect, philosophy as will to power is eminently practical.[15]

Malcolm uses his learning to great oratory effect for the first time in prison during the debates in the old schoolhouse. Here he could debate any topic as a means of satisfying the compulsion he felt while reading to tell the white man to his face that he is the devil; as Malcolm puts it: "And if there was any way in the world, I'd work into my speech the devilishness of the white man" (212). This accusation comes in the form of genealogical knowledge gained through the careful exhumation and consideration of overlooked or suppressed historical fact, combined with the stated desire to advance a contemporary political agenda that at times had merely a tenuous relevance to the subject matter at hand. The subject of mandatory military training for Ethiopians was easily assimilated to a debate about racism, allowing for the supposition that the white man was a force of evil so pure that he inspires an innate desire to combat him, even at the expense of one's life: "'Compulsory Military Training—Or None?' That's one good chance I got unexpectedly, I remember. My opponent flailed the air about the Ethiopians throwing rocks and spears at Italian airplanes, 'proving' that compulsory military training was needed. I said the Ethiopians' Black flesh had been spattered against trees by bombs the Pope in Rome had blessed, and the Ethiopians would have thrown even their bare bodies at the airplanes because they had seen that they were fighting the devil incarnate" (212).

Other topics, such as whether or not Homer actually existed and who was Shakespeare, share a common foundational literary theme where the

identities of the greatest language users in history are called into question
and then related to issues of race and racism:

> They yelled "foul," that I'd made the subject a race issue. I said it wasn't
> race, it was a historical fact, that they ought to go and read Pierre van Paas-
> sen's *Days of Our Years*, and something not surprising to me, that book,
> right after the debate, disappeared from the prison library. It was right
> there in prison that I made up my mind to devote the rest of my life to tell-
> ing the white man about himself—or die. In a debate about whether or
> not Homer had ever existed, I threw into those white faces the theory that
> Homer only symbolized how white Europeans kidnapped Black Africans,
> then blinded them so that they could never get back to their own people.
> (Homer and Omar and Moor, you see, are related terms; it's like saying Pe-
> ter, Pedro, and petra, all three of which mean rock.) These blinded Moors
> the Europeans taught to sing about the Europeans' glorious accomplish-
> ments. I made it clear that was the devilish white man's idea of kicks. Ae-
> sop's *Fables*—another case in point. "Aesop" was only the Greek name for
> an Ethiopian. (213)

Malcolm makes the etymological case via the name Omar that Homer
was a Moor and therefore Black and that he was blinded, as other Moors
were in ancient Greece, to prevent him from finding his way home. This
would mean that Homer was a slave poet unable to find his way back to
Africa, captured and exploited by a racial overlord who sealed off the enslaved from escape by mutilating their bodies such that they had no physical means by which to flee. This would also mean that the Homeric poems would contain within them a poetics of counterdiscursive form and
linguistic performance, which in fact Malcolm sees in Odysseus's attempt
to journey home. The returning, yet lost warrior would be the poet's avatar in his creation, inscribing the longing and pain of the abducted Moor
as he compensates for the hopelessness of his situation with the coded testimony of poetic creation. The true identity of Shakespeare, however, offers a different form of ideologically determined linguistic performance,
where Malcolm surmises through historical conjecture that King James
himself wrote the body of works assigned to the name Shakespeare. He
relates: "In the prison debates I argued for the theory that King James
himself was the real poet who used the nom de plume Shakespeare. King
James was brilliant. He was the greatest king who ever sat on the British
throne. Who else among royalty, in his time, would have had the giant
talent to write Shakespeare's works? It was he who poetically 'fixed' the
Bible—which in itself and its present King James version has enslaved the
world" (214). This would mean that the plays and poems seek to advance

a European, specifically English conception of royal prerogative and, ultimately, in its historical and geographical dissemination, white power, affording Malcolm another example of how linguistic skill and political strength are proportionately intertwined.

Whereas Shakespeare, or King James II as Malcolm would have it, uses a brilliant command of the language to advance the aims of royal sovereignty, Milton poeticizes to a different end, where *Paradise Lost*—and here Malcolm goes so far as to name the approximate edition he read in the penitentiary, volume 43 or 44 of the Harvard Classics series held in the library of a New England correctional facility not far from the university—rhapsodizes the devil's fall and early earthly activities in seeking to corrupt European humanity. As Malcolm describes it: "When my brother Reginald visited, I would talk to him about new evidence I found to document the Muslim teachings. In either volume 43 or 44 of The Harvard Classics, I read Milton's *Paradise Lost*. The devil, kicked out of Paradise, was trying to regain possession. He was using the forces of Europe, personified by the Popes, Charlemagne, Richard the Lionhearted, and other knights. I interpreted this to show that the Europeans were motivated and led by the devil, or the personification of the devil. So Milton and Mr. Elijah Muhammad were actually saying the same thing" (214). This distinction is key for Malcolm in that the poem in his reading of it delimits the satanic field of direct influence as Europe alone, describing great European figures of the church as unwittingly directed by the devil's invisible hand. This is a clear indication to Malcolm that Milton understands the true nature of European humanity as satanic, condemning his fellow countrymen and continental kin while providing a linguistic model, as another blind poet, for the counteroffensive ideological identification of white evil in history and eternity. In this respect, Malcolm understands Milton's and Elijah Muhammad's writings as consonant with one another.

Elijah Muhammad, then, poeticizes the idea of race as a prelude to the demonization of peoples of African descent, where the Black Other in his thought is related to the European devil as Adam in *Paradise Lost* is overcome by Satan. While Malcolm does not extend his reading of the poem beyond these few, highly general remarks, his clear contention is that white Europeans are responsible for the introduction of sin and death into the world through the myth of their racial superiority. Yet, perhaps more importantly, Malcolm introduces *Paradise Lost* into the discussion in order to present Satan, or the white man, as the Father of Lies who prefers the manipulation of language above all other forms of coercion and who, as in Shakespeare and Homer, presents a literary antagonist most like the demonic white European, by virtue of his unparalleled genius in linguistic manipulation. In this respect Milton, too, would be included as an avatar of the satanic power of language and writing, as his poem stands as one of the English language's most profound and beautiful achievements. Along with the devils Milton and Shakespeare, then, must be included the Moor Homer, Elijah Muhammad, and Malcolm X himself, who is well aware that he has sold his soul to the devil for the power to speak as well as the devil can.

In other words, Malcolm deals with the problem of linguistic appropriation in conformity to the master's tongue by negating the sense of dominance that inheres in the use of so-called white speech. He thereby rejects any notion, tacit or otherwise, that African American linguistic patterns in English constitute a language separate from the "standard" American variety. Racial-linguistic difference, while manifest at the material level of the spoken word, is not derived from "nature" but rather from the education that the state allows its citizens. Malcolm learns to speak with institutional political and social power once he gains command of standard English as an autodidact in the former schoolhouse library of Charlestown prison. Here Malcolm escapes the prison house of language by seeing the trace and signature of the structure beneath the surface and learning to navigate the complex interstitial spaces therein. He discovers them by transforming the governing metaphor of its architectural plan into a previously unassigned sociopolitical purpose. For Malcolm, prison, like language, is no longer a space in which he is hindered from developing further and exercising his powerful linguistic abilities. It is rather the opportunity to discover the depths of these talents and hone his skills to the point of absolute mastery.

In other words, Malcolm addresses the problem of adopting the master's tongue by insisting that the devil's bargain one strikes in so doing is not inherently racial but rather specific to language itself as an objective fact. The racial aspects of language are inscribed in it as and through racist ideology that seeks to naturalize the potential potency of linguistic performance to whiteness by infusing the history of its most astounding examples as fraught with racial conflict resolved only by language use itself.[16] That is to say, in the case of Homer, his linguistic gift only allows him to speak of irrevocable loss and the impossibility of returning home. King James II writing as Shakespeare uses his poetic genius to translate the Bible to ensure its place of preeminence among sacred texts and to establish the legitimacy of the divine right he claims over Christians and non-Christians alike, including the Africans being forced into slavery at this time as part of a Christianizing mission. Finally, Milton portrays the Mephistophelian nature of white men in such a way as to celebrate and glorify it while detailing metaphorically the manner in which linguistic power procures mastery through the belief that it belongs naturally to white men.

Malcolm thus recognizes a Habermasian public sphere and posits no Black counterpublic. Through mass media, his public interventions are meant to extend beyond any immediate audience to reach all public constituents. Like James Baldwin, Malcolm subverts "the King's English" in a reversed discourse that realigns signified meaning to speak against the medium of its signification. Malcolm's understanding of social utility, then, is utterly pragmatic; he does not recognize a naturally Black mode of speaking but rather the linguistic product of a specific set of social conditions and relations of power. Because of this, the self can be refashioned in language to take on any linguistically defined, social role and, in it, invert public discourse at will.

In this respect, Malcolm's understanding of language, identity, and power is Foucauldian; yet he diverges from Foucault in one very important aspect. Although he sees language as complicit in the sociopolitical construction of race, Malcolm nevertheless gives no indication he rejects the idea of racial essence. That is to say, unlike Baldwin—for whom race and language are intertwined existentially, making the question of racial essence if not moot then secondary—Malcolm sees Black essence as manifest in historical teleology. For Malcolm does not advance a theory of racial integration and transformation; rather, he posits historically driven racial conflict and political subversion, taking for granted inherent racial difference while assuming the possibility of linguistic infiltration. Malcolm investigates history genealogically to find the continuity of Blackness from Africa to all points in the diaspora, creating social solidarity and political friendship. For him, language does not express essence, it exerts intention.

In Malcolm's philosophy, racial essences are made manifest only teleologically, as historical phenomena. Their traces and trajectories are revealed in the hidden history embedded in language which, once uncovered, can be reoriented. In this respect, Malcolm sees language as the phenomenological site of Blackness, where historical being is revealed without social prescription or political position. This "openness" of language lends itself to ideological manipulation determined by the speaker's linguistic will to power. Language, then, is a single, contested field in which Blackness is revealed in the speaker's practice of signification. Race is a matter of linguistic intention, decided historically. While racially prescribed forms of address and expression exist, they are not prerequisite to utterance. Instead, they determine the historicity of any speech act as political. The historical end toward which any speaker or writer manipulates language signifies racial intentionality, politicizing the signature event context of all communication.

CHAPTER THREE

Black Aesthetic Autonomy

Ralph Ellison, Amiri Baraka,
and "Literary Negro-ness"

I. Invisible Essentialism

Writing to Baldwin in response to his 1962 *New Yorker* article, "Letter from a Region in My Mind," Hannah Arendt, in an unsolicited November 21, 1962, letter to Baldwin, communicates her displeasure. She suggests his essay is "a political event of a very high order, I think; it certainly is an event in my understanding of what is involved in the Negro question. And since this is a question which concerns us all, I feel I am entitled to raise objections." Not certain that Baldwin's essay is a *political* event, Arendt is clear that it is *an* event with regard to "the Negro question." For unlike Gadamer might, Arendt fails to realize that both Baldwin's letter of solidarity and her own to him are political events. That said, Arendt's "solidarity" betrays a hint of the type of racial essentialism that Baldwin's "linguisticism" rejects. For if the Negro question "concerns us all," she believes it does not do so politically, in the public sphere, but rather socially, in the private sphere. As she elaborates in her letter to Baldwin:

> In politics, love is a stranger, and when it intrudes upon it nothing is being achieved except hypocrisy. All the characteristics you stress in the Negro people: their beauty, their capacity for joy, their warmth, and their humanity are well-known characteristics of all oppressed people. They grow out of suffering and they are the proudest possession of all pariahs. Unfortunately, they have never survived the hour of liberation by even five minutes. (2006, 1)

Among other things, she seems to say that without inequality African American beauty, including in literary creation and linguistic improvisation generally, could not exist. In effect she posits that without suffering, African America as an aesthetic complex defined by race, disappears instantly. African Americans dwell in love and aesthetic beauty alone, alien to the politics of the public sphere. From an Olympian height, Arendt imagines African Americans as private aesthetic objects, and therefore incapable of the hermeneutic interpretation of their own aestheticized objecthood.

In "The World and the Jug" (1963) Ralph Ellison criticizes the "Olympian authority" with which Arendt, in her "Little Rock" essay, dismisses racial equality in the public sphere. He expands on this criticism in his 1964 interview with Robert Penn Warren, published a year later in Warren's *Who Speaks for the Negro?* (1965). In the interview, Ellison faults Arendt for failing to grasp that African American parents who send their children into the hostile environments of newly desegregated, "white" schools are introducing them to a social rite of passage required of all African American children.[1] For Arendt, the abstractness of the Constitution, and of federal legislation more generally, renders these forms of legal regulation untenable. "It has been said," she writes in "Reflections on Little Rock" (1959), "I think again by Mr. Faulkner, that enforced integration is no better than enforced segregation, and this is perfectly true" (Arendt 2003, 202). The "truth" of this statement is not "legal" in any positivistic sense; it is social, according to natural law. Arendt suggests that it "is therefore quite possible that the achievement of social, economic, and educational equality for the Negro may sharpen the color problem in this country instead of assuaging it. This, of course, does not have to happen, but *it would be only natural if it did*, and it would be very surprising if it did not" (Arendt 2003, 199; italics added).

To Ellison, in direct opposition to this idea, the goal of altered or invented federal legislation is achieved in order, ultimately, to foster a social climate in which the psychology of white supremacy can be transformed, not affirmed. Evaluating the situation as a literary critic might a novel, Ellison searches for aesthetic aspects of social structure in ritual, seeking to comprehend race relations as a series of acts of literary representations.[2] Effective and widely distributed literary representations depicting the full depth and scope of Black humanity, as well as the acknowledgment of the general possibility of those who create them, directly challenge social inequality with social responsibility.[3] This provocation includes the form in which the structure of the work of art speaks to and of racial injustice.[4] The manner in which the novel, for example, is written contributes to the work's ability to impress on its reader the ethical responsibility demanded by evident social equality.[5] Therefore, the literary work must be understood within the formal continuum in which it intervenes, as well as within the lifeworld of its author who, like Ellison himself, becomes a representative figure in race relations.[6] In this respect, the issue of African American literary form and its consonance with the most avant-garde techniques of aesthetic production have real effects in the struggle for representation in the presentation of Black lives' worth. Literature has the power to present all Americans as independently existing, equal human beings, as opposed to representing Black Americans as phantasmagorical supplements to superior Southern white identity.[7] Because of this, Ellison's conception of literary intervention in the social sphere has little to do with the specificity of a particular event and betrays a deep suspicion of civil rights legislation.

Disagreeing on the proposition that social equality is possible, Arendt and Ellison nevertheless agree that civil rights legislation will not resolve the issues at hand. Ellison shows an early ambivalence about the civil rights movement, reflected already in his second novel, which he was working on in the midfifties (Foley 78).[8] Ambivalence about King's rise to prominence seems to have played a major role in stalling the novel's completion. As Eric Sundquist writes, "*Three Days* was conceived before King became a national figure, as Ellison was constrained to point out when work on the novel stretched into its fourth decade; but the promise that King stood for animates the novel" (Sundquist 2011, 111).[9] A similar uncertainty appears to have compromised Hannah Arendt's view of civil rights legislation. Describing interracial marriage as social custom and potentially lawful act, Arendt writes, "every mixed marriage constitutes a challenge to society and means that the partners to such a marriage have so far preferred personal happiness to social adjustment that they are willing to bear the burden of discrimination. This is and must remain their private business. The scandal begins only when their challenge to society and prevailing customs, to which every citizen has a right, is interpreted as a criminal offense so that by stepping outside the social realm they find themselves in conflict with the law as well" (Arendt 2003, 207). While Arendt seems at first to speak in favor of decriminalizing interracial marriage, she ultimately concludes that the "moment social discrimination is legally abolished, the freedom of society is violated, and the danger is that thoughtless handling of the Civil Rights issue by the Federal government will result in such a violation. The government can legitimately take no steps against social discrimination because government can act only in the name of equality—a principle which does not obtain in the social sphere" (Arendt 2003, 208). Arendt believes this is ultimately because,

> What equality is to the body politic—its innermost principle—discrimination is to society. Society is that curious, somewhat hybrid realm between the political and the private in which, since the beginning of the modern age, most men have spent the greater part of their lives. For each time we leave the protective four walls of our private homes and

cross over the threshold into the public world, we enter first, not the political realm of equality, but the social sphere. We are driven into this sphere
by the need to earn a living or attracted by the desire to follow our voca-
tion or enticed by the pleasure of company, and once we have entered it,
we become subject to the old adage of "like attracts like" which controls
the whole realm of society in the innumerable variety of its groups and
associations. What matters here is not personal distinction but the differences by which people belong to certain groups whose very identifiabil-
ity demands that they discriminate against other groups in the same domain. (Arendt 2003, 203)

II. Baraka's Blues

Amiri Baraka (LeRoi Jones) might not have disagreed with Arendt about
any of this. He was among those African American writers who, like Ellison, were dissatisfied with the tangible results of civil rights legislation.[10]
Because of this tacit agreement between the two, Ellison was, perhaps,
not as critical of Baraka's work in his 1964 review of *Blues People* as is commonly believed. As Kimberly Benston writes, "In dealing with Ellison and
Baraka, the study of their innovativeness must begin in the study of their
attitudes toward the literary and cultural past. Just as their novels are organized by strikingly similar patterns, symbols, and didactic thrusts, so have
their cultural theories been focused upon several common issues. Foremost among these is their attention to Black music, and particularly the
blues, as the core of the Afro-American cultural matrix" (1976, 336–37).[11]
Benston articulates in 1976 what has since become commonplace, that
the blues form a paradigmatic part of African American literary production, including literary criticism and theory. Indeed, the "blues matrix"
makes it impossible to theorize African American literature without consideration of the blues.[12]

For Ellison, the blues are, as Shelby Steele has written, "a unique expression of Black American culture and no less than an artistic ritual of
transcendence. However, this view places him at odds with Black writers
like Imamu Baraka (Leroi Jones) who often view Black culture through the
prism of a particular political and social stance" (1976, 154). This idea is
consonant with James Baldwin's understanding of "the uses of the blues."
In his 1964 essay of that title, Baldwin writes:

"The Uses of the Blues" does not refer to music; I don't know anything
about music. It does refer to the experience of life, or the state of being,
out of which the blues come. Now, I am claiming a great deal for the blues;
I'm using them as a metaphor—I might have titled this, for example, "The

Uses of Anguish" or "The Uses of Pain." But I want to talk about the blues not only because they speak of this particular experience of life and this state of being, but because they contain the toughness that manages to make this experience articulate. I am engaged, then, in a discussion of craft or, to use a very dangerous word, art. (2010, 70)

The blues communicates a "state of being" that could be related by expressions of pain or anguish if not for a "toughness" that only the blues is equipped to portray. While the content of the blues, pain, and anguish is the same, the blues have a representational capacity to signify "toughness" that pain and anguish do not. The blues aesthetic is the formal art of toughness; it is situated in the world as the aesthetic ("rough" or "unflinching") representation of racism's existence. While similar to Ellison's idea of the blues, Baldwin's conception is not that of Baraka, who sees the blues as an aesthetic form of Black transcendence. For Baraka, the blues are a racial category of transcendence, not one of "artistic ritual" alone. Whereas for Baldwin, the blues, and therefore art, provides a hermeneutical analytic for race relations, Baraka hears the blues as positing Blackness in itself along with the material-historical conditions of its existence.

Because he is concerned with the essential or phenomenological expression of Blackness, Baraka grants that this can take any form, including, as Gerald Early once noted, political conservatism (1986, 345). As an early gesture toward both racial essentialism and contingent Black nationalism, *Blues People*, Gennari suggests, reads as "a brief for racial solidarity that anticipated the Black nationalist agenda. But it was also a modernist gesture redolent of the mass-culture critique formulated by 1950s left intellectuals" (2003, 256). The list of intellectuals Gennari gives—including Riesman, Whyte, Galbraith, Mailer, and Packard—should also include the earlier work of the exiled Frankfurt School writers, to whom the American intelligentsia looked for its philosophically reflective critique of the culture industry.

Ellison rejects Baraka's own "theory of reflection," which would see the blues as representing the totality of the African American lifeworld, preferring instead a racially inclusive theory of African American expressive culture that sees the ends of literature in teleologically integrative terms (Parent 2007, 134). Ellison sought to see the blues as an "American musical achievement," whereas Baraka was more concerned with their African American and African background (Tracy 1983, 16). The latter view sought to demonstrate "the existence of a long-standing and vibrant tradition of Black cultural agency" (O'Connell 2013, 64). Baraka believed that the jazz critic needed "native knowledge and understanding of the underlying philosophies and local cultural references that produced blues and jazz in order to produce valid critical writing or commentary about it" (1963, 24). On the surface, Ellison would not necessarily have disagreed with this statement. To have agreed with this statement, however, Ellison would had to have insisted that "native knowledge" be read anthropologically, rather than philosophically. Ellison was not concerned with the "underlying philosophies" productive of the African American cultural forms; he was interested in their generative rituals (Yaffe 2006, 94). Ellison's preference for anthropological discourse over philosophical speculation on the essence of Blackness did not preclude Black nationalism.

Indeed, Ellison "created an alternate nationalist vision predating the nationalism that subsequently rejected him" (Bland 2015, 59). This earlier nationalism was premised on the integrity of cultural exchange and the recognition of African America's contribution to American culture generally. Such a nationalism was at odds with the later, essentialist understanding of Blackness and cultural production. For Ellison, as English has pointed out, when the "trouble was, when it remained singularly Black, the consciousness produced in that assessment did not sufficiently pluralize its own condition" (English 2011, 16). While Baraka perceived in bebop the preliminary results of a fully autonomous blues aesthetic, free of the culture industry's determinative influence, Ellison heard the end of social ritual and the beginning of Black critical theory. His understated antipathy for bebop had to do with the futurity of its posture, which Ellison saw as a rejection of art's commemorative calling as a work of cultural memory (Anderson 2005, 281; Booth 2008, 684). Baraka had added a dimension to the tripartite structure of blues literature, which Gussow aptly sums up as blues form, blues content, and blues effect (Gussow 2018, 45). To the "blues literary tradition" Gussow identifies, Baraka would add the blues' reflection as the synthetic theorization of the total social and spiritual effect caused by the blues matrix, radically increasing its scope.

Ellison praises *Blues People* for its seriousness and scope. *Blues People* attempts to identify and explain the historical forces generating the blues, both in the music and in the culture of those who create it. The book then situates this explanation within the wider American culture, characterized by racial commodification. While Ellison recommends the use of sociology and history in jazz criticism, he notices that recent work by African American writers tends to include critical perspectives derived from the "Freedom Movement." Clearly showing ambivalence about this development, Ellison displays no hesitation when condemning Black militancy in criticism. He accepts as unavoidable, and perhaps commendable, that Baraka's book contains obvious critical views shaped by the Freedom Movement, yet he cannot see the critical value in Baraka's militant views. As a critical position, militancy forecloses on the possibility of objective historical, sociological, and anthropological considerations, in favor of a subjective conclusion selected in advance of the investigation.

Ellison believes that Baraka's militancy precludes him from reading the blues as poetry, forcing the poet to see jazz aesthetics in exclusively sociological terms. The issue, then, is not that Baraka refuses to pay sufficient attention to sociology, but rather that he misses the aesthetic construction and meaning of the blues. Furthermore, Baraka's militancy hobbles his ability to understand the blues both as music and as anthropological disclosure. Indeed, his strong sociological approach appears to preclude anthropological speculation entirely. For Ellison, then, militancy subjects critical views to a disciplinary tunnel vision that betrays the fullness and depth of anthropological phenomena.

From the historicist perspective, Ellison derides Baraka's sense that African Americans have somehow remained, both physically and culturally, isolated from the larger American culture in which they are embedded. He also criticizes Baraka for imagining that an African essence autonomously persists in African American aesthetic culture, to the exclusion of the wider American context in which it has been embedded since long before the United States came into existence. In other words, Ellison categorically rejects the notion that an autonomous African aesthetic obtains in African American expressive culture. He does not deny that African elements were formative in this culture and that they persist in its contemporary forms. However, he denies that any element of the blues aesthetic could exist autonomously from all of its constituent parts. For Ellison, there is no autonomy of African essence surviving in and indeed axiomatically structuring Black art in America.

To be clear, Ellison does see the blues as having aesthetic autonomy as an art form subject to critical appraisal "first as poetry and as ritual." The autonomous aesthetic aspect of African American poetics is translated into cultural action as ritual, after which it elicits a political response. In essence, the Black aesthetic is neither African nor American in American American expressive culture. It is the combination of both, expressed historically as a measure of two, mutually constitutive cultures. Ellison, then, takes issue with Baraka's understanding not of aesthetic autonomy, but rather of the culture industry and the class structure within which it is situated. By suggesting that jazz was appropriated by the culture industry in the 1930s and 1940s, Baraka establishes a racialized essence of African American aesthetic production that is revealed by the autonomous essence of Black art. Categorically rejecting this critical-theoretical understanding of African American expressive culture, Ellison insists on an anthropological, rather than philosophical, view of aesthetic autonomy that rejects racial essentialism, and the intraracial class warfare that is central to Baraka's militancy. For Ellison, this militancy makes Baraka tone deaf to the blues aesthetics' literariness, which is the universal aspect of all Black art.

Baraka, however, is sensitive to literariness as the unifying aspect of the Black arts. That said, his sense of the term is quite different from Ellison's. Baraka uses the word "literary" in two senses, neither of which is found in Ellison. The first relates to an arrangement of aesthetic elements, such that everything seems "premeditated," "definite," and "assimilated." This idea of aesthetic production values seamless improvisation embedded within a compositional strategy that retains the "fire and surprise" of Black art. It is not concerned with anthropological designations of universal cultural phenomena as they are expressed in their historical contingency. Baraka's view emphasizes cultural production over humanistic meaning, focusing on the roles of extemporaneity and revision in achieving arresting social effects of seemingly premeditated inspiration. The literary, then, is studied spontaneity in Black art and life.

Because of this racialized understanding of "literary," Baraka refers to the great jazz musicians of his day—"Trane, Ornette, Sun-Ra, Milford Graves, Tchicai, Brown"—as "the poets of the Black Nation." For Baraka, the artists of the "Black Nation" are all poets, or rather, the aesthetic production of the racialized "Nation" is a poetics. As social phenomena, jazz and poetry are indistinguishable in their effects. This conceit in Baraka's aesthetic theory drove Ellison to criticize the poet's lack of attention to aesthetic detail. He believed that, had Baraka paid this attention *Blues People* would have included a consideration of the anthropological aspects of African American expressive culture. Indeed, insisting on an anthropological mode of cultural criticism, Ellison refused to acknowledge *Blues People*'s primary methodological tactic, philosophical criticism. For unlike Ellison—who does not explicitly include philosophy in his literary and jazz criticism—Baraka openly insists that philosophy be used to comprehend race formation in American culture. In "Jazz and the White Critic," Baraka writes: "It is the philosophy of Negro music that is most important, and this philosophy is only partially the result of the sociological disposition of Negroes in America. There is, of course, much more to it than that" (1963, 17).

In indirect reference to Adorno, the "philosophy of Negro music" is juxtaposed with that of "the new music": "The attitudes and emotional philosophy contained in 'the new music' must be isolated and understood by critics before any consideration of the worth of the music can be legitimately broached" (1963, 19). Baraka's unattributed scare quotes signify the cultural capital of Adorno's work while condemning the coldness of its approach, and the "Olympian judgement" it uses to ascribe, however unconsciously, hierarchical cultural value to works of art. Despite these qualms, Baraka nevertheless integrates aspects of Adorno's philosophy of music into his work, avoiding the German philosopher's jazz essays and concentrating instead on *Philosophy of New Music* (1949) and Adorno's essays on music and language.

Much of Adorno's thought on music was available in translation by the time *Blues People* was published.[13] Although untranslated until 1993, Adorno's 1956 essay, "Music, Language, and Composition," contains much of his philosophy of music already published in English by that time. In it, Adorno insists "music is similar to language in that it is a temporal succession of articulated sounds that are more than just sound. They say something, often something humane. The higher the species of music, the more forcefully they say it. The succession of sounds is related to logic; there is a right and a wrong. But what is said cannot be abstracted from the music; it does not form a system of signs" (1993, 113). Language signifies beyond itself to form the linguistic sign as object of referentiality extending toward material elements obtaining outside the total systematic expression of its being. Music, while functioning in a nearly identical manner to language, does not form signs of reference to objects outside of its own set of elements, and it does not convey concepts beyond what Adorno refers to as a "primitive" version of conceptual signification. Musical concepts are contained in their signification to a self-reflexivity that can only conceptualize musical elements and are otherwise unable to approach the world as a semiotic system for communicating objective information about its contents. In this sense, music is always talking about itself, yet it does not do so essentially. For the innovation of the new music is to thematize this assumption of second nature, in which music abandons all pretense to providing epistemologically valid, objective knowledge about the world and examines instead the referential limits of its own sentence as a self-critical measure.

Furthermore, Adorno believes that music reproduces a specific aspect of language while otherwise distancing itself from language's referential function.[14] For music signifies itself as its organization and fundamental unity as a homogeneous totality in apparent difference, whereas language refers to objects outside itself, leaving its own structure and being beyond of the scope of its semiotic field. Language requires an external philosophy to address its essential being, while music provides its own philosophical explanation. Yet all that music is capable of signifying is itself. Its position as a historical and cultural force can be elucidated philosophically in the same manner as that of language, in so far as the appropriate philosophical understanding of music's material conditions and intervention in the world can be derived from extramusical sources and applied affectively. However, the being of music itself remains elusive, as the cipher for decrypting its signification lies within the enigma itself. In this respect, language and music are mutually constitutive as communicative systems, where language describes the musical event in its effects, and music contents itself with effectuating the phenomenological manifestation of language's form and structure in its essential mode of signification.

For this reason, Adorno rejects the notion of a pure musicality or an ontology of music that would be separate from language entirely. For if this were the case, music would no longer be able to signify anything at all and would instead become the medium of signification for the essence of music alone rather than that of human being as well. He writes: "If the dissonant harmonics had not always also sought the expressionless, it would scarcely have been possible for it to be transformed into the twelve-tone technique, in which, after all, the linguistic values at first recede very strongly in favor of constructive ones. This is how profoundly the antithetical elements are intertwined with each other" (1993, 119–20).

Music does not seek to express itself absolutely, as those composers creating in Hegel's wake believed. Music's expressive purpose is not to make music itself present absolutely and in effect demonstrate nothing other than the pure self-identity of its being, but rather to indicate the constitutive role history plays in musical composition and to measure the force aesthetic affectivity exerts on its social environment. Music, then, is not meant to be experienced outside of history as a transcendent form. Its essence is historical in its self-signifying power. Thus, music is eminently historical as a means of communication similar to language yet concerned with articulating an entirely different set of sociohistorical facts. Music's linguistic values are dialectically intertwined with its ineffable elements. Their tension generates the kinetic torsion of history's vortices balancing composition and informing critical appreciation from the perspective of social value and potential political intervention.

For Adorno, then, the attempt by composers to liberate music from its similarity to language characterizes the history of composition from Beethoven to the present. The rise and development of absolute music is in fact the product of this desire to emancipate music from its mimetic qualities and to differentiate its essence from that of language by denying it a signifying function altogether. Yet this attempt to create an absolute music that signifies nothing neglected to observe music's singular property, namely its self-referential character and the concomitant closure of its mode of signification to articulating objects in the world for reciprocal communication. Music allows for no dialogue outside of its inner dialectic of form and structure. The attempt to separate it from its linguistic capacity was doomed to failure. Serial music comes closest to succeeding by respecting language's inevitability in music and attempting to lay the linguistic character of composition bare by emphasizing the value of music's unique signifying practice as a content in itself capable of finding analogous forms and structures in social patterns and their categorical cognitive apperception. In this respect, the further music and language travel apart, the closer they come together, until they become indistinguishable as the expressive essence of signification itself.

Because music signifies nothing outside of itself, it refers instead to that which it is in its form and structure. Likewise, the form and structure of language are signified by that nonlinguistic element contained within it and which provides the existential shape of its historical materiality. At the center of any linguistic system, holding it gravitationally together is an aspect of signification that, unlike all other referential elements in language, refers to nothing beyond itself. Structurally and formally, this aspect of, or rather in, language is its essential musicality. Just as music contains language within it and becomes one with linguistic essence the further their historical being unfolds, so too does language have music at its center providing the differential basis for its expression in and as material history. The racial essence of language is music. In this regard, Adorno is merely reproducing Rousseau's reflections on the ontological relationship between music and language.

Baraka's "philosophy of Negro music" does this as well, accepting aesthetic theory as the basis of cultural criticism, while providing it with a new, ontological focus. The "philosophy of Negro music" conceptualizes the emotions the blues aesthetic embodies and provokes, rather than the cultural-industrial value derived from compositional technique. Baraka's understanding of the "new Black music" as "the new music," and as "the blues aesthetic," provides a cultural history of strong emotions and the philosophical evaluation of their social causes.

For Baraka in "The 'Blues Aesthetic' and the 'Black Aesthetic': Aesthetics as the Continuing Political History of a Culture" (1991), the blues encompass postbellum African American life, from its constitution as such beyond the oppressed form of socialization formed within slavery to the period immediately following emancipation, when African Americans experienced new freedoms and new repressive measures. He writes:

> The term "Blues Aesthetic," which has been put forward by certain academics recently, is useful only if it is not depoliticization of reference. So we can claim an aesthetic for Blues, but at the same time, disconnect the historical continuum of the Blues from its national and international

source, the lives and history of the African, Pan-African, and specifically Afro-American people.

The Blues Aesthetic is one aspect of the overall African American aesthetic. This seems obvious because the Blues is one vector expressing the material historical and psychological source.

Culture is the result of a "common psychological development." But the common psychological development is based on experiencing common material conditions which are defined, ultimately, politically and economically. (1991, 101)

The blues crystallizes and catalyzes the African musical forms of the plantation and adds to them newly accessible instrumental and compositional materials to create an expressive sound that captures the contemporaneity of its historical conditions. Sonically reflecting both the quotidian existence and the fundamental essence of African American being, the blues provides the baseline of the Black experience in America and forms the basis of any authentic Black music, and of the Black aesthetic more generally.

That said, Baraka premises the blues aesthetic on an essential African influence in order to describe a spiritual continuum in which all Blackness is one.[15] Without modesty, he writes, "If we study Equiano, Du Bois, Douglass, Diop, Robert Thompson, and LeRoi Jones we will see that the single yet endlessly diverse African cultural matrix is the basis not only of what's called the Blues Aesthetic, but any Black Aesthetic" (1991, 102). That is to say that for Baraka, whereas the blues may still encapsulate for dialectic African American history and sociality in terms of their form and function as mutually constitutive and functionally identical, it is now also the embodied spirit of Blackness as manifest in its African origin. It is "the changing same" of "new Black music."

In "The Changing Same (R&B and New Black Music)" (1966), Baraka insists that we "can use the past as shrines of our suffering, as a poeticizing beyond what we think the present (the 'actual') has to offer. But that is true in the sense that any clear present must include as much of the past as it needs to clearly illuminate it" (1966, 188). The suffering of the past informs the present, and is made present, in the new Black music. As part of African American expressive culture, the new Black music is a cultural poetics rather than an isolated art form. This fact of its existence allows it to give aesthetic form to autonomous cultural aspects of African American history, which can be discerned critically as the negation of the culture industry. In this respect, Ellison is right about Baraka's jazz poetics. Baraka is not primarily concerned with the musicological properties of jazz as isolated, purely aesthetic properties, or with its ritualized social construction of race. Rather, the poet reads all Black art, including the new Black music, as the free play of spiritualism at the center of secular, Black literary culture. "Ornette, Archie and Cecil," Baraka writes, are "three versions of a contemporary Black Secularism" (1966, 191).

He goes on to suggest that the

> freedom they, the music, want is the freedom to exist in this. (What of the New? Where?) The freedom of the given. The freedom to exist as artists. Freedom would be the change. But the device of their asking for this freedom remains a device for asking if the actual is not achieved. "Literary Negro-ness," the exotic instance of abstract cultural resource, say in one's head, is not the Black Life Force for long if we are isolated from the real force itself, and, in effect, cooled off. Cool Jazz was the abstraction of these life forces. There can be a cool avant, in fact there is, already. The isolation of the Black artist relating to, performing and accommodating his expression for aliens. (1966, 191-92)

In Baraka's estimate, "they"—Coleman, Shepp, and Taylor—are the music, of one essence with it, and this essence is freedom. The desire of the new Black music is to actualize this freedom in American social existence as recognized historical fact rather than have it remain existentially unfulfilled human potential. Baraka, however, qualifies this freedom as the opportunity to be an artist. Because he sees this freedom as the ontological condition of African American being, to be African American is to be an artist, which is in itself the essence of freedom. African Americans must be allowed to be themselves, as artists, in order to be free, and to be "freedom." Black art, then, is Black being, and the meaning of freedom in America.

"Literary Negro-ness" describes the rigid, strategic expression of this being. It is not of the essence, as is freedom, yet it is indispensable to expressing Black being as freedom, provided its creative idiom is historically appropriate to the matter at hand. In this sense, Baraka calls "Literary Negro-ness" an "abstract cultural resource" because it must possess the plasticity to conform to Black being in any of its historically contingent phases. When it does not, it becomes "isolated" and "cooled off." In other words, it ceases to be relevant to the signification of Black art as freedom, as has occurred to jazz and blues that have been appropriated by the culture industry. For Baraka, "literariness" is the racialized ("Negro-ness") cultural form through which the aesthetic essence of Black being is expressed as freedom in Black art. "Literary Negro-ness" applies to all forms of Black cultural expression, and the Black aesthetic's formal presentation is considered as literary, and not musical. Ralph Ellison's critical thought had both more to fear from, and more in common with, Baraka's blues aesthetic than he cared to admit.

Yet for Baraka, this "Literary Negro-ness," signifying Black being-in-freedom, does not present the same image of African Americans in each type of Black aesthetic product: "Content Analysis, total content. Musical, Poetic, Dramatic, Literary, is the analysis in total, which must come, too. But, briefly, the R&B content is usually about this world in a very practical, where we literally are, approach" (1966, 193). The poet recognizes an order of presentation in which the image of the "Black man" is either more immediate or more abstract. In this scheme of aesthetic representation, R&B possesses the ability to describe the "Black man" with the greatest immediacy, and therefore with the greatest accuracy. As Baraka writes, the "Black Man in R&B is the Black Man you can readily see. Maybe Sadder or Happier or Swifter or Slower than the actual, as with all poetry, but that average is still where the real is to be seen" (1966 195-96). Although each art form belongs to the same totality of representation, the individual presentation of Black life achieved by each particular art form provides an image of the "Black man" at varying degrees of accuracy. R&B uses a model of "Literary Negro-ness" that values the highest degree of accuracy among the Black arts, enabling the "reader" to recognize the "Black man" easily as he is "to be seen." "As with all poetry," R&B signifies in its literariness the being of the poet and the people of which she sings. For Baraka, "literariness" is the phenomenal material of racial ontology in its aesthetic presentation. It is the aspect of racial being open to hermeneutic investigation.

When Baraka praises Sonny Murray's 1963 album, he singles out the last track without specifying that it is called "Black art," for which Baraka provided the lyrics and voice. This track, however, is not an example of literature working with jazz; rather, it is an instance in which lyric participates in the literariness of the music in which it is embedded. Reciprocally, "Black art"—as the representative cut for lyric poetry's reflective relationship with music in the aesthetic totality of the blues—shows the extent to which poetry is part of the same "realist" continuum of accurate representation to which R&B belongs. Indeed, all forms of Black arts are literary, in the critical, hermeneutical sense described, in terms of their racial historicity and their ontological claim to freedom.

As Ellison perceives, Baraka understands Black aesthetics' formal development in relation to "the Freedom Movement." The desegregation of schools is mentioned in this context as the measure and summation of 1950s American racial conflict, where the decision that this antagonism could be "legislated away" has more merit as an index of the aesthetic state of jazz than it does of the logical congruity of foundational ideals animating the American state. Jazz both responds to history and shapes it, in that the refusal of the racial autonomy inherent in authentic African American musical expression both reflects and fortifies a social obstinacy that rejects integration under any terms other than that of unconditional equality.[16] All other measures remain superficial, much like an empty gesture in jazz expression, which is exactly how Baraka understands the dominant jazz style of the latter half of the 1950s, citing 1955, thus giving historical priority of influence to the 1954 Supreme Court decision. School integration found its proper voice and false hope in hard bop. As Baraka writes:

> The Supreme Court was trying to answer James Edwards' interrogator, with its 1954 decision, to integrate the schools "with all deliberate speed." Now in 1963, nine years later, integration has not been fully accomplished, and in a great many cases where it has been, there is mere token integration. But the internal strife in the United States between Black and white has at least been formally acknowledged as a conflict that might conceivably be legislated out of existence, though again it is the sixties that must test the validity of this desperate hypothesis. The fifties was a period of transition, in many aspects, of beginnings and endings. (1963, 217)

Baraka begins his exploration of "the modern scene" with two citations. One is an intentionally tautological statement on the definition of the blues from Ernest Ansermet's early 1918 review of Will Marion Cook's Southern Syncopated Orchestra, which included Sidney Bechet, in *Revue romande*: "The blues occurs when the Negro is sad, when he is far from his home, his mother, or his sweetheart. Then he thinks of a motif or a preferred rhythm and takes his trombone, or his violin, or his banjo, or his clarinet, or his drum, or else he sings, or simply dances. And on the chosen motif, he plumbs the depths of his imagination. This makes his sadness pass away—it is the Blues" (Baraka 1963, 176). Ansermet posits that the blues begin with Black sadness. White sadness does not produce the blues. This means that the blues have a racial point of origin and a racially specific emotional core from within which improvisation and contradiction always and only come to be recognized as blues after the fact of their completion. The tautology lies in Ansermet's insistence that the blues become recognized as such at the moment sadness passes away through the music's intervention. In other words, the blues are simultaneously sadness and the absence of sadness. The blues are the cause, process, and product of catharsis, or the expunging of unwanted emotions through the recognition and transformation of their material-social source. The blues both exist and cease to exist, are present and absent at and in the same musical time.

The second is a quotation from Roger Fry, author of seminal studies of primitivism in modernism, including the one from which Baraka cites the following sentence, *Negro Sculpture*: "It is for want of a conscious critical sense and the intellectual powers of comparison and classification that the Negro has failed to create one of the great cultures of the world, and not from any lack of the creative impulse, nor from lack of the most exquisite sensibility and the finest taste" (Baraka 1963, 176). Here, Fry asserts that "the Negro" has the same innate artistic ability as any other racially representative artist and that Negro art as a whole shows all the characteristics of great aesthetic achievement. However, because the Negro has no indigenous critic to elaborate the universal concerns of art for the Negro according to specific Negro forms of aesthetic production, the art itself falls short of that of other races. Fry here means that there is a universal standard of aesthetic judgment that nevertheless finds specific art historical and epistemologically critical form through the transcendentally qualifying attributes of racial character. The task of the critic is to elaborate both those aspects of art that are universal and the practical, contingent way in which race transforms them in the historical production of art objects. Without this, the artist produces much as a child would, a state of physical and social development that Fry freely associates with the Negro artist. Art has a racially qualified and collaborative world-historical mission, in that it represents both the universal essence of human artistic production and the cultural specificity of race as a formative factor in the genesis and evolution of individual human histories. In this way, art produces epistemologically valid and valuable knowledge through its critically informed production. Without its indigenous critic, the art of the Negro is therefore not yet capable of yielding universal knowledge; rather, it offers only local histories of a childlike race.

These historical characterizations and qualifications of the blues that Baraka traces will return to his discussion in bracing and perhaps unintended ways, their pathways cleared by a sense evolution of the blues out of a socioeconomic context that is both restricted and enhanced by a racial essence expressed historically by the nature of its contingency within the totality of the aesthetic relations that determine the productive interplay between Black and white American cultural praxis. The dominance of the white commercial appropriation of authentically Black musical forms leads to a cultural and indeed existential reckoning for the Black middle class which, even when embracing its status as blues people—or those cultural agents that acknowledge and live within the fact of their social origins—nevertheless must reject this racial truth on an economic basis. For such an acknowledgment of Black culture does nothing to enhance the Black bourgeoisie's cultural capital and may even diminish it. The operative category in Baraka's consideration is economic rather than racial; yet race is an economic force that, through its commercialization, blurs the distinction between racial and class belonging in relation to cultural capital and aesthetic production. Due to their commodification and commercialization by the white culture industry, the blues cannot remain autonomous or "secret" as the art of Black culture. Baraka writes:

> As a folk expression of a traditionally oppressed people, the most meaningful of Negro music was usually "secret," and as separate as that people themselves were forced to be. ("The old blues reminds me of slavery," is the way many middle-class Negroes put it. And they could only think of slavery with the sense of shame their longing for acceptance constantly provided. Their Utopia could have no slaves nor sons of slaves.) But as the secretness and separation of Negroes in America was increasingly broken down, Negro music had to reflect the growing openness of communication with white America. The ease with which big-band jazz was subverted suggests how open an expression Negro music could become. And no Negro need feel ashamed of a rich Jewish clarinetist. (1963, 177–78)

Baraka thus introduces the notion of folk art as the autonomous aesthetic production of a racially and economically construed people. This formulation also includes an understanding of art's autonomy within these registers, such that this self-contained status that the work of art enjoys is contingent on the identification of the race as a biological entity and as an economic reality within and by which the physical essence of this racial being is elaborated culturally. In other words, Baraka jettisons Adorno's reading of jazz while adopting his theories of the culture industry and avantgarde. To these, Baraka adds race as a determinative critical-theoretical factor. For Baraka, peoples of African descent exist biologically as a distinct racial group, apart from those genetic elements defining whites; yet economic circumstances determine the cultural expression of this inherent difference. Where the art of this dialectic between race and economy is isolated so that the race is not undermined by economic imposition on its material culture by another race, the aesthetic product retains its racial integrity. Harding makes a similar point in his reading of Baraka's *Dutchman* (1964) alongside Adorno's review essay, "Wagner, Nietzsche and Hitler," published in English in the *Kenyon Review* in 1947. In this chapter, too, Baraka's understanding of the culture industry and autonomous art is derived from Adorno. Baraka deviates from Adorno's philosophy at the point of race. Race provides art with its autonomous element, allowing it to escape the complete commodification of the culture industry.

For Baraka, where the race is not diluted biologically, its cultural products may in intimate, quasi-private settings reflect accurately the singular beauty, or rather the beauty of the singularity, of the race. For this reason, Baraka does not offer here a reading of race as an economic phenomenon but rather as a real and meaningful biological distinction that is expressed socially through economic means and ends (1963, 185–86). The manner and mode of this expression are the aesthetic properties and products by and through which racial essence is articulated, historically and materially, as intimacy. The privacy of the small band allows jazz to remain "pure," as do the sociopolitically individual and collective attitudes and relations associated with intimacy—so long as the integrity of the economic conditions on which their historical-material articulation is premised remains intact. However, where the closed aesthetic life of the race has been infiltrated by racially eccentric economic interests, its aesthetic-cultural reflection—that which articulates the being of the race—becomes incapable of performing this task, no matter the intellectual commitment the compromised individual and community maintain. For Baraka, the Black middle and upper classes are excluded from authentic racial expression, regardless of their sympathetic social and racial identifications. In this way, Baraka sees the Black proletariat as the revolutionary subject, thus reconciling before the fact the potentially competing interests of race and class within a Marxist critical paradigm.

In other words, Baraka does not, as did Wright, Ellison, and others, dramatize the seeming incompatibility between race and class as codeterminative historical forces shaping the fate of nations because of their inability to reconcile the priority of one or the other as history's prime mover and teleological end. Rather, the elements of cultural production Baraka emphasizes are dialectically identified and informed by their respective domains, each dependent on the other for its sociopolitical expression within the historical-materialist paradigm of critical thought. Race can exist as a historically and ontologically definitive form of social being without being shaped by economic forces. Black culture retains purity of expression, avoiding the invasive precision of industrial commodification that is yet to find a marketable product within the Black body of culture it purports to create. In this way and through the wider, negative economic determinations of alienating commodification, the particulars of the Black socioaesthetic totality only seem to belong to the capital's reifying social process in which African Americans nevertheless participate, regardless of the commodity status of their expressive cultural objects. The two, race and class, come into transformative contact only at the point of the aesthetic product, where expressive culture is bought and sold. This means that Black art is both productive and the product of the race in a way nothing else is. Racial identity is therefore here considered unstable and always in re-action to, as well as productive of, racially recognized arts such as jazz.[17]

In this way, racial identity itself would be the autonomous element of art and not some abstract aesthetic principle or property belonging exclusive to art's domain. Here art and race combine and are indistinguishable outside of the culture industry's commodification of them. Indeed, for Baraka that commodification directly entails the separation of art and race, or rather the creation of a distinction between the two, for marketing purposes. Baraka does not mean to say that race and art are nothing more than sales categories. Rather, he insists that race and art are in their autonomy structurally the same and that the identification of two different sets of cultural products and practices—racial and aesthetic—is the creation of a commodity market in which both will be sold separately and interchangeably. This does not mean that race-art was not for sale as a commodity previously, but rather that its consumption was, as it was, the index of aesthetic-racial achievement. The early production and dissemination of the blues by record companies respected the unity of art and race, yet the appropriation and recommodification of the blues by white musicians split the autonomous work in two, essentially alienating it from itself.

Indeed, Baraka insists that jazz and the blues retain their integrity as Negro music despite their entrance into and embrace by the recording industry and their increasing popularity on radio and at live venues. Black music was able to protect its secret even during this time of expansion and increasing material enrichment. The secret of the blues was that which it held back from, or was simply unrecognizable to, white audiences, with its core of racial Blackness that could not be bought and sold so long as it remained either unrecognized, unacknowledged, or a mystery to its non-Black auditor. The blues possessed an insider's experience absent among whites that prevented it from succumbing entirely to the process of commodification characteristic of the culture that it had entered. In this sense, the Black experience is the autonomous aspect of the blues, qualifying it as an avant-garde art regardless of its sales figures. This also means that art's autonomy for Baraka is not merely bound to the blues: it is its integral yet unblemished racial character. Art is segregated within, giving autonomous life to its production and experience. Likewise, commodification here means the invasive appropriation of this autonomous aesthetic-racial element for white commercial ends.

The appropriation of race's aesthetic autonomy suits the needs of the culture industry and the larger ideological-political complex it serves. Unlike Ellison, Baraka believes that the culture industry's ideology of race intervenes as a powerful economic and ideological weapon in American social relations and determines much of jazz production. For Baraka, the shift from jazz's aesthetic autonomy to the jazz commodity occurred during the midcentury war years, which necessitated yet again African American participation in foreign combat and greater inclusion and earning potential in a depleted domestic workforce. When the promises of social and political integration and advancement extended by these needs were not honored in the war's immediate aftermath, civil unrest was met by brute force combined with a subtler and more invasive cooptation of Black culture as a means of neutralizing racial resentment and its expression as open revolt. The first attempt to achieve a radically increased appropriation of Black racial autonomy can be heard clearly in the swing music of the 1940s, which incorporates increased elements of African American expressive culture while still allowing its autonomous aesthetic essence to remain elusive.

Swing's appropriation of all elements of African American musical expression, aside from the autonomous core of racial-experiential identity, is facilitated and solidified by the existence of the Black middle class as a culturally assimilated elite that nevertheless became alienated from, yet still attached to, the center of its essential racial being. The dialectic of race as social essence and class as the historical modulation of this essence for its cultural-political legibility within the wider American socioeconomic scene continues even in the swing era, because the blues had yet to be appropriated and reified by commercializing capital for the purposes of profit and the political suppression of violent revolutionary impulses awakened by the broken promise of equality. Assimilation was not equality; rather, it was a form of social control practiced because this autonomous racial essence remains elusive to the culture industry. Count Basie was able to retain blues elements in his swing orchestrations that were able to speak to the younger generation of Black musicians who could not be heard by white practitioners, allowing for the racially coherent development of bebop as the new home of autonomous Black music in America. Baraka thus links the survival of this autonomous aspect of the blues in the 1940s and in the face of the rapidly increasing commercialization of the big band to the rise of the saxophone as the primary instrument of jazz, as well as to the proliferation of smaller, individual-oriented complements of jazz musicians.

Highlighting Coleman Hawkins and Lester Young, Baraka shows that their movement away from the big band format to small groups of musicians allowed them to preserve the aesthetic autonomy of the blues that eventually came under threat from the mechanized nature of swing production in large orchestras. Indeed, without this retreat into smaller, more intimate ensembles, the swing orchestra's market hegemony and concordant mode of aesthetic production might have erased the essence of the blues from jazz altogether. This essence was revived and kept alive in small bands that eschewed such commercialization at the level of musical arrangement, if not always at that of intent. For Baraka, the centrality of the saxophone soloist among a few other players could not accommodate the scale of the culture industry's factory-like jazz (re)productions. The direct progenitors of bebop dropped out of the swing system; in so doing they saved the aesthetic autonomy of blues people, for here Baraka is concerned with ordinary people as much as he is with music and extraordinary musicians. Indeed, in his understanding of jazz and its history, there is no way to distinguish the folk from their music.

The Great Migration and the establishment of Black life in urban centers shifted the parameters of assimilation's negotiation between acceptance in equality and submission to white supremacy under altered economic conditions. By the 1940s, according to Baraka, it was clear to both urban and rural Black populations that no matter the attainment, African Americans would never be accepted in equal partnership due to the very fact of their Blackness. In other words, Blackness itself, and not some level of socioeconomic and educational achievement, was the barrier imposed by white America against blacks to assimilation in terms of equality and social responsibility. This meant that commercial success in swing, for instance, was premised on race, where only the white composer and bandleader could enjoy unmitigated financial success. Baraka understands equality economically as racially equal earning potential from cultural goods that are otherwise equal in quality. Furthermore, while the "quality" of their jazz might be equal, Black jazz retains an autonomous, aesthetic-experiential element that resists commodification in this way, and thus becomes universally valid.[18] Black jazz is therefore philosophically superior to and more critically vital than its white counterpart. Yet, this aspect of the music must necessarily remain invisible to market forces and their price estimate of quality.

That is to say that blues autonomy, and that of avant-garde art more generally, is the essence and substance of racial experience outside of its commodification and commercial classification in the culture industry. Race is therefore an aesthetic experience articulable in music and other art forms outside the industrial complex of its mass production in the small, semiprivate venues in which the public sphere is limited in expression to a self-selecting audience drawn by racial affinity recognized through similar socioeconomic circumstances. The Black middle and upper class are doubly alienated from the autonomous element of bebop, in that, though the racial component of the music may still speak to them as an echo of an earlier, less commercialized period in the history of the blues, their economic status withholds the unmediated utterance of the blues sentence while simultaneously closing them off socioeconomically from the community capable of both hearing and responding to the blues call. The Black bourgeoise loses her authentic relation to the essence of Blackness and the African American community as it is conditioned economically. The bourgeoisie both conceptually and historical-materially is a thing of whiteness. To enter it as an African American is to embrace and become utterly determined by racial despair—a type of philosophical ennui akin to what Kierkegaard describes in *The Sickness unto Death* (1849).

Bebop, however, is still susceptible to white appropriation, for according to Baraka, the Great Migration caused a certain unavoidable level of urban integration that enabled white consumers to hear the otherwise enclosed, private sound of Black blues autonomy, allowing them to ape it to a certain extent.[19] This means that white beboppers could talk and walk the part of their Black counterparts, to be certain; however, Baraka denies that this appropriation entailed the assimilation of Black aesthetic identity as a means to the imperialist commercial ends of white popular culture. Instead, Baraka follows the social logic of this appropriation to the logical conclusion that whites talking or playing bebop attempted to reproduce nonconformity as a borrowed mode of rebellion that was the fundamental socioracial condition of all African Americans. While the white bebopper can evince this imposture at will, Black Americans never cease to be beboppers in this essential way (Baraka 1963, 189). For Baraka, then, the ontology of bebop's fundamentally counterpositional social relations is absolute and absolutely African American. All authentic American sociopolitical resistance reflects the existential nature of Black rebellion in America.

Black music in the 1940s maintained its status as autonomous by insisting on a new conception of the Black musician as an artist rather than a sui generis product of the folk. Baraka understands that the folk label became a branding tool for hot music and that as such it attempted successfully to commodify and commercialize the notion of Blackness as an aesthetic principle. This product of Blackness in the culture industry entering the 1940s was thus a parody of that which it purported to be. Unable to assimilate fully Black racial essence at the source of its canned entertainment, blues reproduction for radio and phonograph, and the sale of swing both live and in recorded form, thus occurred along the lines of approximation, much like the technology on which it relied. Indeed, for Baraka, all attempts by white musicians or by Black entertainers working within the culture industry are doomed to parody. Only the work of an artist escapes this fate, and such creators work according to the dictates of their art, outside the system. Bebop is outsider art. Even at its most commercially successful, bebop keeps its "secret" from white executives, audiences, and practitioners. As Baraka sees it, "For the first time critics and commentators on jazz, as well as critics in other fields, attacked a whole mode of Afro-American music (with the understanding that this attack was made on the music as music, and not merely because it was the product of the Black American). The point is that because of the lifting of the protective 'folk expression' veil from a Negro music, the liberal commentators could criticize it as a pure musical expression. And most of them thought it hideous" (1963, 190).

This autonomous, "secret" element is responsible for the attacks on bebop levied by cosmopolitan white art critics. Such critics "instinctively" react ferociously to music that is unable to be reproduced as Dixieland folk sound or smooth big band swing by white musicians as part of the culture industry, yet which is nevertheless still impossible to ignore or reclassify as something other than blues based. Arriving on the art scene by pathways paved by the culture industry, bebop introduces the Black avant-garde to the white public while still retaining blues autonomy. Bebop's rejection of the white appropriation of Black racial identity by the expressive means appropriate to its objective essence signifies the aesthetic intervention and elaboration in the field of racial representation regardless of the relevant and singular race thereby actuated and represented. In other words, bebop demands recognition as equal to all other modes of autonomous self-representation with regard to race in its apparitional field, that of commerce. Bebop's critics come forth, for the first time condemning an art derived from Black culture, because the music had the audacity to stay Black, resisting all forms of the culture industry's racial commodification.[20]

Ultimately, Baraka focuses and reflects on the negative critical appraisal bebop received when it first appeared, which emphasized what sounded to the white critical ear like musical nonsense, or the end of art itself, rather than avant-garde jazz's grand entry on the world-historical stage. Rejecting the label of "mere" folk expression, bebop takes its place among the avant-garde of the forties regardless of the white critic's acknowledgment, hence Baraka's epigraph on criticism's need for organic intellectuals sufficiently capable of appraising what white critics cannot. Furthermore, the self-determination of bebop is thus fueled by its racial essence in and as aesthetic autonomy, which remains independent due to the inability of the white critic to appropriate it to a Western critical paradigm for the historical elaboration of art. For at the moment jazz announces itself to be or contain an autonomous art form rather than exist in and for the culture industry as the product of an easily assimilated folk expression, its critical comprehension ceases, and the music is heard as un- or antimusic. To these critics, Black artistic expression cannot exist because blacks cannot be artists in the sense of art's autonomy beyond the commodification of folk productions. When Black art appears unmistakably as art, it is labeled nonsense or as an inartistic and thus offensive parody of authentic autonomous art. This statement on criticism again brings Baraka consciously back to the chapter's epigrams, which in this light he refers to as "lugubrious."

This excessive, indeed ostentatious, mournfulness is directed toward two aspects of the blues at once. The first is the incapacity of the music to provoke and provide a suitable form of criticism due to the nature of its unreflective, undialectical origin, that of abject sadness. In this respect, the critic mourns her own lack of a responsive, interrogative field of inquiry and the impossibility of a properly equipped and requisitioned stream of data with which to investigate the musical form. The second is the origin of the blues itself in mourning as a lugubrious reaction to objective social conditions. By limiting the blues at the point of the music's origin to sadness with no other critically constructive element present at inception and allowing for further elaboration in any other but the most emotive expressions of unreflective pain, the blues are denied any type of critical function whatsoever, regardless of a critical idiom's ability to recognize and expound on the music in sociopolitical critique. The approach to the blues that confines its subject to cathartic sadness alone fails to grasp the music as art, seeing it only as the commodity of a white counterculture.

Baraka focuses on the white appropriation of bebop's countercultural attitude in order to explain how the music comes to be popular without compromising the autonomous aspects of its racial core. To Baraka, the racial roles in the reproduction of art are now reversed. Previously, blacks were denied the status of "artist" due to the racist assumption that artistic achievement was congenitally impossible for them. Any evidence of artistic achievement was understood as the imitation or parody of authentic aesthetic production. This racist fantasy fueled the belief that blacks could never be fully assimilated to white culture as producers. This exclusion includes the ability to produce art's autonomy and thus the aspect of it necessary for offering the proof of "true" artistic ability and mastery. This evidence is essentially white and therefore impossible for blacks to manifest in any authentic way. Bebop's aesthetic autonomy is essentially Black and therefore the white musician's attempt to reproduce it falls into the same parody of which Black artists were accused.[21]

The distinction between folk and autonomous art is of decisive value in Baraka's thought, in which folk cultural production can be adequately assimilated by another folk or race for economic purposes, without a fundamental loss dealt to the site of the intervention's cultural origination. The commodification of folk music does not necessarily betray the racial origin in which the folk product in its first, untainted form abides. This is because, as the product of the folk, folk art is always collaborative and open to influences derived from outside the otherwise closed circle of its racial being. Folk culture itself is not racially pure but rather the product of the folk, which must not be confused with the race. The individual expresses the race in and through her autonomy as a racial subject drawing aesthetic forms and patterns from within, instinctually and in dialectical tension with a lived experience that is also based in part on the same racial instincts. The interplay of economy and racial disposition that produces the authentic lifeworld of the races, making them impossible to penetrate fully as the economically assimilating yet racially alien subject, also provides the basic formal structure of art's aesthetic autonomy as the articulation of racial authority. Folk music could never offer this, as it specifically suppressed this racially autonomous element of art in order to strive for the universality of expression as that of all "folk" and not of the particularity of one race in contradistinction to all others.

Music presents an essence of identity that transcends the materiality of its folk designation, naming instead the inherent rhythms of the "race" that reveals the sociopolitical continuum in which all races appear both as they are and as the dominant modes of economically determined aesthetic and cultural reproduction. These basic rhythms in African music were at odds with those present in the economically and culturally dominant polka and military marches, such that they ceased to play a decisive role in African American musical expression. Yet the echo of African rhythmic necessity is at the origin of jazz, expressing natural rhythms and covering them with the artifice of the polka and the military march. This mixture produces bebop while shrouding and protecting its recalcitrant African essence as the autonomous—because unexpressed yet formative—core of its artistic achievement. Bebop presents the negation of African rhythm as racial essence. This African racial essence itself is for Baraka the negative dialectical moment of authentic aesthetic production. He believes

by borrowing the principle of a two- and four-beat bar first from hymns and then from polkas and military marches, the American Negro made a sharp break with his African ancestors. However, his sense of rhythm was not completely at home in this rigid framework. An opposition arose between the container and the thing contained. Half a century after the birth of jazz, this opposition has not been smoothed away, and it probably never will be. The Negro has accepted 2/4 and 4/4 bars only as a framework into which he could slip the successive designs of his own conceptions ... he has experimented with different ways of accommodating himself to the space between measure bars. (1963, 193)

The text of this African authenticity is then read back into the history of jazz beginning with the blues as a layering of non-Western rhythmic patterns at the expense of a preciously hegemonic emphasis on melody. Indeed, Baraka seems to suggest that the primacy of melody racially characterizes Western music, raising the specter of classical music's infiltration of jazz in the 1940s and 1950s as a means to introduce and elaborate on this idea. Baraka is quick to assert the maintained integrity of bebop in the face of this pervasive threat of influence yet concedes that later developments in jazz in the 1950s consciously incorporate classical melodic themes as a means of musical exaggeration to kaleidoscopic yet critical effect. In it, the intentionally parodic element of transracial musical influence is reversed, as Black musicians openly mock the stilted and anodyne nature of Western, white melody. This allows Baraka to localize complex rhythmic patterns as the non-Western, autonomous musical element of African American aesthetic production, which he then is able to link to the blues, understanding it as the transhistorical, racial-aesthetic essence of blues expressivity.

This expressivity connects across time and musical form through a common approach to rhythmic progression and innovation, which according to Baraka has its foundation in African music. He hears in early blues a steady rhythmic instrumentation that extends or shortens according to the vocalization and lyrical phrasing of the singer, where rhythm is interpreted in its mutability to conform, complement, or conclude the artist's dexterity in improvised versification in combination with her carefully composed sense of lyrical rhythm and metric time. These fundamentally African aspects of the music transformed under the weight of historical contingency and socioeconomic expediency manifest throughout the history of African American music as inaugurated with the blues in this emphasis on polyrhythmic lucidity and improvisational variation at ever increasing levels of compositional complexity and sonic density. This leads Baraka to articulate his contemporaneity with free jazz and other forms of avant-garde jazz experimentation of the 1960s, which realize the latent autonomy of African American expressive musicality in its formal achievement in coordinating the free play of rhythms from all instruments dedicated to a single score. For Baraka, free jazz is the highest expression of the racial ideal that is the autonomy of African American art. This development, however, begins as bebop: "Bebop also re-established blues as the most important Afro-American form in Negro music by its astonishingly contemporary restatement of the basic blues impulse. The boppers returned to this basic form, reacting against the all but stifling advance artificial melody had made into jazz during the swing era. Bop melodies in one sense were merely more fluent extensions of the rhythmic portions of the music" (1963, 195).

Bebop, then, began this movement that would culminate in free jazz's polyrhythmic liberation of all instruments, yet which nevertheless conforms to a coherent compositional whole. Because it began the breakaway from mainstream jazz as fully realized by the culture industry in swing, bebop was bound to be heard originally as "weird," countercultural, and even dangerous by both the Black and white middle class, the traditional consumers of swing. The "weird" label is another way for Baraka to emphasize the aesthetic value of bebop, where art in order to be such must exist autonomously outside of the culture industry even when it is bought and sold as commodities circulating in the racial marketplace of culture. Bebop departs from the Black bourgeoisie and returns to the Black proletariat while remaining among the African American middle class, utterly impractical to the Black worker. Likewise, the white middle class sees this new form of African American aesthetic self-assertion as too odd to be entertaining and too Black to be of use to the white working-class masses. The question then becomes, who bought this music? Or rather, who sponsored it? Baraka's presentation does not clarify who consumed bebop, preferring instead to allow the thought that somehow bebop existed organically in nightclubs that operated as if part of a system of patronage from some past era of ascendant aristocracy. Indeed, it seems its connoisseurs are not consumers, in any proper sense—they are addicts. Baraka writes:

> The terms of value change radically, and no one can tell the "nodding junkie" that employment or success are of any value at all. The most successful man in the addict's estimation is the man who has no trouble procuring his "shit." For these reasons, much of the "hip talk" comes directly from the addict's jargon as well as from the musician's. The "secret" bopper's and (later) hipster's language was the essential part of a cult of redefinition, in terms closest to the initiated. The purpose was to isolate even more definitely a cult of protection and rebellion. Though as the bare symbols of the isolated group became more widely spread, some of the language drifted easily into the language of the mainstream, most of the times diluted and misunderstood. (There is a bug killer on the market now called "Hep.")

> The social and musical implications of bebop were extremely profound, and it was only natural that there should be equally profound reactions. One of these reactions, and one I have never ceased to consider as

socially liable as it was, and is, musically, was the advent and surge to popularity of the "revivalists." (1963, 201–2)

Baraka suggests that somehow this music not only *jes grew*, it also paid for
its own adolescence. Indeed, he posits a radical independence and isola-
tionism among bebop and subsequent Black avant-garde musicians that
he claims derives from the desire to present the Black artist as neither
house nor field slave, but rather as something utterly outside the realm of
slavery's axiomatic characterizations, signified instead by lifestyle choices
from type of dress to sort of recreational drug, with heroin addiction being
the pinnacle of social success in securing a position of righteous solitude
in a segregated society. Somehow, jazz artists are able to sidestep entirely
the need to support themselves economically. In so doing, they maintain
their standing as independent agents creating and supporting an economically autonomous art. In this respect, Baraka's notion of aesthetic autonomy indulges in pure fantasy, as indicated by its use of heroin addiction to
posit radical racial freedom rather than extreme dependence and destruction by means other than directly economic ones. Indeed, Baraka's bebop
artist exists outside the system entirely, yet somehow still has no trouble
procuring his "shit" (1963, 204–5).

To be clear, Baraka must posit an economically independent condition
for the "real jazz" artist in order to make the claim that the continuum
of race and economy as reflected at once in the culture industry and its
autonomous aesthetic Other ceases to apply to African American music as avant-garde jazz. Because of this, the dialectic of racial expressivity that previously prevailed in salable forms of Black expressive culture
grinds to a halt in bebop and has remained standing still since. In other
words, where jazz artists are dependent on white patronage of some sort—
understanding here that the Black bourgeoisie qualifies to some extent as
this because of their economic dependency on white culture—aesthetic
autonomy dies at the hands of the culture industry's racial appropriation
of authentic Blackness. However, where the jazz artist has no ties of patronage, or finds other ways to reject the cultural claims made on him by
white economic sponsorship, such as heroin, aesthetic autonomy becomes
possible. In other words, the economic structure of jazz has remained the
same; however, the music itself has opened new cultural means by which
to combat the economic imperialism of the culture industry's racial appropriation of racial essence. For

unlike Dixieland, this music did not conjure up any memories of minstrelsy
or blackface; in fact, quite the opposite, progressive jazz was probably the
"whitest" music given the name jazz to appear up until recent times. It was

a music that was at its best vaguely similar to what contemporary classical composers were doing. It was a self-consciously "intellectual" and intellectualized music, whose most authentic exponent was Stan Kenton, with compositions like Bob Graettinger's *Thermopylae*, *City of Glass*, and *House of Strings*. (Raeburn's music, for all his ambitions toward a "serious popular music," as titles like "Boyd Meets Stravinsky", "Yerxa" or "Dalvatore Sally" would indicate, still sounded quite a bit like bucolic mood music; "Mickey Mouse music" is a musicians' term for it.) (1963, 206)

After this assertion, Baraka then outlines the historical phenomenon that concerns him as much as any aspect of the culture industry. He notes that the reaction to bebop's self-asserted racial autonomy was a reactionary revivalist tendency that recapitulated the historically moribund New Orleans Dixieland jazz tradition, and in so doing raised questions about the origin of jazz generally. The ambiguity of origin the revivalists created in their reaction against bebop was seized on by white jazz critics "collecting hot," who began to develop a theory of two separate jazz traditions, one to which bebop belonged and the other characterized by a more authentic Dixieland jazz lineage. Bebop was so strange and threatening to white critics that they exploited an opportunity to disown it as jazz, making of bebop an unfortunate, racially parodic development in classical music rather than a phase in the logical evolution of Dixieland jazz itself and as a preliminary step in the aesthetic articulation of racial autonomy as a social force. This view of bebop allows for the formation of a legitimate white bebop tradition, because from this perspective the music originally derives from white sources. Bebop is thus a deviant form of classical music, while Dixieland returns the focus on jazz to its authentic being not as autonomous art but rather as folk expression.

The rise of progressive jazz—which Baraka understands as the white imitation, as opposed to appropriation, of bebop—serves to reinforce the notion of an autonomous racial element present not in its parodic negation in Dixieland jazz, but rather as revealed in the direct line of polyrhythmic associations that could be drawn through bebop to the current moment of free jazz. Unable to alter this essential racial core, white musicians taking up bebop's innovations in both musical form and social style remain a question for Black and white audiences alike, despite the fact that their product is still consumed in financially lucrative quantities. Granting that white artists continue to profit from the trade far more than their Black counterparts, the salient critical point Baraka wishes to make is that sales figures and contractually awarded dollar amounts do not define the appropriative work of the culture industry. Indeed, Baraka's great innovation, in the system of cultural criticism devoted to the culture industry as it pertains to race appropriation, innovation, and elaboration, is the insight that race as aesthetic autonomy exists and prevails in its purity depending on the intellectual reception of the consumer and not merely on money spent and profit won. In this way, Baraka sidesteps the question of patronage, transforming it into one not even of taste but rather of knowledge. The book *Blues People*, then, is meant to ensure the racial integrity of the current moment of African American cultural production by illuminating its true origins and thereby naming the stakes of its autonomy. The knowledge *Blues People* imparts is meant to protect Black music from appropriation by the white middle class.

A tension and resistance appear in Baraka's argument when he comes to cool jazz, in that it seems to derive from bebop and yet is dominated by white musicians, despite recognizing its founding father as Miles Davis (1963, 209). Indeed because of cool jazz's perceived formal beginning in Charlie Parker's rhythmic textures, it has achieved success while being associated with the blues tradition. However, Baraka states as an axiomatic given that cool jazz comes to prominence on the commercial basis of Dixieland jazz and through white performance, regardless of the prominence of Miles Davis and a few other Black cool artists. This means that the fault line separating the commodification of the culture industry and autonomous art characterizing and authenticating the aesthetic product of Black composers and musicians lies at the heart of cool, the origin of which is claimed by both Dixieland jazz, as the "arthouse" wing of a commercially vibrant music scene, and by the blues as the passage of certain bebop artists from the lesson of Charlie Parker and other boppers to the commercially successful yet still racially untainted and aesthetically autonomous Black musician experimenting with racially pure rhythmic expression from within the culture industry through conscious parody of the premises on which Dixieland achieves its popularity. Miles Davis masters the role of the racially compromised creator in order to weaponize conformity to the culture industry.

He does this by elaborating and extending Charlie Parker's rhythmic complexity, helping it to evolve by forcing it into recognizable standards that demand proven melodic patterns while still allowing for the free play of the sonic density that acts as a foil to easy compositional solutions based in traditions other than that of the blues. For Baraka, Davis is essentially a blues musician invested in the production and contemplation of the purity of sound through its defilement and ultimate absence. Those musicians under the spell of Lester Young's union of melodic enchantment and conjuration of sound purity depart from the realism of Parker's demanding polyrhythmic scheme in order to create objects of sound rather than reflect critically on the historical contingency and materiality of social sub-

stance as represented in multiple dialectical encounters of rhythmic relations. Young's followers produce an untroubled world of sound, whereas
Davis, and Young himself, display a world fraught with contradiction, distortion, and uncertainty, held together ultimately by the glory of the medium itself as a means of assuaging doubt by accurately articulating suffering. Where cool jazz closes its eyes, the blues are unflinching.

Combining racial history, essence, and constitution with asymmetri-
cal rhythmic stances understood to originate in the same triumvirate of
phenomenologically deduced experiences, Baraka describes and decries
the logic by which a bifurcated notion of blues beginnings is disseminated
to the Dixieland traditions and not to those of bebop. This distortion and
eventual exclusion of bebop's beginnings allows white critics to label it as
a grotesque parody of white classical music, whereas Dixieland jazz and its
most sophisticated variant, the cool style, represent the truth of essential
"Negro" expressivity. Against this, Baraka lauds the knowledge and mastery with which Black composers and performers reference the superficial aspects of the classical tradition in jazz. He also laments the extent to
which cool jazz has succumbed to its desire to assimilate to this tradition
while still presenting itself as the legitimate heir to the African American
musical heritage.

This lament is both part of and caused by Baraka's explanatory model
for shifts in style and substance in the history of jazz, here limited to the
twentieth century, which takes as its leitmotif and organizing principle the
dialectical interplay of a specific history as reflected as innovation in a particular aesthetic tradition. In this way, jazz history's variations and pro-
gressions authentically reproduce the truth of political economy from the
perspective of its material history. Baraka thus tacitly posits the priority of
popular entertainment as the proper site for the elaboration of social representation in its essential relation to political economic becoming, as well
as the central role that African American expressive culture plays in this
process. For African American art is the only autonomous aesthetic form
capable of withstanding the racially identified culture industry's commodification of all cultural forms, such that Black art can be seen as the only
legitimate source of cultural-historical knowledge, as given in and through
popular entertainment. The African American, therefore, is the true subject of American history, as she is the only racial subject capable of providing objective knowledge of the socioeconomic forces shaping historical
being (1963, 220–21).

Here Baraka substitutes Lukács's theory of the proletariat as the privileged subject of history through increasing revolutionary class consciousness with African America as the identity of a race-based subject of labor
that, through its aesthetic "secrecy," comes to know itself as the revolu-

tionary race that is shaped socially by the forms of labor imposed on it historically.[22] In its autonomous form, aesthetic labor rejects all other forms of labor entirely, making do on the dividends of an uncompromising art as offered up by the community itself rather than through the profits of the culture industry. Baraka thus presents a financial model of racial-aesthetic autonomy not as charity but rather as the proper monetary representation of the community for an essential function, undermining any sense of commodification by those for whom the music, as is the case, has meaning as a mode of the critical unveiling of self-consciousness. In other words, African Americans still consume bebop or free jazz within the structure of production and distribution provided by the culture industry. However, the way in which the music is heard determines its true value as either a commodity or an asset of awakening to revolutionary racial consciousness. This critical choice is not provided by "jazz" forms devoid of the autonomous racial element characteristic of the blues, without which Black art becomes white commodity.

Be that as it may, Baraka understands that esoteric, mystical, or rigorously and recognizably epistemological proclamations on the autonomy of Black art will fully explain its ability to circumvent conscription in the culture industry as one white commodity among others, even when produced exclusively by Black artists. He thus suggests a mode of social signification that subverts white racist stereotypes about African Americans by accepting them on the surface in order to keep white America at arm's length. The breathing room found in "Negro smell" and other odious attributes assigned to African Americans by a racist white public allows Black artists to keep their secret, which is the origin and strength of Black music and Black social being itself. The blues remain elusive to the white cultural-industrial complex as this racial essence is kept hidden behind a wall of racist tropes preventing whiteness from desiring to tear the veil and assimilate Black being. In this way, Blackness is left alone to plan, organize, and execute the task of social justice in America.

Notions of law and justice underlie the entirety of Baraka's presentation of blues people, in that the aesthetic outlined has as much to do with formal musicological attributes as it does the social and political concerns of a racially determined economic collective. The blues are not merely a catalog of elemental African American expressivity confined to the sphere of culture. Rather, the music is the direct articulation of a sociopolitical disposition determined by the material history of a race, where "race" has a combined aesthetic, biological, and economic meaning. Where the legality of racially determined governance established as constitutional right deviates from the authentic attributes of racial character, revealed in their legitimacy by authentic autonomous art and social being, any amendment to this constitution oriented toward aligning it more correctly with nature must in part answer for why the misalignment existed in the first place. That is to say, for Baraka positive law has no necessary connection to the cultural sphere in which the natural law of race is revealed. This revelation can be distorted by interference from legislation and judicial intervention, which need to be rejected, in favor of a Black hermeneutic of equality. Interpreting the union of "word and culture" is far more effective in the struggle for racial recognition.

The Revolutionary
Will Not Be Hypnotized

CHAPTER FOUR

Eldridge Cleaver and Black Ideology

I. Marcuse and the Minister of Information

Despite his deep admiration for Malcolm X, Eldridge Cleaver radicalizes Black ideology to exclude linguistic performance under the racial terms of the public sphere. Maintaining the idea of separate and unequal spaces, he rejects the desire to gain recognition from within the white-dominated public sphere and concentrates instead on intraracial acknowledgment. Looking at the work of its minister of information, this chapter shows that Black Panther Party ideology is centered on a project of racial enlightenment that rejects white recognition as a matter of course and focuses instead on African American self-perception. The cult of the Black self is, however, qualified. This Black lumpenproletariat are generally young, male, impoverished, imprisoned, and prepared to commit violent acts in the name of Black liberation. This subject rejects universal humanism and any notion of "brotherly" love in the name of the revolutionary embrace of Blackness.

Eldridge Cleaver's *Soul on Ice* (1968) advances a cosmology for sexuality—gleaned mostly from Marcuse's *Eros and Civilization* and Plato's *Symposium*—that encompasses a universal history with the material teleological goal of utopian harmony in social oneness. In *Eros and Civilization* (1955), Marcuse writes in this vein about different forms of violence. Criticizing the "strange myth according to which the unhealing wound [that] can only be healed by the weapon that afflicted the wound [and that] has not yet been validated in history," Marcuse concludes, "the violence which breaks the chain of violence may start a new chain" (1955, xxi). He goes on to speculate that "in and against this continuum, the fight will continue. It is not the struggle of Eros against Thanatos, because the established society too has its Eros: it protects, perpetuates, and enlarges life" (xx). Here, Marcuse differentiates two different types of violence. The struggle between Eros and Thanatos produces one type of violence, while the quest for justice engenders another. The former type is ultimately instinctual and ontological; the latter conforms to the social and historical patterns of the affluent society even while attempting to correct their oppressive imbalances. In other words, one order of violence obeys natural law and the other obeys the positive. Nature causes authentic, instinctual conflict, while the violence of the affluent society endeavors to suppress natural aggression. Violence within the continuum of the second order can only be met with more violence, yet this increase in violence will never redress the prior wrong, as both acts of violence belong to the same genre of aggression. Only violence that abolishes second order aggression completely can unleash the natural violence between Eros and Thanatos, which for Marcuse is the force of freedom, or freely flowing libido.

Marcuse frames his Freudian concept of Eros philosophically by recalling the psychoanalyst's explanatory reference to Plato. Following Freud, Marcuse notes that in Platonic philosophy sexuality is considered the atomic striving for reunification in matter's original state of oneness. The world was formed when matter was smashed into atomic particles, which sexual desire then seeks to reintegrate. Eros, then, is "the great unifying force that preserves all life." Nevertheless, for Marcuse "the ultimate relation between Eros and Thanatos remains obscure" (1955, 27). This is in part because Marcuse reads Freud as a dualist who only at the end of his career began to see the ontological polarity that defines the life and death instincts in nonoppositional terms. That said, the obscurity defining the relation between Eros and Thanatos that Marcuse attempts to penetrate may not lie in his reading of Freud, but rather in this secondary, indirect encounter with Plato.

Marcuse sees Plato as the starting point of Western philosophy's subjugation of nature in the name of reason. Plato initiates this campaign against nature with the antagonistic formulation of the relation between the *ego cogitans* and the *ego agens*. The "scientific rationality of Western civilization" pits the subject against the object, as nature comes to be seen as serving the purpose of the knowledge of the subject and the mastery that it enables. For Plato, base human nature needed to be overcome and mastered by reason, which existed apart from the realm of instinct as the element of divinity in the human being. Included in the base, instinctual life of humanity, yet still an essential aspect of the human being's higher purpose of cosmic reunification, sexuality was not to be denied but rather redirected toward proper sexual unions. For Marcuse, the assignment of sexual partners for philosophical purposes begins the repression of the instincts in the name of instrumental reason.

Marcuse sees Freud as recuperating "the early stage of Plato's philosophy, which conceived of culture not as the repressive sublimation but as the free self-development of Eros" (1955, 125–26). This means that, for Marcuse, Plato's thought is divided into two stages of development. In each, Platonic philosophy makes direct use of Eros differently, depending on the phase of Plato's career to which one refers. Concentrating on Plato's early work, the late Freud of the metapsychology adapts the idea of Eros as "free self-development" absorbed by logos, seeing it as a constituent part of reason. For Marcuse, the "repressive sublimation" of Eros reflected in the "history of ontology" begun in Plato's later thought rejects this understanding as irrational and excludes it from reason as "an archaic-mythical residue."

The philosophical categories that begin to appear in Plato and persist in the present are structured conceptually and linguistically to perpetuate the opposition of Eros and reason. Eros is suppressed by means of an "every-day language" that takes its sense from logos as the character of reason structuring quotidian life. The subject as a linguistic construction is constituted as a rational being whose integrity is apprehended ontologically as incompatible with the instincts. From Plato on, "the defamation of the pleasure principle has proved its irresistible power; opposition to such defamation easily succumbs to ridicule."

Marcuse's preference for Freud's later work is evident in his emphasis on the psychoanalyst's eventual use of the term Eros to describe the life instincts. Using Plato to underscore the sexual value of this term, Freud sees Eros as beyond sexual gratification in the sense that the life instinct becomes imbricated with the pleasure principle against the oppressive regime of the reality principle. Before adopting the, to some extent, Platonic sense of Eros, the pleasure principle in Freud could be distinguished from sexuality, with sexual behavior comprising one aspect of the wider apparatus of life instincts. In the late work, the network of life instincts is bound by libidinal sexuality, whereby instances of life expression are modulated by erotic energy. In this model, sublimation becomes the survival of unregulated, erotic impulses within the repressive order of the reality principle, a structural conceit that speaks against any Platonic idea of the reality principle. Freud appropriates Platonic Eros in order to undermine Platonic logos.

For Marcuse, then, Freud advances a later theory of nonrepressive sublimation to counterbalance that of the earlier theory of repressive sublimation. In the latter theory, sublimation acts in collusion with the reality principle, helping to constitute the subject in accordance with its laws. Erotic attachments are surrendered and transformed into acceptable objects and modes of social behavior. In this way, the Platonic logos attains social ascendancy over erotic irrationality. However, according to Marcuse, Freud's later theory of nonrepressive sublimation allows these unruly sexual attachments to survive in detached, obscured form. Here sublimation is not transformation to the point where the impulse cannot be recognized but rather a type of masking that leaves beyond recognizable traces of the impulse's true intent. Such impulses are then expressed in a way that lacks overt sexual intent and yet contain, because of nonrepressive sublimation, a strong, even if veiled, erotic aspect.

The consequences of this reading of Freud's late introduction of Platonic Eros into psychoanalytic theory are far reaching. They suggest that sexuality is polymorphous and socially productive, as the repressive order of the reality principle contains thinly veiled erotic bonds that help hold society together. This bond is sexual in nature, as the desire for any particular body speaks to the general desire for any body, by virtue of the desired body's shared characteristics with others of its type. The polymorphous sexual identification of others with a form of desire creates the social bonds on which the reality principle is premised, in effect conflating two types of love: Eros and Agape. For Marcuse, the "notion that Eros and Agape may after all be one and the same—not that Eros is Agape but that Agape is Eros—may sound strange after almost two thousand years of theology." Marcuse then departs from the letter of Freud's text for evidence of this, looking to Plato's *Symposium* instead for evidence "that Agape is Eros."

That said, the erotic impulse as Eros remains sublimated. While access to it is possible, it cannot be attained freely. Marcuse then asks: "How can civilization freely generate freedom, when unfreedom has become part and parcel of the mental apparatus?" (1955, 225). Being free to generate freedom means the end to repressive sublimation and the social clarification of that which was sublimated without repression. From "Plato to Rousseau," Marcuse complains, this could only be attempted through the "educational dictatorship" of the elite, who believed they alone possessed "knowledge of the real Good." To satisfy the needs of contemporary society, Marcuse instead calls for education's liberation, which would begin with an inclusive understanding of those who, in terms of intellectual capacity, could acquire the knowledge of the Good, or Truth. For implicit in Marcuse's reading of education "from Plato to Rousseau" is the notion that only the elite had the natural intellectual ability to acquire the truth. This prejudice must change, if "civilization" is to "freely generate freedom."

For Cleaver, this "freedom" would entail the return to humanity's original state, recognized as a single, homogenous identity. In *Soul on Ice*, he describes a "weird mitosis of essence" occurs at the moment the "Unitary Self" crawls out of the muck of the "Primeval Sphere," splitting in two, thereby dividing into male and female. Presumably, gender existed in this Unitary Self before its division or mitotic action, yet it reproduced asexually, or more accurately, through comprehensive autostimulation. Once gender segregated, these now-split creatures seek to return to their original state in an Apocalyptic Fusion. The use of the term "apocalyptic" indicates that history begins with this gendered schism and that it may only end with the elimination of the division. This means that material history begins with and is a record of heterosexual activity teleologically directed toward its own obviation. Given the centrality of sexuality in and as history, the Unitary Sexual Image of the normative heterosexual couple entails the historicity of the social response to material temporality, with the Unitary Society as the sought-after end of human self-alienation.

For Cleaver, the splitting and self-alienation that takes place primevally causes antagonisms to arise between individuals of each sex and between the sexes. Competition to determine and become the ideal human types or Unitary Sexual Images of each sex generates conceptions of gender and race. Yet the initial antagonism produced by the primeval mitosis itself is between classes, meaning that this division into sexes also entails the a priori appearance of class as a result of sexual separation. Class and sex are thus inherently linked, insofar as the primeval mitosis achieves both the creation of two sexes and the production of class as a biological reality. Distinctions such as gender and race form subsequently and as a result of the alienation that results from the initial, essential division of sex and class, or sex as class. For Cleaver, this also means that any deviation from the ideal Unitary Sexual Image is the manifestation of fundamental antagonisms within sex and between classes. Homosexuality would be, then, a perversion of alienation from both natural and teleologically vital sexual drives.

Within the alienated sphere of class society, the sexual images produced are those that reflect the social purpose of each class. Unlike homosexuality, which is a priori against nature, heteronormative sexual images are misaligned with that of the Unitary Sexual Image due to class differentiation and distortion, yet not as a result of a natural perversion. The labor each class performs determines its sexual image, which, despite being a deformed conception of the Unitary Sexual Image, is nevertheless appropriate to this primeval Unity. For Cleaver, then, those classes that perform intellectual labor project a sexual image reliant on the valuation of mind, whereas those classes that are consigned to physical labor present sexuality as strictly of the body. The former class of image belongs to the "Omnipotent Administrator," with the latter category representative of "The Supermasculine Menial."

The Ultrafeminine and the Amazon correspond to the masculine categories of mind and body defining the class society. These distinctions are for Cleaver alienated positions within an instrumental society separated from its own essence in unity. All societies possess the basic gendered class structure and corresponding sexual images described, yet the "racial caste system" is not requisite. That said, when a racial caste system is present in society, it becomes associated with the normatively gendered, mind/body division of labor, naturalizing sexual antagonisms. In essence, the addition of race to an otherwise normatively established class- and gender-based society creates an alternative natural history to that of the primeval unity, confusing society's proper teleological goal. In this respect, race both enhances and nullifies the historical purpose of sexual difference. On the one hand, it naturalizes it by making its distinctions essential to human being and becoming. On the other hand, it neutralizes it by distancing human being and becoming from its true goal: the unity of humanity in its original equality of all members.

For Cleaver, primeval unity is regained "naturally" through the alienation of class, which is overcome sexually. This redeeming sexuality chooses its images and attractions also "naturally," according to the division of labor, as represented by each class. However, where race is associated with class distinction, a false conception of nature is introduced into the system of restitution Cleaver envisions. Race, then, is unnatural, as it allocates some bodies and minds to the wrong class, creating category errors throughout the system provided by nature to return to it. The first antagonism that needs to be overcome is race, where present. If this is not done, race will be mistaken for nature, making it impossible to realize the primeval unity due to the proliferation of category errors in sexual imaging and attraction. All class conflict in a racial caste system must consider heterosexuality as a primary, normative, and integral part of its critical approach.

In "The Land Question" (1968b), Cleaver makes explicit that any discussion of Black liberation in America must be held in light of colonialism. African America is a "Black colony" in the "white mother country." Because of this, the only way to decolonize America is through violence, following Fanon's understanding of the historical relationship between colonizer and colonized in The Wretched of the Earth (1961). Indeed, Cleaver recommends the type of urban guerrilla warfare in the United States that is being fought in other nations in the global battle for decolonization.[1] He does not, however, here endorse uniting these struggles. This is not because he sees them as unrelated, but rather because they are a priori the same in his thought. His conspicuous gendering of "whiteness" as "mother" and the Black masculinist representation of resistance through its all-male cast indicate that the struggle for decolonization is to establish the racial hegemony of the Black Supermasculine, in effect clearing the field of racial caste by reducing race to one, and then allowing nature to take its course. For in the United States, African Americans have both mind and body, whereas whites have only mind.[2]

After King's assassination, Cleaver wrote a "Requiem for Nonviolence" (1968d), in which he makes clear that Black militants hated the civil rights leader just as racist whites did. Civil rights leaders were content to accept the logic of the white mother while Black (male) militants sat back and watched as the movement of nonviolence ended in the only way possible. Indeed, Cleaver sees the murder of King as the catalyst for revolutionary violence and liberation achieved as it must be, in blood.[3] For Cleaver, King's death exposes the civil rights movement once and for all for the sham that it was, a corporate-sponsored public relations pitch that catered to those who profited most from its life and demise. As Cleaver understands events, King had ceased to be profitable, politically and financially, and his death was one last cash grab, with the greatest beneficiary being Lyndon B. Johnson. That said, Cleaver writes a requiem for nonviolence, and not for King, who means little to him beyond his role as figurehead for nonviolent protest and the civil rights movement more generally. Cleaver sees nonviolence as complicit with the established, oppressive, racial regime, and believes that where the racial caste system prevails, violence must follow. Were it a natural matter of class alone, sexual instinct would achieve the elision of difference and the return to primeval unity.

Here Cleaver is again not far from Marcuse. As Marcuse remarks in "Problem of Violence and the Radical Opposition" (1967),

> opposition is concentrated among the outsiders within the established order. First it is to be found in the ghettos among the "underprivileged," whose vital needs even highly developed, advanced capitalism cannot and will not gratify. Second, the opposition is concentrated at the opposite pole of society, among those of the privileged whose consciousness and instincts break through or escape social control. I mean those social strata that, owing to their position and education, still have access to the facts and to the total structure of the facts—access that is truly hard to come by. These strata still have knowledge and consciousness of the continuously sharpening contradictions and of the price that the so-called affluent society extorts from its victims. (2005, 58)

Marcuse identifies the "underprivileged" of the New Left as geographically classifiable national and global minorities "found in the ghettos" and possessing "vital needs" mediated sociopolitically by colonialist and imperialist discourses. As a discursive formation, these "ghetto" communities have no internal cohesion and no demonstrable, active sense of organized resistance. Yet these same communities function effectively as a revolutionary "class" within a global conglomerate agitating against colonialism and imperialism as a coherent organic unit. Old Left Marxist designations of class confined to Europe and white America are no longer relevant by themselves to the critical conception of the revolutionary subject of history. The new proletariat is a mass of minority ethnicities and races where each alone is powerless. However, as part of the global-historical subject of revolution they unite to become the most powerful political force for human liberation. For example, minority communities in the United States are structurally incapable of effective political organization and agitation in isolation. In this respect, Marcuse takes the sheer weight of numbers to be decisive in both revolutionary ends and means, where an isolated minority community has no opportunity even to become politically aware of the radical social ontology of its political community. In other words, a single race alone is relevant in the sphere of revolutionary politics only in relation to other races. These races represent "mostly groups that do not occupy a decisive place in the productive process and for this reason cannot be considered potentially revolutionary forces from the viewpoint of Marxian theory—at least not without allies. But in the global framework the underprivileged who must bear the entire weight of the system really are the mass basis of the national liberation struggle against neo-colonialism in the third world and against colonialism in the United States" (2005, 58).

In this understanding of the social construction of this new revolutionary subject, Marcuse describes the global composition of the authentic apostles and adherents of the New Left, which entails for him a discarding of Old Left ideology construed narrowly as the Eurocentric, class-oriented calculation of the revolution's proper instigation. Marcuse's New Left leaves behind this limited conception of revolutionary history's geopolitical locus and the segregated human geography it implies in favor of a diverse, inclusive and global evaluation of the teleological development of human liberation, the evolution of which now agitates against the common enemy of oppressed minorities as created and characterized through colonialism and economic imperialism. The civil rights movement has its partisans among the New Left, yet it itself is not a product of and creative participant in the New Left in isolation in the United States. It can only be considered part of this wider movement when its means and ends align in solidarity and objective focus with those of oppressed minorities across the world. Any noninternationalist resistance of an isolated, segregated minority population is not part of the New Left and not considered by Marcuse to be political in nature.

Marcuse points out that the current focus of opposition is not on the traditional revolutionary groups and historical paradigms in Marxist thought but rather, as in the case of the civil rights movement, on artists, poets, and intellectuals. Unable to attain a position of political power through elected office or other means, the revolutionary forces of the New Left rely on agitative tactics appropriate to positions outside the political order proper, commensurate with these groups' standing within one-dimensional society as the administered yet unsatisfied subjects of monopoly capitalism. In other words, Marcuse here extends his presentation of "one-dimensional" man to include a depth within this single plane of being that, because of its racial difference within the homogeneous zone of satisfied desires, enables one-dimensional man to perceive a fundamental lack in the social being provided by monopoly capitalism in its strategic satisfaction of the base-level wants and needs of those whose lives it controls. Revolutionary resistance must come from social positions unaccounted for fully by monolithic monopoly capitalism as it eliminates difference in favor of an ideal global subject for exploitation.

In this vision of revolution, the civil rights movement becomes both the ideal mode of resistance to this inherently racist process and, simultaneously, doomed to failure if it remains isolated. For such isolation leaves it vulnerable to capitalist appropriation precisely through the means of its resistance, at the level of art, poetry, and intellectualism. The culture industry becomes the front line in the war of liberation (2005, 59–60). For Marcuse, this liberation is facilitated by the newly awakened student movement. Collegiate youth are finally aware of the realities of their democratic system, now that these facts have been revealed to them from behind a veil of ideological state apparatuses, capitalist commodification, and interpolation through market participant consent and consumption. Once the students awaken to these realities, they drop out of school to organize against recurrent and rebarbative instances of injustice, concentrating on two geopolitical contained, discordant relations between putative democratic practice and racial inequality: racial injustice and oppression in the segregated South and the destructive imperialist aggression motivating the carnage of the Vietnam War. These two events, the civil rights movement and the war in Vietnam, mobilize the student, motivating her to cease to be a ward of the state and become instead an activist warrior fighting on behalf of racial others and the dream that was lost to the nightmare of American democratic praxis. The student dropouts themselves are overwhelmingly white; therefore, the student movement is a rebellion against whiteness as much as it is outrage over insidious inconsistencies in the rhetoric and practice of American policy, foreign and domestic. The student movement is a protest against whiteness understood as racist violence, imperialism, and judicial oppression.

While Marcuse sought to find a language for a form of racial and sexual liberation that transcended heteronormativity and incorporated violence, Cleaver reinforced the homophobic claims of the revolutionary Black male subject. Although Cleaver lauded Marcuse and the New Left's ability to associate and galvanize several points of sociopolitical resistance, such as antiracism and antiwar protests, he drew the line where free love compromised the structure of heterosexual Black male potency as a revolutionary principle. In characterizing white men as effeminate and envious of Black male sexual potency, as he did in *Soul on Ice*, Cleaver makes use of Marcuse's concept of "surplus repression," or as Marcuse puts it, "the restrictions necessitated by social domination."[4] Surplus repression normatively reshapes the instincts to conform to the "performance principle" of totalitarian control, whereby each subject performs unnatural duties as if from nature. While Cleaver grants the reality of surplus repression, he rejects the indeterminacy of race and gender implied in Marcuse's understanding of nonpathological, or "basic," repression. Instead, Cleaver limits Marcuse's field of reference with surplus repression in order to exclude Black male same-sex desire as "natural" and therefore potentially liberating. Indeed, for Cleaver the embrace of any revolutionary position that does not extol the supremacy of Black male heteronormativity is a betrayal to the race and the racial class.

Because of the revolutionary consanguinity of erotic attraction, Cleaver in "A Letter from Jail" (1968c), claims that he "fell in love" with the Black Panther Party one night in February 1967. At a meeting to plan a commemoration of Malcolm X's death, Cleaver is awestruck when Huey Newton, Bobby Seale, and other Panthers walk into the room and he meets them for the first time. He is enamored of their uniforms, their weapons, and their readiness to commit violence in the cause of revolution. Cleaver identifies them, and Newton in particular, as the rightful heirs to Malcolm X's legacy of unified Black resistance. He writes that whereas Malcolm used language as a sword, Newton was the physical manifestation of this violence. Newton marked the choice of the bullet over the ballot and, for Cleaver, the fulfillment of Malcolm's movement to violent revolution.[5] Cleaver thus falls in love with Newton as the embodiment of Black revolutionary violence. His attachment to the revolution is one of love, even if he did not feel revolutionary love.

In three published "love letters" (1968) to his attorney, Beverley Axelrod, written along with *Soul on Ice* in 1965 while he was in jail, Cleaver spends most of his time emulating a demurring, sensitive, caring individual, only to reveal at the end of the third letter that he has been misrepresenting himself all along. Indeed, Cleaver unveils a type of monster that is simultaneously self-loathing and world-hating, to the point that he calls for a Black finger—his own—on the nuclear trigger, so that he may act out his nihilistic fantasy of apocalypse. Tellingly, he hates the Watts "insurgents" for showing the world that he is a sham, a "Tom," smiling for the world while having no interest in Black liberation. Indeed, for Cleaver, "liberation" means the annihilation of all. Empty, save for hatred, Cleaver confesses to being a conman in the context of a love letter, allowing him to consolidate the ruse, and power, by telling the truth to complete the lie. Cleaver's true love could only be the Black Panther Party.

This was not the only time Cleaver betrays someone he loves while in prison for the sake of Black nationalism. In "The Guru of San Quentin" (1967), Cleaver relates that his time in San Quentin was spent studying under its guru, Crist Lovdjieff. The "Saint of San Quentin" was a former schoolteacher who came to the prison to educate any and all who would care to learn, and Cleaver was perhaps his most engaged student. Under Lovdjieff, Cleaver studied intensely primarily Western and Eastern philosophy, reading Aristotle, Confucius, Marx, Lenin, Mao, and Merton, among others. Indeed, Cleaver he was "more exposed to Lovdjieff than to Watts," which means that the Watts exposure Cleaver mentions in one of his love letters is really that of a Lovdjieff student pretending to be a revolutionary. The instruction ends, however, when Cleaver's teacher asks him to write on universal love. Cleaver turns in an essay inspired by Malcolm X, indicating that, for historical reasons, it was impossible for him to love a white person. This leads to a conflict between mentor and mentee, ending in Lovdjieff slowly disappearing from the prison. Cleaver does not relate specifically why Lovdjieff stops teaching there, leaving instead the impression that both the fact that he taught interracial love, and Cleaver's rejection of it, made it impossible for him to continue instruction at San Quentin. Cleaver's revolutionary zeal had claimed its first victim.

Cleaver's time in prison is perhaps not as radically formative as that of Malcolm X or other Black activists of the period. Indeed, Cleaver seems to suggest that his prison education was decisive for his intellectual development as a radical philosopher open to a diversity of traditions. His perception of other inmates accords with a notion of life in prison as far from idyllic, yet without crime. That is to say that nothing anyone has done has earned this form of incarceration and that, as Cleaver stated at the rally before his parole revocation hearing, all African Americans should be released from jail, regardless of the crime committed.[6] This radical view of the carceral state agrees with the idea that police action against African Americans is never warranted because the state that authorizes it, or rather that creates the conditions for its possibility, is itself illegitimate. Nevertheless, this understanding of racialized "criminality" would suspend any thought on crimes against nature, or inherent criminality, labeling all law the dissemination of state power and ideological force.

II. The Black Subject of History

Returning to his true love to write a very brief introduction to Bobby Seale's account of Huey Newton, Cleaver adds "An Aside to Ronald Reagan" (1968a), then governor of California. While the Cleaver of the introduction is self-effacing in deference to Seale, the writer of the "Aside" celebrates the self in opposition to "Mickey Mouse," Cleaver's name for the future president.[7] Reagan had attempted and at first failed to exercise some control over the University of California's Board of Regents to prevent Cleaver from delivering a series of ten lectures. Defiant, Cleaver taunts Reagan for having the temerity to try such a thing, believing that, while the governor may have legislative powers, he should have no say in the intellectual and political content of university-sponsored courses and events. This bold presentation stands in odd tension with the introduction just below it, separated only by another, buffering introduction by Robert Scheer, explaining that Cleaver compiled the Newton texts only in conjunction with Seale. Scheer as editor cedes editorial control to Cleaver, who then disavows his own work in preference to Seale, who bows before Newton. At the end of the editorial chain, only Newton is left to bear responsibility for the publication and the ideas therein. Cleaver's betrayal is complete.[8]

There are hints of this two-facedness already in Cleaver's "On the Ideology of the Black Panther Party" (1967), written as the Black Panther Party's minister of information, stating and situating the influences and goals of the movement in relation to those of Marxist-Leninists.[9] Cleaver cites the party's minister of defense, Newton, as the movement's key interpreter of Marxism and Leninism, writing: "However, we must place heavy emphasis upon the last part of that definition—'interpreted ... by our Minister of Defense....'—The world of Marxism-Leninism has become a jungle of opinion in which conflicting interpretations, from Right Revisionism to Left Dogmatism, foist off their reactionary and blind philosophies as revolutionary Marxism-Leninism. Around the world and in every nation people, all who call themselves Marxist-Leninists, are at each other's throats. Such a situation presents serious problems to a young party, such as ours, that is still in the process of refining its ideology" (1969, 1). Cleaver continues with this critical observation: "For too long Black people have relied upon the analyses and ideological perspectives of others." Looking to Newton for the proper understanding of the same forces Marx and Lenin interpret, Cleaver alludes to the minister of defense's *Revolutionary Suicide* when he states: "Our struggle has reached a point now where it would be absolutely suicidal for us to continue this posture of dependency" (1969, 1). Reiterating Newton's thought, Cleaver insists: "No other people in the world are in the same position as we are, and no other people in the world can get us out of it except ourselves" (1969, 1). The obstacle to this is these facts, according to Cleaver: "There are those who are all too willing to do our thinking for us, even if it gets us killed. However, they are not willing to follow through and do our dying for us. If thoughts bring about our deaths, let them at least be our own thoughts, so that we will have broken, once and for all, with the *flunkey-ism* of dying for every cause and every error—except our own" (1969, 1). Preventing this deadly interference begins with the embrace of Newton's thought. For Cleaver, Newton "gave the Black Panther Party a firm ideological foundation that frees us from *ideological flunkeyism* and opens up the path to the future" (1969, 1).

In this way, Cleaver posits that Newton's thought is more vital to African America than that of Marx and Lenin, because Newton speaks to the specificity of four hundred years of racial oppression perpetrated against peoples of African descent, while Marx and Lenin do not. Furthermore, Cleaver insists that the state of Marxist-Leninist discourse is no longer viable even in relation to its own limited interests, as it has fallen into infighting and self-contradiction. Ultimately, Cleaver claims that Newton's Marxist-Leninist critique and wider revolutionary program of armed resistance has more to say to the African American freedom struggle than it does to any contemporary revolutionary ideology derived from the traditional sources of Marxist-Leninist social and philosophical intervention. As Cleaver states, "the many other mass activities that we have been forced to indulge in in order to build mass support for our comrades who have gotten captured by the pigs. We are absolutely correct in indulging in such mass activity. But we are wrong when we confuse our mass line with our party line. Essentially, what Huey did was to provide the ideology and the methodology for organizing the Black Urban Lumpenproletariat. Armed with this ideological perspective and method, Huey transformed the Black Lumpenproletariat from the forgotten people at the bottom of society into the vanguard of the proletariat" (1969, 2).

Cleaver thus takes a similarly charged yet ultimately opposed causative approach to global revolution as Marcuse, in that he sees the locus of world revolution as the regional conflict, centered around the African diaspora in the United States.[10] Through self-education and intellectual and historical self-assessment of African Americans, a blueprint for successful armed resistance can be established and exported to other oppressed minorities. The necessary philosophy for the attainment of this goal is produced in indigenous intellectuals within African America, in that the African American is uniquely positioned both inside and outside of the West to be the revolutionary subject of history, as dictated by the material conditions of her sociopolitical reality. In other words, the Black Panther Party is not interested in integrative nonviolent change from within the legal sovereignty of white America. Rather, the party wishes to establish a new state and thereby possess a priori lawmaking violence as the rejection of the white state. The Black Panther Party is a political party because it rejects the white political sphere and seeks instead to establish its own state as a political organization in clear opposition to a specific enemy.

Citing the suicidal nature of their revolution—as it encompasses the point of no return in a war of annihilation in which extinction is the only response to failure—Cleaver insists that with such stakes only those directly affected by the daily conditions and teleological end of the struggle can be existentially invested in it to such an extent as to be able to offer authentically viable strategies for and solutions to the conflict. In other words, Cleaver states that the war being fought has a specificity of cause and combatant that requires an indigenous intellectual response, for it is only those belonging to the groups in armed conflict who can understand and respond to the conflict in the authentically visceral sense required. Each such conflict is therefore unique and cannot be subsumed under a general theoretical understanding of revolution as and of the global totality of oppressed minority positions.[11] The concept of revolutionary suicide articulates the isolated specificity of each minority movement of armed resistance, where to take up arms locally confines the armed conflict to the unique sociopolitical conditions of its creation. Nonindigenous leaders are detrimental to the cause, as they have not a priori "committed suicide" by becoming committed to the revolution. For Cleaver, he, Newton, and indeed all Black Panthers are already dead, having committed to the cause.

Indeed, Newton's philosophy is the core of the Black Panther Party, and it is to be considered the exclusive property of African America.[12] As such, it is the only authentic philosophical position of resistance available to African Americans and is by the substance of its position unavailable to any minority resistance group outside of the in situ context of its autochthonous existence. That said, should this message be distorted or prevented from reaching African America, any movement derived from it would effectively lose the intellectual shape of its ends and means. For this reason, Cleaver laments that the full scope of Newton's philosophy has yet to reach the wider African American public, as it is either contained entirely in prison with Newton's incarceration or diluted and distorted as it is carried through prison walls and delivered into the hands of the media by the Panthers themselves in the attempt to sanitize Newton's thought for the legal apparatus in which he is trapped. This leaves the minister of information as the only, albeit self-proclaimed, outlet for Newton's authentic philosophy. Cleaver's audience must take his word for it that what he writes accurately reflects Newton's thought and not just his own, if and where the two diverge.

In other words, as the minister of information, Cleaver claims a unique, nearly oracular relation to the truth of Newton's thought, which he introduces in his pamphlet as authoritative above and beyond any other source. Cleaver then suggests that the versions of Newton's philosophy in circulation, as espoused by the Black Panthers themselves, are inaccurate because they have been tailored to the legal battles Newton wages to gain release from prison. By this logic, no one currently has the knowledge and/or opportunity to relate to the wider public the substance of Huey Newton's revolutionary beliefs—except for Cleaver himself who, as the party's minister of information, now has total control over its message. Cleaver speaks with Newton's authority while Newton is behind bars and even when Newton is free, because, according to Cleaver, the party founder's legal troubles are endless and will thus constantly affect Newton's presentation of his own philosophy. In this way, Cleaver becomes the de facto leader of the Black Panther Party, as the only source of information pertaining to the substance of its beliefs and objectives.[13]

So positioned, Cleaver speaks in Newton's name in order to outline the philosophical nature of his achievement, stating that the party founder provided the intellectual basis for the organization of the African American lumpenproletariat into the vanguard of the proletariat as a whole. Newton does this "armed with ideological perspective and method," such that these elements and attributes are themselves weapons not dissimilar to the rifle he is pictured conspicuously carrying on the cover of the pamphlet. Newton's rifle is philosophy, which he teaches the African American lumpenproletariat to use by first identifying them as such, or as those members of the proletariat for whom his appropriation of Marx and Lenin can be used, as the vanguard of a movement, to violent revolutionary effect. In other words, Newton has appropriated Marx and Lenin for the purposes of placing race at the front of what those philosophers had perceived to be a class war, revealing instead that the economics of labor oppression and class conflict cannot be dissociated from racism, and indeed are ideologically determined by it. For this reason, Cleaver sees the role of ideology, or information, as central to the struggle for liberation. In Newton's name, he writes: "Ideology is a comprehensive definition of a status quo that takes into account both the history and the future of that status quo and serves as the social glue that holds a people together and through which a people relate to the world and other groups of people in the world. The correct ideology is an invincible weapon against the oppressor in our struggle for freedom and liberation" (1969, 3).

For Cleaver, ideology names two definitions of separate yet related phenomena. The first, "power," is prefaced by Newton's name and given as a direct quote of the Black Panther Party founder. According to Cleaver, Newton believes that "power is the ability to define phenomena and make it [*sic*] act in a desired manner" (1969, 3). This straightforward understanding of the all-important term is then followed by an authorial exercise of power in which Cleaver now defines "ideology." It is a definition that he does not attribute to Newton at all and that requires considerably more textual space to unfold. While Cleaver's definition certainly evinces the requisite understanding of ideology's fundamental relation to the status quo, he adds an element to it that makes the position and practice together far more powerful than an agent of sociopolitical stasis. Ideology binds a people, as a people. It is the "glue" that holds a people together. It will therefore manifest differently depending on where and by whom it is devised. For this reason, Marxism cannot be imported into the United States without serious revision. Cleaver writes:

> Marxism has never really dealt with the United States of America. There have been some very nice attempts. People have done the best that they know how. However, in the past, Marxist-Leninists in the United States have relied too heavily upon foreign, imported analyses and have seriously distorted the realities of the American scene. We might say that the Marxism-Leninism of the past belongs to the gestation period of Marxism-Leninism in the United States, and that now is the time when a new, strictly American ideological synthesis will arise, springing up from the hearts and souls of the oppressed people inside Babylon, and uniting these people and hurling them mightily, from the force of their struggle, into the future. The swiftly developing revolution in America is like the gathering of a mighty storm, and nothing can stop that storm from finally bursting, inside America, washing away the pigs of the power structure and all their foul, oppressive works. (1969, 3-4)

Cleaver understands Marx's statement on the inevitability of violent conflict between the proletariat and bourgeoisie as the mightiest weapon in the history of ideology, as he puts it. This assumes that this facet of Marx and Engels's writing is the most lucid and important from the perspective of revolutionary bellicosity; that the totality of their writings primarily advocates such revolutionary violence; and that there is a coherent history of this strain of ideology in which these writings intervene as weapons.[14] Cleaver takes from Marx and Engels a call to arms to the oppressed proletariat rather than a historical analysis of the proletariat's creation and condition. The importance of the particularity of this reading becomes strikingly clear when Cleaver immediately goes on to conclude that this great weapon requires refitting if it is to be used in the United States, where conditions are not the same as those prevailing in Europe at the time Marx, Engels, and Lenin wrote. Furthermore, in addition to being limited by the geopolitical situation, the thought of Marx, Engels, and Lenin was also defined temporally and historically. Because of this, Cleaver believes, "We must emphasize the fact that Marx and Lenin didn't invent Socialism. They only added their contributions, enriching the doctrine, just as many others did before them and after them. And we must remember that Marx and Lenin didn't organize the Black Panther Party. Huey P. Newton and Bobby Seale did" (1969, 5).

This last point seems obvious enough, and Cleaver's overall analysis would have to grant a body of philosophical writings from all times and places that "contribute" to the specificity of Black Panther ideology. In this sense, Cleaver appears to contradict his own assertion that the vanguard position of Newton's philosophical thought is of crucial importance to provoking the revolution. He writes that the impending uprising is like a coming storm that cannot be stopped, placing it within a teleological understanding of a natural sociopolitical order that requires no intellectual intervention to instigate its events. The revolution will occur no matter what, as it is naturally, instinctively fated to do. However, Cleaver avoids any real self-contradiction by displacing the intention of his intervention. He does not wish to foment revolution with his pamphlet as Newton seeks to with his writings and speeches. Rather, Cleaver's pamphlet attempts to provide the appropriate method and tools to comprehend critically the inevitable events to come. Cleaver thus presents a racial-critical theory of revolution in contradistinction to those currently in circulation, as represented by the Marxist-Leninist thinkers he continues to reference without explicitly naming. In other words, unlike Newton, Cleaver does not attempt to incite revolution, which would be a crime. Rather, he presents a theory by which to grasp and analyze the revolution for which Newton acts as a natural catalyst.

Cleaver's essay turns Newton's tangible objective of revolution inside out in the sense that, for Newton, writing is a means of self-defense and education meant to provide the proper orientation in a conflict facilitated and indeed made possible by his philosophy. Recognizing this, Cleaver too decries the shapelessness of African American life with regard to property, employment, and belief in basic institutions. Yet he does not understand his work as minister of information in the same sense as Newton does his theoretical writings and wider revolutionary philosophy. For Cleaver, the dissemination of information means the evaluation of Newton's philosophy in the world and in history, placing it in relation to that of Marxist-Leninists as a mode of social-racial justification and exultation that transcends any interracial notion of proletarian struggle. As Cleaver is quick to point out, it is the white "working class" who form the lynch mobs, not the landed white bourgeoisie.

Insisting that Marx and Lenin were racists who, despite their great achievements in advancing the cause of socialism, spoke about European problems strictly for a European audience, Cleaver dismisses their priority in the development of socialist economic theory and revolutionary socio-political analysis in non-European communities. He suggests that much more exact models of Marxist-Leninist revolutionary action can be seen in North Korea and China, where Kim Il-sung and Mao Zedong have re-fashioned the writings of Marx and Lenin to fit the specific racial needs of their respective nations. Blacks in the United States must do the same, rejecting the authority of Marx, Lenin, and Marxist-Leninists as "white" and embracing instead the philosophies of Newton and Bobby Seale as racially and therefore socially relevant.

This exclusion is not a rejection of Eurocentrism alone. Cleaver writes:

And even Fanon, in his published works, was primarily focused on Africa. It is only indirectly that his works are beneficial to Afro-Americans. It is just easier to relate to Fanon because he is clearly free of that racist bias that blocks out so much about the Black man in the hands of Whites who are primarily interested in themselves and the problems of their own people. But even though we are able to relate heavily to Fanon, he has not given us the last word on applying the Marxist-Leninist analysis to our problems inside the United States. No one is going to do this for us because no one can. We have to do it ourselves, and until we do, we are going to be uptight.

We must take the teachings of Huey P. Newton as our foundation and go from there. Any other course will bring us to a sorry and regrettable end. (1969, 5)

Fanon's work enters Cleaver's discussion as an archive for Newton's thought without leading the minister of information to the judgment that the Black Panther Party's philosophy is derivative of the French West Indian psychoanalyst's. Indeed, Cleaver believes Fanon to be the first philosopher of African descent in the post-Marxist-Leninist tradition to break from the Eurocentric model of its origin and discursive history. Yet Fanon nevertheless focuses almost exclusively on Black Africans, making, for Cleaver, little of his analysis relevant to the lives of African Americans. That said, Cleaver does concede that Fanon developed the idea of the Black diasporic lumpenproletariat, to which African Americans belong, as a potent category of labor pertaining to third-world worker-subjects who are, however, primarily determined by race and racism. This connection allows

Cleaver then to explore the definition of African American Blackness as produced by colonialism, providing a recognizable theoretical determination that nevertheless will have to be altered to suit the specific historical-material circumstances of this subcategory of lumpenproletariat.

Giving credit where it is due, Cleaver writes:

> Fanon unearthed the category of the Lumpenproletariat and began to deal with it, recognizing that vast majorities of the colonized people fall into that category. It is because of the fact that Black people in the United States are also colonized that Fanon's analysis is so relevant to us.
>
> After studying Fanon, Huey P. Newton and Bobby Seale began to apply his analysis of colonized people to Black people in the United States. They adopted the Fanonian perspective, but they gave it a uniquely Afro-American content.
>
> Just as we must make the distinctions between the mother country and the colony when dealing with Black people and White people as a whole, we must also make this distinction when we deal with the categories of the Working Class and the Lumpenproletariat. (1969, 6)

The existence of the lumpenproletariat as it is defined in Fanon divides the Marxist-Leninist working class into that of the "mother country" and that of the colony. The lumpen of the colony experience a different history of capitalist oppression than do those of the mother country, making it impossible to consider them theoretically and historically as one. This means, then, that the teleology pertaining to each group cannot be the same. The theory propelling each of the separate groups forward in history has to differ from one another and will therefore be based on different historical and philosophical sources. Written from the white European perspective and thus that of the mother country, the writings of Marx and Lenin and those invested in this tradition speak only to the lumpen of the colonizer. Those of the colonized require an intelligentsia derived from within their geopolitically determined social space and that is a product of the race, as defined economically by colonial oppression, yet recognized culturally through the biological categories of inherent racial difference. Divergence in racial characteristics among the lumpenproletariat does not, for Cleaver, result in inherent variation in base intelligence. Rather, it pertains to physical prowess and sexual potency such that colonization becomes the means by which to secure a form of labor physically unavailable in the mother country while simultaneously containing a sexual threat in a world ever increasing in its global interconnectedness.[15]

The failure of the lumpenproletariat as configured in the United States is its embrace of the "racial caste system." Cleaver insists that the so-called "Criminal Element", those who live by their wits, existing off that which they rip off, who stick guns in the faces of businessmen and say "stick'em up," or "give it up"! Those who don't even want a job, who hate to work and can't relate to punching some pig's time clock, who would rather punch a pig in the mouth and rob him than punch that same pig's time clock and work for him, those whom Huey P. Newton calls "the illegitimate capitalists." In short, all those who simply have been locked out of the economy and robbed of their rightful social heritage.

But even though we are Lumpen, we are still members of the Proletariat, a category which theoretically cuts across national boundaries but which in practice leaves something to be desired. (1969, 7)

This interconnectedness does not reach inward within the domestic political scene, for Cleaver expressly rejects the notion of a single American working class and lumpenproletariat in which Black and white laborers share the same concerns and benefits through federated trade unions organized and functioning on a principle of social equality for and responsible to all. The status of Black America as colonized situates the relationship between racial groups as one determined first and foremost by racial distinction, where colonization becomes the primary mode of economic engagement and political participation in all social relations is racially determined. Indeed, these essentially racially determined modes of social belonging indicate that all social totalities are identified as such by the capitalist enterprise, in conjunction with the juridico-political institutions that support it unreservedly, and are mediated entirely by relations of colonial subjection and mastery. The worlds of Black and white workers are separate and unequal, because the initial determination deciding their sociopolitical ontology is defined by purely racist conceptions and is executed in systems of domination conceived exclusively for these purposes. The historical-material contingency of the selective process of socialization in relation to the political economic structures of internal and external colonialism creates radical differences in the nature of the lumpenproletariat in terms of its social attitude and function, as Newton is well aware. Indeed, speaking in his name once again, Cleaver reminds his readers that Newton understands the designation of the Black lumpen's "Criminal Element" as "illegitimate capitalists."

In other words, Cleaver is using the "lumpen" category in order to designate that portion of the working class that does not work. Here unemployment is caused not by material economic factors specific to the historical development of capital considered as the willful yet disembodied, absolute agent of world-historical becoming. Rather it is caused solely on the basis of irrational, economically inimical forms of racist belief and action. That is to say that the lumpenproletariat formed by colonial structures of economic exploitation have little to do with historical reason, functioning instead, and exclusively, according to racist precepts and not strictly according to the location of available resources. The issue is not that a specific, valuable crop such as sugar can be grown only in a particular place and therefore requires a particular physical type of worker to withstand the working conditions there. Racist determination preexists the need to cultivate sugarcane and protect plantation owners from being forced to consider, implement, and finance one of a thousand other ways to arrange labor on their sugarcane farms. Cleaver posits, then, an instrumental racist reason as that which shapes economic practice and thus the working class. As a consequence, the working class as such is constitutively racist. For this reason, African Americans require a different form of intellectual armature and organized resistance to capitalist aggression.

This distinction between the employed as the working class and the unemployed as the lumpen extends beyond the racial divisions within and determining the notion of the proletariat to antagonisms within the Black colony itself.[16] Here Black workers and the Black unemployed are at odds due to the structural assignment of roles within the social totality, as decided by employment status alone. In identifying the lumpen distinction of unemployment in all areas of socioeconomic formation and relational existence, Cleaver prioritizes employment status above race, indicating that white and Black cooperation within the categories of general groups distinguished could in fact occur. This non-working-class proletariat, or lumpen, because it must exist within the Black colony by virtue of employment status alone, transcends racial distinction in any rigorous ontological sense, creating the categorical opportunity for interracial collaboration in a revolutionary project designed not to end racism but rather meant to restructure the meaning and function of employment in capitalist society.[17] For Cleaver has made no argument against employment. Instead, he attacks the fact that unemployment exists and is assigned disproportionately yet not exclusively to African Americans.

In fact, for Cleaver the working class has become the parasite on humanity that the lumpen had always been accused of being on the working class itself. The notion of parasitical exchange between lumpen and working class with regard to economic survival as sufficient sustenance drawn from the class or social body directly above it transforms when applied to the working class. Here the proletariat is no longer content to draw its life from within the class and class system, thriving instead within the economic ecosystem of the whole beyond capitalism as a naturalized state of social being. In other words, Cleaver has made a moral argument against the existence of the working class rather than confining his criticism to historically contingent political economic necessity. The working class is a parasite on humanity itself and not merely on a subclass within that of human being. The lumpen then is also qualified absolutely as a moral agent on the world-historical stage, where the local character of the African American unemployed—a subcategory within a separate racial-economic class—takes on the dialectically opposite character of the universally parasitical working class and acts as the ideal medium of human being for all of humanity. Against the dehumanization produced by labor of any kind within capitalism's oppressive socioeconomic regime, human freedom can only be found in life among the "illegitimate capitalists," rejecting both labor unions and student protests. Cleaver writes:

> It is because of Black people's lumpen relationship to the means of production and the institutions of the society that they are unable to manifest their rebellion around those means of production and institutions. But this does not mean that the rebellions that take place in the streets are not legitimate expressions of an oppressed people. These are the means of rebellion left open to the Lumpen.
> The Lumpen have been locked outside of the economy. (1969, 7)

Because they are unemployed, these illegitimate capitalists wage their war against capitalism in spaces other than those of the white working class. Indeed, Cleaver is quick to point out that, as wage earners, the white working class belongs to workspaces and other social institutions such as the university. In these spaces, the leftist wing of the white working class—which itself is divided between right and left political affiliation—agitates for the amelioration of its socioeconomic condition as a desire to improve the prevailing conditions of labor under capital. In this sense, protests within the institutions that support the capitalist regime serve only to seek redress to specific aspects of that regime rather than to overturn it entirely. White student protesters and labor unions remain invested in the capitalist superstructure and all of the social conceits that buttress it. The Black lumpen, however, have no such investments. Without access to institutional space, lumpen protest and revolt take place in the streets and thus in a form radically different from that of the white working-class left. The Black lumpen, then, seek to oppose and overthrow a clearly delineated enemy, whereas the white working class on the right and left ultimately work toward the same general goal, the improvement of socioeconomic conditions for white wage laborers under the capitalist regime.

Because of this, the

Lumpen finds itself in the position where it is very difficult for it to manifest its complaints against the system. The Working Class has the possibility of calling a strike against the factory and the employer and through the mechanism of Labor Unions they can have some arbitration or some process through which its grievances are manifested. Collective bargaining is the way out of the pit of oppression and exploitation discovered by the Working Class, but the Lumpen has no opportunity to do any collective bargaining, The Lumpen has no institutionalized focus in Capitalist society. It has no immediate oppressor except perhaps the Pig Police with which it is confronted daily. (1969, 10–11)

The police represent the oppressive regime to the lumpen. That is to say, the Black lumpen have no investment in the political economic life of the society that oppresses them. They have no institutional standing and therefore no platform from which to agitate for change. The lumpen cannot, for example, engage in collective bargaining the way the working class does, because they have no employment at which to find a labor union through which to participate in collective bargaining with the goal of improving their situation under capitalism. In other words, the institutional face of capitalism is veiled before the lumpen and not before the working class, hence the situations, sites, and methods of resistance available to the lumpen are different from those of the Left. This is so because it is able to face the representatives of capitalist power in any institutional forum where capital legally determines the terms of the labor performed and can alter those terms to the extent the law allows. The lumpen's only direct encounter with a representative of the capitalist regime comes in direct conflict with police.[18] The nature of lumpen resistance is determined by the site of their contact with the sole institution of capitalism with which they are confronted. Lumpen resistance is always therefore violent and revolutionary as it seeks to found new laws by first destroying those charged with protecting and enforcing the old laws.

Indeed, Cleaver makes it clear that the forms of resistance employed by the lumpen respond directly to the state of unemployment and disenfranchisement from the basic institutional structures of capitalism, such that the lumpen revolution has categorically different ends than those of the capitalist working class. He writes:

So that the very conditions of life of the Lumpen dictates the so-called spontaneous reactions against the system, and because the Lumpen is in this extremely oppressed condition, it therefore has an extreme reaction against the system as a whole. It sees itself as being bypassed by all of the organizations, even by the Labor Unions, and even by the Communist Parties that despise it and look down upon it and consider it to be, in the words of Karl Marx, the father of Communist Parties, "The Scum-Layer of the Society." The Lumpen is forced to create its own forms of rebellion that are consistent with its condition in life and with its relationship to the means of production and the institutions of society. That is, to strike out at all the structures around it, including at the reactionary Right Wing of the Proletariat when it gets in the way of revolution. The faulty analyses which the ideologies of the Working Class have made, of the true nature of the Lumpen, are greatly responsible for the retardation of the development of the revolution in urban situations. It can be said that the true revolutionaries in the urban centers of the world have been analyzed out of the revolution by some Marxist-Leninists. (1969, 11)

The lumpen do not seek to alter the conditions of labor; rather, they wish to abolish labor as such, as it is alien to its socioeconomic being. This Scum-Layer of Society wishes instead to reproduce the conditions of its existence as without labor. They do not seek to supplant the white working class within the capitalist system; the goal is rather to end the capitalist system as such, not in confrontation with the institutions of capitalist society but rather in conflict with the forces of physical coercion in compliance with its laws. In this respect, the lumpen revolution has nothing to do with the abolition of private property as the first legislative step in the creation of a rational society designed to promote general well-being. The lumpen instead and through their direct assault on the police seek to annihilate all forms of violent authoritarian oppression, regardless of the nature of the totalitarian system they serve. In this respect, Cleaver advances anarchist rather than Marxist-Leninist-inflected revolutionary goals.

Perhaps this is why the goals and platform of the Black Panther Party listed at the end of Cleaver's first pamphlet as minister of information includes among their demands the unlikely and jarring insistence on full employment for all African Americans. While the insistence on this aspect of the oppressed lumpen is highly logical and indeed necessary, it is nevertheless inappropriate to the intellectual and ideological assessment of the Black lumpen's meaning as Cleaver just elucidated it. For the pamphlet takes great pains to establish the lumpen's difference from the white working class—and indeed its basis for antagonism toward it and its intellectual arm, Marcuse's New Left—as premised on unemployment, where the lack of gainful employment names a constitutive element of the lumpen's racial identity and historical mission outside of white capitalism. In other words, if the demands of the Panther platform presented were to be met, the lumpen would cease to exist as a racially defined entity, and African Americans would enter the system of capitalism as invested partners rather than as its internal contradiction and dialectical negation. Cleaver presents a prescription for economic assimilation and not for the anarchic destruction of capitalism that is the ontological reason and justification of the Black lumpen's existence.

In his first official published communication, the minister of information speaks out of both sides of his mouth. Cleaver claims that unemployment determines the structure of lumpen existence; yet his list of demands seeks to integrate the lumpen into the white working class, as it demands full participation in the employment structure characterizing capitalist totalitarianism. This contradiction would not be rectified by the revolutionary and indeed anarchic philosophy Cleaver affirms as the true yet unknown substance of Newton's thought. Rather, it reflects the more careful, conciliatory ideas Newton expounds in conflict with the courts. This battleground area of agitation goes unexplored by Cleaver, as he denies the revolutionary potential of legal activism in favor of a romanticism of the gun.

Cleaver's ideal revolutionary is thus an armed Huey Newton, the image of which adorns the cover of the pamphlet. This picture of Newton, where the rifle he holds at his waist appears to spring from his loins and to stand erect as he steadies it with both hands, plays up the masculine potency of armed resistance that Cleaver seeks to convey. Firmly gripping the firearm, Newton is portrayed as anything but a lawful subject, causing the pamphlet again to deliver a mixed message that only seems to be reconciled by the list of demands that seeks inclusion while threatening annihilation. Yet the pamphlet roundly condemns that into which it wishes to be introduced, doing so on ontological grounds rather than on a strictly historical-materialist basis, making the suggestion that Newton is the "naturally" armed leader of the lumpen both problematic and decisive. For in order for the lumpen to cease to conform to this revolutionary category, Newton must be removed from his position of leadership, as his ideas are by their nature inimical to capitalist oppression. This is evidenced by the very legal troubles that pervert his philosophy for public consumption. For the philosophy of Huey Newton does not call for economic assimilation but rather for the anarchical separation of the races. The minister of information, however, does look to the integration of racial communities as the key not to revolution but rather to survival. The armed figure of the pamphlet's cover seeks to conjure an image of self-defense and not aggressive, "unprovoked" racial destruction.[19]

Unrepeatable

CHAPTER FIVE

Angela Y. Davis and
Black Critical Theory

I. Davis and the Negative Dialectics of Black Liberation

The image of the armed Black resistance fighter was fundamental to Angela Y. Davis's philosophy in the 1960s and was embodied for her narratively in Frederick Douglass. Davis's training in critical theory at Frankfurt in the mid-1960s and her subsequent embrace of Black militancy combine to create a revolutionary philosophy centered on the self-defense Douglass showed in his struggle with the slave breaker Covey. Davis's position rejects "the human condition" as Hannah Arendt imagined it and the idea of a public sphere premised on human equality. She posits instead the violent interruption of the master-slave dialectic as ideologically determining public reason and the superiority of the slave's sense of being that this violence produces. Ultimately, Davis's philosophical intervention accounts for the operative existence of the negative in universalist discourse, positing its superiority of philosophical truth.

In an often-overlooked passage from her autobiography (1974), Davis states that "Frankfurt was a very intensive learning experience. Stimulating lectures and seminars conducted by Theodor Adorno, Jürgen Habermass [*sic*], Professor Haag, Alfred Schmidt, Oscar Negt. Tackling formidable works, such as all three of Kant's *Critiques* and the works of Hegel and Marx as well (in one seminar, we spent an entire semester analyzing about twenty pages of Hegel's *Logic*)" (1974, 142).[1] Seemingly downplaying her training in critical theory, Davis concentrates in the account of her time in Frankfurt on her life as an activist. While it may appear that Davis prefers to emphasize activism over philosophy, the descriptions of her activism in Germany bring into relief the connection between the study of philosophy and radical political activism, with the goal of "overturning the enemy system" (1974, 142–43).[2] The students' interlinking of philosophical training with domestic and international political intervention is striking, not least because it is the direct teaching of her mentor Marcuse that philosophy led to action. Indeed, Davis moves so quickly yet fluidly from the introduction of her philosophical studies at Frankfurt to participating in street demonstrations and minor forms of guerrilla activism in West Germany that it becomes hard to differentiate the two, from the point of view of the autobiography's structure of intentionality. In order to understand the philosophical aspect of her actions, it is important to be familiar with the work of the critical theorists she mentions in her autobiography that she worked with and the extent to which she engaged with critical theory and Hegel's philosophy while in residence at the Frankfurt School.[3]

Davis worked with Habermas as he delivered the 1965 lecture that would become *Knowledge and Human Interests* (1968). In it, Habermas argues that the negative dialectic nature in the positive sciences provides the critical model for understanding all unspecified and illegible being in the critical theory of society. This means that, despite his reservations and outright criticisms, Habermas has not yet deviated far from Horkheimer and Adorno's discussion of the matter in their *Dialectic of Enlightenment* (1944). That is to say that Habermas identifies the problem of the negative as the primary concern of critical theory, and that the object of this concern is in fact nature, regardless of its manifestation in social thought. In other words, the problem of racism from a critical-theoretical perspective is one of negation without recuperation. The slave in Hegel's master-slave dialectic, for instance, exists under erasure, along with nature as a whole, for the cognitive means to perceive him socially are compromised by a naturalized yet ultimately alienated and reified philosophical understanding of nature. Freedom as a natural fact cannot exist for the slave because he is not part of the natural order as conceived from the standpoint of alienated, instrumental reason. Replaced by second nature, nature is signified in negative terms alone. The recuperation of nature includes the natural truth of human freedom. The means by which this is done are those of liberation. The slave provides, then, a unique critical-theoretical opportunity to discover the path to freedom in universal acts of human liberation.

Davis also mentions that she worked with Alfred Schmidt, whose *Concept of Nature in Marx* ([1962]; in English, 1971) is still considered required reading today. Positing "concrete freedom" as the achievement of mastery over social necessity, Schmidt writes, "Concrete freedom, for Marx in close accord with Hegel, consisted in conceiving and mastering social necessity" ([1962] 2014, 133). Indeed, much of Schmidt's discussion of nature in Marx is mediated by Hegel. "Concrete freedom, for Marx in close accord with Hegel," would be the elimination of the ideological construct of nature in the first place, whereby freedom becomes a project without ontological qualification in strict definitions of human being. From this "follows the famous sudden leap from the realm of necessity to that of freedom. Marx, however, was both more skeptical and more dialectical in seeing that the realm of freedom does not simply replace that of necessity, but retains it as an inextinguishable internal moment. A more rational organization of the economy can certainly limit the labour-time necessary for the reproduction of life, but can never wholly abolish labour. This reflects the dialectical duality of Marxist materialism. It is capable of being transcended in non-transcendence. Marx reconciled freedom and necessity on the basis of necessity" ([1962] 2014, 135). This necessary "realm of freedom" as Marx refers to it can only be attained when necessity no longer plays the decisive role in the social organization of labor. Schmidt is also quick to point out that, unlike Engels in the *Anti-Dühring*, Marx does not understand freedom solely in terms of the reorganization and rationalization of production through socialization. Rather, Marx retains the element of necessity in his idea of freedom as a means of explaining the fact of labor in itself. Necessity dictates labor, regardless of the social organization of its productive forces. The realm of freedom is reached when the social understanding of labor is not oppressive but rather that of the rationally necessary. In other words, Marx, Schmidt believes, transcends necessity in nontranscendence. That is to say, Marx calls for a better social understanding of labor rather than its abolition in some utopian gesture. Necessity, then, is transcended dialectically in its negation, followed by the meaningful renegotiation of its terms according to its synthesis with the concept of freedom, or simple reason. Freedom is necessity made rational.[4]

While in Frankfurt, Davis studied under Oskar Negt shortly after he published *Strukturbeziehungen zwischen den Gesellschaftslehren Comtes und Hegels* (1964). Here, Negt finds much in common methodologically between Hegel's Idealism ad Comte's positivism, writing, "Für Comte und Hegel ist die Geschichte ein gesetzmäßiger Zusammenhang, durch den die Einzelerscheinungen untereinander und in Beziehung auf das Ganze bestimmt sind. Dem Comteschen fundamentalen Entwicklungsgesetz, das die Hauptstufen der gesellschaftlichen und logisch-begrifflichen Entwicklung wiedergibt, entspricht bei Hegel die notwendige Folge der Volksgeister" (96). (For Comte and Hegel, history is a coherent structure through which the individual phenomena are determined in relation to one another and according to the whole. Comte's fundamental law of development, which reflects the main stages of social and logical-conceptual development, corresponds in Hegel with the necessary unfolding of the Volk's spirit.) This difference leads Negt to conclude that "Die Erklärung der Gesamtgesellschaft als ein System wechselseitig voneinander abhängiger Kräfte, bis zu der die positivistische Soziologie allenfalls sich vorwagt, ist nach Hegel noch nicht bis zum wirklichen Begreifen des Zusammenhangs zur inhaltlichen Vermittlung von Wesen und Erscheinung gekommen" (69). (According to Hegel, the explanation of society's totality as a system of mutually interdependent forces, up to the point at which positivist sociology intervenes, has not yet come to a real understanding of this totality as the substantive mediation of essence and appearance.) Affirming the value of Hegel's dialectic for examining the relation between history and freedom, Negt's work of the mid-1960s is strongly indebted to Adorno's, and that of the Frankfurt School generally.

It is also strongly influenced by the most important among the four philosophers Davis mentioned, and the one who is the least well known in the English-speaking academy, Karl Heinz Haag. In "Das Unwiederholbare," published in 1963 as part of a volume celebrating Adorno's sixtieth birthday and reprinted as part of Haag's seminal work on the history of Idealism in philosophy, *Philosophischer Idealismus: Untersuchungen zur Hegelschen Dialektik mit Beispielen aus der Wissenschaft der Logik* (1967), Haag transforms the history of philosophy into the narrative of identity as produced in the interaction between subject and object and as productive of subjectivity and objectivity. In this sense, philosophy as a whole is definitionally concerned with the problems of Idealism, in which the priority of subjective thought requires mediation in authenticating objects-in-themselves. The dialectic in which the subject comes to know the object reflects the structure of objectivity in its epistemologically valid apprehension and expression. The identity presented by dialectical thought is apprehended, however, only at the expense of the concept of nonidentity. In other words, all that escapes or is excluded from the dialectic of subject and object as initiated and directed categorically as a constitutive element of subjectivity does not exist in any objective sense. The subject takes hold of the nonidentical in an act of complete possession, and in so doing does violence to the object of nonidentity by divesting it of its potential for freedom. Here Haag and Adorno express a similar understanding of the history of philosophical thought. Indeed, Adorno dedicates his *Drei Studien zu Hegel* (1963) to Haag.

In his 1964–65 lecture course on history and freedom, Davis's direct advisor, Adorno, plays devil's advocate, suggesting that the simple disjunction between theory and historical fact in Hegel's understanding of freedom authorizes the historian to disregard the philosopher entirely (2006, 84). Indeed, Adorno suggests that because Hegel simply gets history wrong, particularly with regard to China, his notion that modern Western society was defined by the availability of freedom to all of its subjects rings absurd. Hegel makes this absurdly inaccurate claim, Adorno suggests, for the sake of the formal symmetry of philosophical presentation. Having recognized this, the student of history is free to move on to more responsible, relevant readings. The student of philosophy, however, is not so lucky. For, Adorno concludes, there is still something of great value in Hegel's formal presentation, and his understanding of history and freedom may have been at first glance misapprehended. A closer examination is required, for those who would still care to investigate.

Adorno asks that Hegel be understood in a less literal sense and read for his emphasis on individual freedom. For Hegel, according to Adorno, freedom is the meaning of history, and its teleological realization in absolute spirit is the work of the individual. The right to individuality, or even the existence of the concept of the individual, predicates the end of history, insofar as this concept can be developed and expanded to become universally valid for all. Hegel differentiates between absolutist states and societies and modern parliamentary democracies in the philosophical sense of individuality's priority in history. Here the state that possesses a single individual, the emperor or king, exists at an earlier historical stage than one in which a universal sense of individuality pervades social understanding, if not practice. In terms of antiquity and the history of Western philosophical thought, the Greeks—while originating the idea of the individual—had no understanding of its universalization with regard to noncitizens. The slave and the barbarian were outside of history, and therefore rightfully unfree.

Adorno is careful to speak of "formal freedom" in relation to the historical end of slavery.[5] This understanding of freedom signifies the degree to which philosophy, as a theory of society, shows both how indispensable it was in articulating historical changes in social organization and relations and the extent to which it itself has become "purified" as a formal exercise in metaphysics.[6] For Adorno, even and especially Hegel shared the insight that philosophy had come to possess a "revolting purity" in its alienation from that which it was created to explain. Philosophy cut off from social action generates in its analytical conclusions its own historical reality. The world picture philosophy describes becomes aspirational rather than experiential, indicating an ideal realm of action in which the reality of freedom is exchanged for the promise of human perfection. Philosophy's revolting purity is, then, the ideological gesture of its ideal world in which experience counts as the substantive shadow of a "formal freedom" (2006, 149).

The formal concept of freedom arises from the idea of progress conceived as a means of understanding humanity's struggle with nature. The terror of nature is assuaged and eventually overcome through the progressive demythologization of the initial presentational means used to situate human being in its natural environment. The means that humanity develops to achieve mastery over nature are imposed on all nonidentical elements of social relations, leading to the oppression of the nonidentical in all its forms. The dialectical result of this "enlightened" development in which nature is demythologized and the nonidentical is oppressed is the creation of formal freedom. In it, freedom exists as a structural necessity for the demythologization of nature, yet it cannot be granted to nature, or anything considered alien to the realm of human being in its epistemologically prescribed, ontically known form. Any being that falls outside the definition of human being as provided by the epistemological rigor of reflective modes of Enlightenment is subject to the oppression reserved for nonidentical being. For, having

> arisen from within society, progress calls for a critical confrontation with society as it actually exists. The element of redemption it contains, no matter how secularized, is indestructible. The fact that it can be reduced neither to actual reality nor to ideas points to its own contradictory nature. For the element of enlightenment in the concept, the impulse towards demythologization which, by assuaging the terrors of nature, ends up in reconciliation with it, is twinned with the element of the domination of nature. The model of progress, even if transposed into the godhead itself, represents the control of nature, both inner, human nature and nature outside man. The oppression practiced by such control and mirrored in the mind in the identity principle of reason, reproduces this antagonism. The more identity is postulated by the spirit that dominates, the more injustice is meted out to the non-identical. Injustice is passed down to the non-identical, feeding its resistance. (2006, 150)

The question of nature as nonidentity is an important one in Adorno's presentation of history and freedom. Concentrating largely on Hegel's philosophy, Adorno suggests against a surface reading of Marx that labor alone is the source of all wealth. In fact, as Adorno would have it, labor is impossible without nature, from which it derives and by the material means of which it becomes possible. Nature is the source of all wealth, with the notion of labor as wealth's producer acting chimerically to obscure nature's independent value. Because labor is seen as creative in this sense, it appears to authorize of itself ownership of nature. By this belief, anyone who has no creative talent for the creation of value is his own value as labor alone. This would, then, by right render him the property of those for whom labor is the medium through which they express the force of their creativity in dominating nature. In other words, the bourgeoisie's inverted dialectic of labor and nature justifies slavery as the creative necessity in subduing nature for the greater good of all.

The idea of the greater good has animated the history of the concept of freedom. Indeed, Adorno sees freedom as the expression of its historical context and not as an immutable universal law or natural right. In this respect, freedom can be contested as it is awarded to a limited minority in totalitarian and slaveholding societies. Acknowledging its character of contingency, the concept of freedom can come under siege from those to whom it is not granted or does not apply. When not manifest in a state of open revolt, freedom can be negotiated in the public space, and indeed the public sphere exists for the sake of such negotiations. Adorno's discussion of history and freedom, in which freedom has a history and cannot exist outside of it, leads to a preliminary description of the public sphere as a space where inconsistencies in the conceptualization of social reality are debated and resolved. This idea of the public sphere provides a different notion of freedom, one in which the movement of bodies and the pursuit of ideas is determined in advance according to its ideal by political deliberation. Political freedom names public space as the site of social freedom's definition through comprehensively participatory democratic deliberation.

Adorno's discussion of the dialectical relation of history and freedom is, then, also the presentation of a philosophy of history in which philosophical concepts can be considered neither immutable nor changeable but rather as the starting points for contingent historical expression.[7] In this respect, while the concept of freedom present in philosophy from at least Plato forward is schematically valid and authentic to its historical moment, its articulation at other points in history can only be grasped by a critical-theoretical practice sensitive to the fluctuating universality of concepts. The concept of freedom as applied to the citizen of ancient Athens will maintain a philosophical bond with its contemporary iteration, yet it could not be called on to explain its current expression in atemporal, universal terms. For Adorno, this is the substance of dialectical criticism and the lesson of Hegel's philosophy of history.[8]

In the short sentences of Davis's autobiography between introducing these thinkers and narrating her time listening to Rudi Dutschke speak publicly, the ostensible reason for her stay in Frankfurt has disappeared entirely, with a purely contemplative mode of philosophical engagement instead becoming philosophy as acts of resistance. Davis is also quick to note that Dutschke's would-be assassin was inspired by Martin Luther King Jr.'s murder, a connection Davis exploits to bridge the struggle in Germany and the American civil rights movement. This link is made, however, through violence, and by means of the negative political consciousness awakened not by King's words but rather by the manner of his death. King's assassination is important to Davis's narrative only insofar as it sheds light on tactics used by a white supremacist in attempting to suppress the liberation movement in Germany, Davis's account of which ends with the killing of first-time student demonstrator Ben Ohnesorge by police. Davis then shifts national political contexts by explaining that she had left the United States in 1964, at a time of relative tranquility, and that in the intervening two years America had erupted in revolutionary violence. This period of rupture begins for Davis with the Watts riots, from which, "Phoenix-like, a new Black militancy was born." Given that Davis describes the time of the King and Kennedy assassinations as characterized by the "tranquility" of the status quo, it becomes clear that disruption, for her, comes only through armed Black resistance. While such resistance is not new, the iteration of its rise from Watts's ashes is. The "metamorphosis" of the Black Liberation Movement into Black Power marks the turning point in Davis's own transformation from observer to revolutionary participant.

In essence, Davis excludes King's work from consideration in the account of her radicalization, yet she includes his assassination—not as a wounding moment of outrage but rather as an event that taught her the necessity of violence in enacting change. Furthermore, when she laments being away in Frankfurt studying philosophy during the flowering of the Black Liberation Movement, she does not do so as a means of denigrating philosophy. Rather, she regrets not being in the United States to see and analyze, firsthand and philosophically, the liberation movements springing up across the country, and in particular in California. Davis wants to be close to the Black Panthers to gather data through proximity and to analyze philosophically yet in sympathy with their cause in order to present a new, authentic theory of liberation that transcends race by destroying false consciousness, or what she refers to here as "the collective coming to consciousness of my people."[9] She writes:

> My decision to study in Frankfurt had been made in 1964, against the backdrop of relative political tranquility. But by the time I left in the summer of 1965, thousands of sisters and brothers were screaming in the streets of Los Angeles that they had observed the rules of the game long enough, too long.
>
> Watts was exploding; furiously burning. And out of the ashes of Watts, Phoenix-like, a new Black militancy was being born....
>
> Adorno had readily agreed to direct my work on a doctoral dissertation. But now I felt it would be impossible for me to stay in Germany any longer. Two years was enough. I arranged for an appointment with Adorno at the Institute and explained to him that I had to go home. In my correspondence with Marcuse, he had already agreed to work with me at the University of California in San Diego, where he had accepted a position after having been practically pushed out of Brandeis for political reasons. I wanted

to continue my academic work, but I knew I could not do it unless I was politically involved. The struggle was a life-nerve; our only hope for survival.
I made up my mind. The journey was on. (1974, 143–45)

Davis extends the reach of this Black revolutionary consciousness to all
African Americans living abroad at the time, who she assumes must be
feeling as she is.[10] While it is unlikely that all African Americans outside
of the United States in 1965 felt the express need to philosophize the Black
Liberation Movement up close, it is nevertheless the case that Davis is assuming an instinctual need to consider freedom for what it is, a philosophical question. She does not reject her studies at Frankfurt, or philosophy
in general. Indeed, she wishes to continue on with them and complete her
dissertation, work that Adorno has already agreed to direct. However, for
Davis, part of philosophizing is action, and while she takes such action
in Germany, the locus of her struggle is in African America, among "her
people." She meets with Adorno to tell him that she is leaving Frankfurt
to study with Marcuse at San Diego; the philosophical tie with Frankfurt
School critical theory is never severed. Indeed, the continuity of Davis's
thought is striking.

II. The Inhuman Condition

Davis begins her fall 1969 UCLA lecture course, "Recurring Philosophical
Themes in Black Literature," with Frederick Douglass's autobiographies.
The lectures were published while Davis was in prison, and Marcuse was
asked to provide an introduction. If he felt no hesitation introducing Davis
to Adorno before the arrest, he experiences some trepidation about introducing these lectures.[11] In fact, Marcuse admits in an open letter to Davis published in *Ramparts* in February, 1971, to feeling "uneasy" about introducing Davis's published *Lectures on Liberation* (1971) for reasons that,
while perhaps obvious, require direct articulation:

> I felt uneasy when I was asked to introduce the publication of your first
> two lectures on Frederick Douglass, knowing that "under normal circum-
> stances" you would not have authorized their publication in the form in
> which they were delivered, and recognizing that they dealt with a world to
> which I am still an outsider—could I say anything about it in an authentic
> manner? And lastly, you were my student in philosophy, and I taught phi-
> losophy; your thesis was to be on a problem in Kant: what does your life for
> the liberation of the Black people, what does your present plight, have to
> do with the philosophy of German Idealism? (1971, 22)

Davis's mentor confesses that, aside from the trepidation he knows his former student would have about the publication of work she did not oversee, he himself is hesitant to say anything about Frederick Douglass and a "world to which I am still an outsider." In other words, Marcuse points to a racial barrier that leads to exclusion from the cultural and historical knowledge that would authorize him to say something about Douglass. That said, Marcuse does feel confident in speaking to Davis herself and, for his introductory purposes more importantly, the philosophical tradition reflected in her critical thought. Wondering again about the incommensurability between the African American and German experiences, Marcuse questions what German Idealism might be able to contribute to the struggle for Black liberation. He then lights, however, on a passage from Davis's lectures about Kant's concept of freedom and sees in a flash the connection between Idealism's understanding of it and the first act of liberation.[12] Douglass's violent resistance to Covey shows Marcuse that freedom begins with liberation and is not merely its goal. Within Black critical theory is a reading of Kant truer to sociopolitical experience than is commonly thought.

Marcuse next introduces into the letter's body, directly at its center, a reminiscence that serves a dual purpose yet still fits only awkwardly:

> The abstract philosophical concept of a freedom which can never be taken away suddenly comes to life and reveals its very concrete truth: freedom is not only the goal of liberation, it begins with liberation; it is there to be "practiced." This, I confess, I learned from you! Strange? I don't think so.
>
> There is more to it. Years ago, we had a seminar on Hegel. We read, among other texts, the famous chapter on the dialectic of Master and Slave in the *Phenomenology of Mind*. It ends with the recognition of the Master's dependence on the Slave, which outweighs the Slave's dependence on the Master. In your lecture, you discuss the *Phenomenology* and Hegel's philosophical analysis comes to life in the struggle in which the Black slave establishes his own identity and thereby destroys the violent power of the master. (1971, 22)

He recalls, without elaboration, that some time prior to her incarceration Davis had participated in his seminar on Hegel, in which was closely read the *Phenomenology*'s passages on the master-slave dialectic. Without reference to Davis's reactions to this material, Marcuse notes that for Hegel the slave eventually comes to a greater consciousness of freedom than the master, who remains dependent on the slave's labor and recognition.[13] Providing no further explanation, Marcuse then moves abruptly to the circumstances of Davis's imprisonment by relating how often he is asked to explain how it is that someone as intelligent and accomplished as Davis could have gotten herself into her predicament: "The world in which you grew up, your world (which is not mine), was one of cruelty, misery and persecution" (1971, 22). Carefully refusing to acknowledge her involvement as anything other than alleged, Marcuse suggests that because of the conditions in which she was raised—those of African Americans generally—philosophy could only mean something to Davis if translated into action. While the white male philosopher can consider his object in the abstract, for those born into oppression philosophical thought must lead to its concrete realization in social relations.

Marcuse's assumption, then, is that racial difference cannot be transcended merely through the exchange of narratives, and that there is something historically and socially irreducible in racial experience that prevents any form of unmediated understanding between different races. This mediation requires a specific form of universal thought, one which is not provided in literature, as Marcuse does not find that Frederick Douglass's autobiographies in themselves bridge this distance. Literature is incapable of offering interracial understanding as its mode of cognition cannot extend beyond the race of its producer in any authentic way. In other words, Marcuse can certainly read and understand Douglass's experiences, yet he cannot identify with them in any positive sense without a nonliterary form of mediation. Assuming that German Idealism would not furnish him with a mode of mediation appropriate to Douglass's text, Marcuse is amazed to discover through Davis's intervention that indeed African American literature and European thought can be profitably put together when the particulars of social experience are read as instances of practical tests and proofs of philosophical positions advanced by German Idealism and Western philosophy as a whole. In other words, Douglass offers a practical example of abstract Idealist thought as action. In this respect, Davis's introduction of Douglass and African American literature into German Idealism, and vice versa, allows for the experiential adjustment to universal propositions that have gone untested with regard to the full scope of human condition, or otherwise excluded it.

Indeed, it is with an implied reading of Arendt's *Human Condition* that Davis introduces the struggle for Black liberation. She writes:

The idea of freedom has justifiably been a dominating theme in the history of Western ideas. Man has been repeatedly defined in terms of his inalienable freedom. One of the most acute paradoxes present in the history of Western society is that while on a philosophical plane freedom has been delineated in the most lofty and sublime fashion, concrete reality has always been permeated with the most brutal forms of unfreedom, of enslavement. In ancient Greece, where, so we are taught, democracy had its source, it cannot be overlooked that in spite of all the philosophical assertions of man's freedom, in spite of the demand that man realize himself through exercising his freedom as a citizen of the polis, the majority of the people in Athens were not free. Women were not citizens, and slavery was an accepted institution. Moreover, there was definitely a form of racism present in Greek society, for only Greeks were suited for the benefits of freedom: all non-Greeks were called barbarians and by their very nature could not be deserving or even capable of freedom. (1971, 110)

While not naming Arendt directly, Davis's brief characterization of the philosophical concept of freedom neatly summarizes *The Human Condition*'s basic presentation of the origin and meaning of the polis. Davis does so to take issue with the historical practice of freedom in relation to its idea as expressed in ancient Greece and, more important, contemporary reading of the Greek polis. In other words, her concern is not for the truth of Greek slavery and ethnic bias; it is, rather, with contemporary philosophy's inability to account for these obvious contradictions to human freedom precisely because it defines "the human condition" from a theoretical position defined by racism. In a few lines Davis condemns the entirety of Western philosophy from Athens to the present as compromised by a definition of the human condition that is compromised by racism. Whether Athenian or American, the presence of slavery presents a constitutional crisis. As Davis puts it:

> In order not to mar the beauty of the Constitution and at the same time to protect the institution of slavery, they wrote about "persons held to service or labor," a euphemism for the word slavery, as being exceptional types of human beings, persons who do not merit the guarantees and rights of the Constitution.
>   Is man free or is he not? Ought he be free or ought not he be free? The history of Black literature provides, in my opinion, a much more illuminating account of the nature of freedom, its extent and limits, than all the philosophical discourses on this theme in the history of Western society. (1971, 110)

In this way, Davis indirectly addresses another of Arendt's shibboleths of freedom, Thomas Jefferson. Taking Jefferson as the embodiment of American constitutional rationality, Davis recalls his euphemism for slavery, "persons held to service or labor," when he defined not freedom but rather the conditions for its right, that of being human.[14] For Jefferson and the Constitution's framers, the slave was a person of a specific sort. This meant in turn that there are specific sorts of people, some of whom do not have access to the basic human rights guaranteed by the Bill of Rights and by constitutional protection. In this respect, Davis's concern is freedom as the basic condition of human being, where certain persons are qualified as being human on the basis of the rights granted them by political freedoms. For Davis, dialectically the statement is not tautological: it is nonsensical.[15]

Importantly, her stated method of philosophical analysis is dialectical in a recognizable sense: that of the Frankfurt School, where she studied under Adorno for two years, and that of Marcuse, who was her mentor in the United States as well as a close friend and supporter. She writes: "Black people have exposed, by their very existence, the inadequacies not only of the practice of freedom, but of its very theoretical formulation. Because if the theory of freedom remains isolated from the practice of freedom or rather is contradicted in reality, then this means that something must be wrong with the concept—that is, if we are thinking in a dialectical manner" (1971, 110). Davis uses the dialectical method to examine the philosophical concept of freedom in African American literature. She begins with the negative experience of freedom, or that of the slave, as presented in Frederick Douglass's autobiographies. Indeed, the "pivotal theme of [the] course will thus be the idea of freedom as it is unfolded in the literary understanding of Black people. Starting with Frederick Douglass, we will explore the slave's experience of his bondage and thus the negative experience of freedom. Most important here will be the crucial transformation of the concept of freedom as a static, given principle into the concept of liberation, the dynamic, active struggle for freedom" (1971, 111).[16]

The dialectical method is thus used in literary analysis, targeting the work of literature as the phenomenological cite of freedom's dialectical unfolding. In this respect, Davis reads African American literature as the medium of reflection making the history of philosophy visible from the negative perception of unfreedom, or the oppressed. Through African American literature Davis hopes to present from within philosophy in its positive expression of freedom a more thorough philosophical understanding of the human condition in relation to the history of freedom's negation. Because of its origin in slave writing, African American literature is uniquely constituted to present a full dialectical understanding of freedom, whereas before Frederick Douglass, according to Davis, Western philosophy had only been represented positively. For Davis, African American literature is essentially philosophical because it embodies the negative experience of freedom, which she understands as the struggle for liberation, or freedom's positive manifestation.

Davis reduces this dialectic to a question of freedom's definition as either psychological or physical. At first defining freedom in terms of a rigid either/or, Davis then suggests that the two, thought and action, may not be mutually exclusive, and indeed they may be constitutive of one another. In order to demonstrate her point, she begins by questioning Sartre's belief that even the slave is free to choose death over enslavement. Davis finds this understanding of freedom unacceptable, as the choice to terminate one's existence is not the dialectical negative of enslavement, which is liberation. Because the "freedom" Sartre sees in the slave's suicide is a false dialectical counterpart to freedom, Davis posits instead liberation as the necessary formulation of enslavement's dialectical negation. The slave, then, is free while enslaved only insofar as she has the possibility to liberate herself. Indeed, it is important to Davis's understanding of freedom that the slave be responsible for the removal of her chains if she is to realize the latent freedom within her. For if she were to be emancipated by the will of another, that same will could again enslave her, making her freedom conditional, rather than the unconditional state of freedom necessary for absolute liberation. She recapitulates to her students that "throughout the course, I have said, the notion of freedom will be the axis around which we will attempt to develop other philosophical concepts. We will encounter such metaphysical notions as identity, the problem of self-knowledge. The kind of philosophy of history that emerges out of the works we are studying will be crucial. The morality peculiar to an oppressed people is something we will have to come to grips with. As we progress along the path of the unfolding of freedom in Black literature, we should retrieve a whole host of related themes" (1971, 111).

Davis begins from the premise that the slave knows the definition of freedom as the negation of the condition of being enslaved. This understanding of freedom is fundamentally different from that of the master, who exercises his freedom only insofar as he possesses the ability to force another to labor for him. In this sense, the slave also realizes intuitively what must be done to achieve freedom as the negation of enslavement. From the slave's perspective, liberation is freedom. The slave achieves a higher, more authentic consciousness and state of being free than the master, whose freedom depends on the enslavement of another and who is therefore not free from the other who must obey the master's commands. Slavery creates the conditions for the realization of true freedom. Put this way, Davis combines the dialectical conclusion of Hegel's master-slave dialectic with Arendt's presentation of the origin of the public sphere of the polis as the freedom from labor and the right to slaves. She uses Hegel to condemn Arendt's reading of Greek political thought on freedom and slavery, insisting that only the slave can know true freedom as liberation and the state of being and having been liberated.

This consciousness of true freedom is both individual and collective. Davis writes:

> The collective consciousness of an oppressed people entails an understanding of the conditions of oppression and the possibilities of abolishing these conditions. At the end of his journey toward understanding, the slave finds a real grasp of what freedom means. He knows that it means the destruction of the master-slave relationship. And in this sense, his knowledge of freedom is more profound than that of the master. For the master feels himself free, and he feels himself free because he is able to control the lives of others. He is free at the expense of the freedom of another. The slave experiences the freedom of the master in its true light. He understands that the master's freedom is abstract freedom to suppress other human beings. The slave understands that this is a pseudoconcept of freedom and at this point is more enlightened than his master, for he realizes that the master is a slave of his own misconceptions, his own misdeeds, his own brutality, his own effort to oppress.
>
> Now I would like to go into the material. *Narrative of the Life of Frederick Douglass* constitutes a physical voyage from slavery to freedom that is both the conclusion and reflection of a philosophical voyage from slavery to freedom. We will see that neither voyage would have been possible alone; they are mutually determinant. (1971, 112)

Douglass's first autobiography, then, is for Davis the paradigmatic representation of the dialectical process of freedom, as embodied in the self-liberated slave. She posits his narrative as the account of the physical movement from slavery to freedom, which is itself a reflection of and on the philosophical nature of liberation in dialectical relation to forced labor. In this respect, the *Narrative* as text enacts a twofold process mediation whereby a physical journey both signifies and is enabled by the philosophical truth of freedom. This means that true freedom begins in slavery and can therefore be qualified as liberation. For Davis, true freedom and liberation are synonymous. Indeed, the philosophical truth of freedom cannot be told by anyone other than a former slave and can only be appreciated by those in a similar state of bondage or social oppression. Douglass is not exceptional in the philosophical presentation and experience of true freedom's possibility. Rather, he represents the paradigm of a general experience among those similar to him in composition and condition. As Davis puts it:

> His critical attitude when he fails to accept the usual answer—that God had made Black people to be slaves and white people to be masters—*Lectures on Liberation* is the basic condition that must be present before freedom

can become a possibility in the mind of the slave. We must not forget that throughout the history of Western society there is an abundance of justifications for the existence of slavery. Both Plato and Aristotle felt that some men were born to be slaves, some men are not born into a state of freedom. Religious justifications for slavery are to be found at every turn. (1971, 112–13)

Freedom as liberation begins when the slave resists the condition of slavery. This occurs as a sequence of questions the answers to which contradict both the physical and intellectual reality of the slave. Certainly, the slave conforms physically to the appearance of a human being. However, the definition of human being as given in philosophy is not dependent strictly on physical state. It is, rather, a condition of self-conscious freedom. The slave's awareness that she is not free also indicates a self-conscious understanding of freedom, in a negative dialectical sense. This means that the slave fulfills both the physical and intellectual requirements for freedom, and yet is not free. The justification for resistance is, therefore, manifest, insofar as liberation would mean newly won freedom for both master and slave. For the master rules under a false understanding of freedom, which is derived philosophically rather than theologically. Davis makes the source of the error evident when she locates the site of Douglass's negative recognition of freedom in his complaint that God could not have made slaves, and yet proceeds to explain the history of slavery's logic as beginning with Plato and Aristotle.

The rejection of this logic initiates the slave's journey to freedom through the struggle for liberation. Turning to Douglass's narrative, Davis reads the slave's physical confrontation with the overseer Covey philosophically as the refutation of slavery as a universally valid condition. As she describes it:

His first concrete experience of the possibility of freedom within the limits of slavery comes when he observes a slave resist a whipping. Now he transforms this resistance into a resistance of the mind, a refusal to accept the will of the master, and a determination to find independent means of judging the world.

Just as the slave has used violence against the violence of the aggressor, Frederick Douglass uses the knowledge of his owner—i.e., that learning unfits a man to be a slave—and turns it against him: he will set out to acquire knowledge precisely because it unfits a man to be a slave. Resistance, rejection, on every level, on every front, are integral elements of the voyage toward freedom. Alienation will become conscious through the process of knowledge. (1971, 116)

Douglass's defeat of the overseer signifies more than the individual slave's assertion of his rights as an individual; it also portrays the universal moment of liberation beginning in the denial of slavery's basic philosophical assumptions. In beating Covey, Douglass shows that the universal path to freedom begins with the violent act of liberation as the recognition and assertion of the universal human rights owed all slaves. That is to say, Davis makes clear her belief that freedom is won only in the violent struggle for liberation. Freedom begins in insurrectionary violence that rejects the foundations of the legal system that could allow unfreedom. In this respect, Douglass's act is more akin to natural or divine violence than the criminal act of a rebel slave.

For Davis reading Douglass, freedom is a matter of identity, as mediated by nature. It is by nature that human beings are free. The recognition of this humanity historically as the way in which the individual is freedom is the individual's identity as a human being. This identification is provided by nature mediated by authentic human activity, or free labor. Alienation from nature refuses the recognition of individual freedom, and thus the humanity of the alienated. Because the system of slavery alienates both master and slave from nature, neither master nor slave is free. Unable to identify oneself in nature, and thus incapable of apprehending the authentic identity choice of labor, master and slave lead inauthentic lives, or lives of nonidentity. Only consciousness of this condition presents the opportunity to escape this situation of negation in alienation, through the violent liberation of the slave. As Davis theorizes:

> The slave is actually conscious of the fact that freedom is not a fact, it is not a given, but rather something to be fought for; it can exist only through a process of struggle. The slave master, on the other hand, experiences his freedom as inalienable and thus as a fact: he is not aware that he too has been enslaved by his own system....
>
> Here the problem of freedom leads us directly into the question of identity. The condition of slavery is a condition of alienation. In a later autobiography he wrote, "Nature never intended that men and women should be either slaves or slaveholders, and nothing but rigid training long persisted in, can perfect the character of the one or the other." Slavery is an alienation from a natural condition; it is a violation of nature that distorts both parties—the slave and the slave owner. Alienation is the absence of authentic identity; in the case of the slave, he is alienated from his own freedom. (1971, 114)

Indeed, it is only the act of violence that penetrates the veil of nonidentity in which the slave is enveloped. Alienated from nature by slavery and experiencing humanity only through the definition the master accords himself, the slave has no possibility of becoming cognizant of freedom's existence from within its negation alone, having accepted the master's imposition of nonidentity or freedom's negation without resistance, which is to say by consent. This term means here by means of physical and intellectual violence, where no other option is known to exist. In other words, Davis understands "consent" as the imposition of a singular reality on the slave by violent means perceived as natural. It is only through violence that the slave comprehends the fact of another mode of being, as it was violence that established her reality as a slave ontologically and empirically. Without violence as the fundamental cognitive gesture, the slave would have no possibility of recognizing any condition beyond that of her own alienation and negation and that of the master's humanity.

The master's humanity consists in his positive knowledge of freedom. The moment the slave becomes aware of freedom in its positive sense, she begins the process of her liberation. Liberation begins with a transformative act of violence in which consciousness is altered from its manifestation as "the negative counterpart of freedom" to its positive realization in and as human being. In this respect, while an act of violence raises the slave to the awareness of her negative state, the apprehension of freedom in its positive incarnation, that of human being, occurs in stages as a result of knowledge's cultivation. Being human means that the slave is both educable and engaged in the progressive acquisition of knowledge. Freedom is the right to knowledge and the liberty of its pursuit. Resistance thus begins in violence yet proceeds according to pedagogical principles leading to the subject's instruction in and edification of being human as a form of action. For the act of resistance is here learning as a mode of self-conscious, self-directed self-fashioning.

Freedom as the right and ability to pursue the highest development of the self begins with the consciousness of alienation. Alienation functions such that it precludes consciousness of its work. In this respect, alienation is a form of consciousness; indeed, it is false consciousness. In order to experience true freedom, false consciousness must be overcome. The slave to false consciousness must, in a Platonic sense, loose his chains and rise out of the cave to the surface to see objects in their true light. The act of violence that breaks these chains is such that the world perceived through false consciousness is unveiled for what it is. False consciousness itself, however, must be dismantled and replaced by a process of self-cultivation that allows an education to populate the spaces in consciousness abandoned by false consciousness in retreat. In this way, liberation is as much a matter of *Bildung* as it is freedom, where the two can only be distinguished if the consciousness to be educated is shrouded in the darkness of false consciousness or has been touched by the light of true human being. Davis relates to her students that

> Marcuse likes to point out that we often ignore the fact that Karl Marx also said that religion is the wish-dream of an oppressed humanity. On the one hand, this statement means, of course, that wishes become dreams projected into an imaginary realm. But on the other hand, we have to ask ourselves: Is there anything else implied in Marx's statement about the notion of wish-dreams of an oppressed humanity? Think for a moment. Real wants, needs, and desires are transformed into wish-dreams via the process of religion because it seems so hopeless in this world: this is the perspective of an oppressed people. But what is important, what is crucial, is that those dreams are always on the verge of reverting to their original status—the real wishes and needs here on earth. There is always the possibility of redirecting those wish-dreams to the here-and-now.
>
> Frederick Douglass redirected those dreams. Nat Turner placed them within the framework of the real world. So there can be a positive function of religion because its very nature is to satisfy very urgent needs of people who are oppressed. (We are speaking only of the relation of oppressed people to religion, not attempting to analyze the notion of religion in and for itself.) There can be a positive function of religion. All that need be done is to say: let's begin to create that eternity of bliss for human society here in this world. Let's convert eternity into history. (1971, 119)

Davis highlights the role of Christianity in Douglass's thought, attributing to it both the worldly and the supernatural form in which to learn about freedom in human equality and to imagine his liberation. In other words, Christianity provided Douglass and other slaves a means by which to envision their own human being through liberation and freedom. This idea is contrary to Marx's condemnation of religion as the opiate of the masses; yet, as Davis points out through reference to Marcuse, Marx also described religious thought as a repository for worldly wishes and the hopes and dreams of an oppressed people. Focusing on this understanding of religion, Davis extols the value of Christianity for slave liberation as the intellectual and spiritual means by which to first picture freedom from the perspective of its positivity. In effect, Davis adopts Marcuse's more Freudian reading of Marx on religion, in which religious thought is a type of wish fulfillment, as in a dream, without investing in the sexual aspects of psychoanalytic thought that so attracted Cleaver.[17] Davis is impressed by Marcuse's analytical rigor yet rejects his incorporation of Eros in liberation.

While Davis's discussion of religion is by her own admission limited to its practice among oppressed peoples, it is nevertheless an instructive account of censorship within the peculiar institution. For as Davis notes, pro-slavery advocates selected passages from the Bible according to their content concerning docile servitude. The religion presented from a highly censored Bible taught that the highest form of obedience to God was obedience to the slaveholder and his proxies. The key to fashioning a Christianity devoted to plantation slavery's flourishing was, as Davis notes in regard to Frederick Douglass, maintaining a nearly 100 percent illiteracy rate among slaves so that they could not read the Bible for themselves. Had they been able to do so on a mass scale, revolt would certainly have broken out across the slave-owning states and territories, as the widespread lesson of civil disobedience in the Bible would have become evident. This understanding in Davis's thought of forced illiteracy on New World slaves also places literacy on equal footing with violence as a means to achieving self-consciousness as a slave in relation to freedom as a positive dialectical value. Literacy alone is a form of violent revolt, as it allows the slave to read all that is written in the Bible and elsewhere. As Davis reminds: "Thus, those passages in the Bible that emphasized obedience, humility, pacifism, patience were presented to the slave as the essence of Christianity. Those passages, on the other hand, that talked about equality, freedom, the ones Frederick Douglass was able to discover because, unlike most slaves, he taught himself to read—these were eliminated from the sermons the slave heard. A very censored version of Christianity was developed especially for the slaves" (1971, 120).

With literacy comes self-development through education, the end of which is the ability to think critically about the new possibility of freedom presented by the violent act of liberation, be it physical or literary. Davis spends a few moments at the beginning of her second lecture discussing the nature and meaning of Black studies, which she softly divides into the permeable categories of history and literature. Indeed, distinguishing between the two in name only, Davis goes on to suggest that the purpose of studying either under the disciplinary heading of Black studies is to learn from the past to replicate its successes and avoid its failures. The only way to do this is by grasping the way in which the past is relevant to the present. The study of history and literature are the sites at which the past can be evaluated for its inevitable effect in its reproduction as the present. This evaluation is philosophical, as it is philosophical ideas that provide the structural and conceptual basis for the reproduction of the past as present and the means of intervention to prevent the return of prolongation of the very unfreedom philosophy helped to create. Davis advocates for a thorough knowledge of philosophy's history and a critical-theoretical posture and attitude toward its recurrent principles and primary categorical assumptions.

In particular, Davis posits the dialectical method not merely as a philosophical device by which to analyze a static history of philosophy. This allows her to see that "the master is thought to be free, independent; the slave is thought to be unfree, dependent. The freedom and independence of the master, if we look at it philosophically, is a myth. It is one of those myths that, I was saying at the last session, we have to uncover in order to reach the real substance behind it. How could the master have been independent when it is the very institution of slavery that provided his wealth, that provided his means of sustenance? The master was dependent on the slave, dependent for his life on the slave" (1971, 130).

Dialectical method is for Davis also the manner in which contradiction in philosophical thought is revealed as contradiction, indicating the first step toward liberation and its reconciliation in resistance. Douglass realizes a contradiction in the concept of freedom as developed ideologically in the history of philosophy and practiced in slavery. Likewise, he apprehends another contradiction in the religious practice of his master, which stands in direct opposition to the Christian faith Captain Auld professes. This means that not only is the moment of contradiction or negation in dialectical method crucial to liberation in thought and practice, it also indicates the innate philosophical mode of cognition by which freedom can be said to be the fundamental characteristic of human being. Freedom is the human condition in which beings attempt to resolve the contradictions of their social circumstances. Freedom is possible in slavery, if only as a mode of cognition that demands liberation.

Part of this freedom in slavery is won within and through religion. Davis subscribes to the idea that religion is ideological and intended in its contradictory presentation by and to the master to confirm slavery as the will of God and a natural fact. Yet Davis maintains that within religion, that is to say within ideology, freedom can be found when alienation is confronted in terms of contradiction and dialectical correction according to the ideal intent of the institution. That is to say, Davis does not wish to abolish religion because she does not see it as wholly ideological. Like the concept of freedom itself, religion possesses truths that are not metaphysical but rather practical and theoretical in nature. The very contradictory structure of its logic as formulated by the master provides enlightenment to the slave in the negation of the negation. Religion's deconstruction offers the slave a moment of clarity and self-conscious recognition that enables the first step in liberation and thus in resistance. Davis's list of slave revolutionaries and resistors each, according to her, remain within religion and use it as a potent force in the freedom struggle. She does not, however, detail the positive aspect of religion's dialect in slavery and freedom. In other words, Eros is absent from the letter of her discussion and is not even assumed.

Instead, alienation features so prominently that Eros would seem impossible in any authentic sense. The slave's alienation, however, is not that of the master. Both master and slave find themselves alienated from freedom, yet not in the same way. The slave's alienation is that of being property rather than human being in the sense defined by freedom. As an exchange value, or "money," as Davis puts it, the slave is alienated from freedom, and therefore from human being. The master is not alienated from human being, and therefore is not property. On the contrary, as a property owner, the master is alienated from nature in his inability to acknowledge the full scope of human being. The master's understanding of nature, and therefore himself, is incomplete, indeed intentionally so. Unable to perceive the full breadth of human nature, the master subverts and perverts his own nature through the denial of freedom to the other. Nature as a concept is important for Davis's understanding of freedom, as the master, too, is in a condition of unfreedom, albeit for different reasons than the slave.

Because of this, Davis concludes that the master is always on the verge of becoming the slave, and the slave the master. As evidence, she cites Douglass's fight with Covey, which forms nearly the totality of her engagement with Douglass's texts, and Hegel's master-slave dialectic. In the context of the latter, she provides some speculative remarks on the contradictory yet productive nature of thought's dialectical movement. Introducing these remarks only to dismiss them as too speculative for the practical application of philosophy she seeks to describe, Davis then suggests on the basis of an understanding of dialectic as contradiction alone that Hegel presents the master's condition as one of slavery, and vice versa. While Hegel is aware that the master depends on the slave to meet life's necessities for him, he does not insist that the master does not understand necessity as a concept. This is not the case with the slave, who toils without a sense of the superfluous, and therefore without pleasure. Despite being necessity's dialectical partner, pleasure as superfluous is absent from Davis's account of Hegel's *Phenomenology of Mind*. Davis does not account for desire, its frustration, and its satisfaction. Her rejection of Marcuse's emphasis on Eros leads to a misreading of Hegel with consequences for her critical theory of Black liberation.

For the exclusion of desire from Hegel's master-slave dialectic also leads to its elimination from consideration in Marxist thought on dialectical subjectivity and freedom. In effect, Davis forecloses on the ontological aspect of the initial confrontation between master and slave, in which subjects of desire engage in a struggle for identity as driven by each's desire for the Other as the self. The desire to be oneself is the desire for master. The slave must renounce this and all desire, indicating that freedom and desire are intimately, indeed definitionally connected. This aspect of Hegel's phenomenology of mind in and as dialectical method and subject constitution informs Marcuse's psychoanalytic presentation of liberation yet is absent from Davis's. This has a schematizing effect on Davis's thought in which the origin of slavery and the engine of liberation cannot be accounted for in her dual discussion of liberation and freedom. The dialectical method she extols as the substance of history has no motivating factor setting it in motion beyond a notion of greed that passes without interrogation. The liberating violence perpetrated by the slave comes about in response to an incompleteness in dialectical logic rather than as the desire for freedom or anything else.

For Davis, Eros is absent from her presentation of dialectical thought because desire plays no role in its ultimately mechanistic function. The master-slave dialectic is propelled forward by the natural sense of domination supporting white supremacist thought rather than the desire for identity intrinsic in Hegel's phenomenology of mind. In other words, Davis posits white supremacy is the cause of slavery rather than presenting the desire for identity in Hegelian dialectical thought as the origin of white supremacy. This enables her to avoid the fraught subject of mutual desire between the races and thus any compromise of the slave's integrity with regard to freedom. For in Hegel's account of mastery's dialectical origin, the slave consciously concedes his freedom as a result of his desire to avoid death, thereby acknowledging freedom's objective definition. For Davis, the slave comes to know freedom's meaning only through the movement of liberation and is therefore a subject without desire. The slave's constitution as a conscious object thus obeys the formal principles of dialectical thought without regard for the law of "libidinal" force that sets it in motion.

This is an important distinction in Davis's thought, for it forecloses on the possibility of Eros as a mode of communal liberation. In effect, all subjects must come to freedom individually, through a universally patterned yet singularly structured experience of liberation. The individual slave may revolt as instigated by highly subjective, if not idiosyncratic, experience that nevertheless provokes the universal response of violent resistance. However, this insurrectionary action cannot be coordinated by anything other than chance or fate. In this respect, while the slave's individual act of revolt is intentional, any movement of mass resistance would have to be instinctual or natural, as no affective bond exists between slaves that would coordinate their insurrectionary action as anything more than a collection of revolutionaries each acting in her own interest. Without Eros or any affective mode of identification between subjects of liberation, no communal movement of liberation is possible beyond that which is provided by fated divine violence.

Davis's version of critical theory incorporates a philosophy of history that privileges the slave above the master in the experience of freedom. Because of this, Davis has not yet abandoned the universality of the human condition, a conceit for which any conception of a specifically Black public sphere would still be necessary. Her understanding of history and freedom is, then, derived from an Idealist perspective reliant on dialectical materialism for its teleological conception of social liberation. It depends on an idea of nature that comprehends all that humanistic thought excludes, including the political role played by slave labor in economic production.

For Davis, the social reality of the slave as outside of history contradicts the definition of freedom that subtends the production of self-knowledge. The slave's freedom would mean that of the master, from an epistemological standpoint. Ontologically, the slave redeems history, where the historicity of being is understood teleologically as absolute slave subjectivity. Davis thus retains a sense of the Idealist absolute as the slave coming to knowledge of herself teleologically through the experience of *her* bondage and *her* freedom. The slave's initial awakening to history occurs in reaction to her first intuitive act of violent resistance. This would also mean that the slave's entrance into historical consciousness is instinctual, as the violence that suddenly erupts from the newly resistant slave is otherwise inexplicable. For Davis, this impulse to commit liberating violence comes from an instinctual longing for freedom that defines the African American experience. It drives the initial act of violent liberation and continues to operate in Black history, and it is historiographically recorded by Black expressive culture. The asocial existence of the slave becomes in history the record of private struggle generated by the individual lives and longings of African Americans.

In this sense, the rigorous universalism of critical-theoretical reflection on freedom, revolutionary violence, and liberation cannot accommodate race-specific essentialism. Black Power philosophers could not fully, and in some cases even partially, accept theories of Black liberation reliant on the same universalist notions of human being that created conditions of racial inequality in the first place. Here Black liberation is not part of the unfinished project of the Enlightenment. Rather, it is the destruction of this project. Black Power philosophers such as Davis and Cleaver looked to, and then through, critical theory for inspiration. There they originally found substantive essentialist theories of human difference and segregated becoming that, with significant alteration, explained the unique historical presence of Africans and people of African descent in a teleological narrative of racial domination. Cleaver's rejection of what he refers to as Marxist-Leninist thought, and his later conversion to Mormonism, show a longing not for proletarian revolution but rather for hierarchy in the social order of salvation.

Black Aesthetic Theory [CONCLUSION]

In *Knowledge and Human Interests* (1968), Habermas describes philosophy's "classical tradition" as "theory," a mode of ontological inquiry related to the discovery of "Ideas." Habermas understands "Ideas" as "constellations of concepts" that provide ethical force and significance to social existence. Theory, then, uncovers the ontological framework of the Idea, revealing the constituent elements of its ethical intervention in society. For this reason, it is important to know what theory is in order to understand how social relations are determined within the power of its ethical force.

To best do this, Habermas traces the etymology of the Greek word *theoria*, or "looking on," which in classical philosophy indicated the contemplation of the cosmos ([1968] 1971, 301). However, this act of contemplation entailed the internal conformity of the subject to the object contemplated. In order for the early astronomer to obtain knowledge of the heavens, it was first necessary to transform internally to conform cognitively to the physical activity of transmitting information about the stars, which was thought to be identical to that of the heavenly bodies themselves. This means that while nature functioned according to the same general principles regardless of the object under investigation, human being as the observational subject possessed the natural ability to reproduce or mimic in thought functions in nature. To obtain objective knowledge of nature, the subject need only surveil her own thought process while contemplating an object in nature. This double activity of thought and its critical appraisal formed the basis of theory.

According to Habermas, the classical understanding of theory also holds that the reflective aspect of the subject engaged in contemplation of the cosmos forms her thoughts in harmony with the natural movement of the object investigated. These thoughts in turn shape the existence of the investigating subject, whereby a life is fashioned that conforms to the natural order observed. At this point, theory and ethics meet, and the pursuit of knowledge ethically determines the lifeworld of the investigator. The effect of this is the creation of social relations established according to ethical positions derived from nature and formulated in theory. Theory, in the classical sense, is the ontology of ethical precepts as objective human knowledge. Modern philosophy could not maintain this distinction, as "objectivism is eliminated not through the power of renewed *theoria* but through demonstrating what it conceals: the connection of knowledge and interest" ([1968] 1971, 316–17). Unable to deny the extent to which self-interest determines the "objective" disposition of the observer, or *theoros*, Habermas posits that "philosophy remains true to its classical tradition by renouncing it. The insight that the truth of statements is linked in the last analysis to the intention of the good and true life can be preserved today only in the ruins of ontology" ([1968] 1971, 317).

Thought of in terms of classical *theoria*, "thinking literature" produces an objectivist ontology of both "thinking" and "literature," as well as of the ethical structure giving value to all the social relations they describe. For this reason, Black aesthetic critics writing in the late 1960s to mid-1970s accepted the ontology outlined in Baraka's 1963 *Blues People* and used it to construct a theory of Black liberation. However, the book's difficult union of aesthetic universalism and racial particularism made its theoretical position difficult to maintain. The qualified acceptance of aesthetic universalism in Western poetry is evident in Hoyt Fuller's "Towards A Black Aesthetic" (1968) in which—after quoting Joseph Bevans Bush's "Nittygritty," a poem dedicated to Baraka (Jones)—he claims that "Black revolutionaries" do not "reject the 'universal' statements inherent in Shakespeare's works; what they do reject, however, is the literary assumption that the style and language and the concerns of Shakespeare establish the appropriate limits and 'frame of reference' for Black poetry and people" ([1968] 1994, 203). Fuller refers to Black poets as revolutionaries, and he writes of poetry as street-level revolutionary insurgence that recognizes universalist themes—yet not as they are presented in Western poetry. Instead, Fuller suggests that the racially superior subject at the center of Western universalism is Black, not white. He then gives Baraka's ontologically informed aesthetic of Black exceptionalism explicit revolutionary goals. Whereas Baraka's philosophy identified and classified autonomous Black aesthetic singularity, Fuller and others mobilize "Black art" for battle.

This "radical reordering of the western cultural aesthetic," as Larry Neal referred to it, moved beyond a more speculative mode of Black being, taking for granted Baraka's ontological grounding of a separate, superior

Black community (1968, 29). Instead, Neal articulates the terms of critical engagement for African American literary theory and criticism. His task is epistemological, involving the adumbration of aesthetic categories in which the Black literary critic works, identifying "Literary Negro-ness" according to a new set of criteria. Neal's "Literary Negro-ness" is oriented toward a categorical expression of Black aesthetic practices that reassign racial value to Western aesthetic forms, rather than merely rearrange them. The form these practices take is determined by the Black community rather than Western traditions as they have been valued traditionally. This conceptually reconfigured constellation of aesthetic practices yields a new, racially specific critical vocabulary derived from the discursive field of its cultural expression, the Black community itself.

Addison Gayle characterized this struggle for the "Black Aesthetic" as the attempt to break free even of Neal's radical revaluation of the "western cultural aesthetic." Calling it the "white aesthetic," Gayle's 1971 *The Black Aesthetic* rejects Western philosophy in toto as racist ideology by which peoples of African descent were denied the status of "beautiful." In addition to "pleasing," "beautiful" also signified "good." As "ugly" and "bad," blacks could be dehumanized according to a rule of human differentiation and hierarchy determined by arbitrarily determined aesthetic norms. For Gayle, therefore, the union of ontology and aesthetics in Western philosophy had to be refuted in its entirety. The Black aesthetic was not a matter of the reorganization of Western philosophical categories but rather their utter destruction and replacement with "Black is Beautiful" ([1971] 1994, 212).

Writing in "After LeRoi Jones," Don L. Lee claims that "Black art of the sixties, on the national scene, started with the advent of LeRoi Jones (Amiri Baraka) and the Black theater" ([1971] 1994, 221). By the 1970s, however, the hermeneutic understanding of Black art has transformed. For Lee, the essential substance of Black art is constant and universal; however, its critical apprehension is subject to historical development, as the "Black sensibility" "grows" and becomes more capable of discerning Blackness obscured by the white aesthetic. The critic of heightened Black sensibility perceives Blackness, seeing that "it cannot be defined in any definite way." In the early 1960s, Jones attempts to define Blackness in a definite way, philosophically; in the early 1970s Amiri Baraka, Lee believes, has seen, along with other critics of heightened Black sensibility, that Blackness is inscrutable. As a mystery, Blackness cannot be defined through the concepts and categories of Western philosophy. Knowledge of Blackness is negative and ineffable, experienced first as a feeling and then given a critical vocabulary that will forever be unable to define the being of Blackness. At this point, a Black hermeneutic is no longer possible.

In her later work *Blues Legacies and Black Feminism: Gertrude "Ma" Rainey, Bessie Smith, and Billie Holiday* (1998), Angela Y. Davis appears to return to the "aesthetic dimension" of African American life and to the theoretical assumptions of a Black hermeneutic. In so doing, Davis indirectly offers a critical reason for her lack of interest in revolutionary love over violence in her early years, when she concentrated on the continuity of racist oppression between slavery and the present—and despite her close ties to Herbert Marcuse. While Marcuse's theory never disappears from her work, the later work makes a more overt, if still disavowed, gesture toward the role of Eros in his thought:

> In examining Billie Holiday's love songs, I find it useful to employ Herbert Marcuse's notion of the "aesthetic dimension," first explored in his work *Eros and Civilization* and later elaborated in *The Aesthetic Dimension*.... While Marcuse's notion of "aesthetic form" is anchored in a conception of "authentic" or "great" art informed by eighteenth- and nineteenth-century European literature, aspects of his theory of the subversive potential of art, developed as a critique of orthodox Marxist aesthetics, can be invoked not for the purpose of assimilating Holiday's music into the canon of "great" art, but rather as a way of understanding the persisting power and appeal of her performances. (1998, 163–64)

At the time of the Douglass lectures, Davis treated Black life as entirely public, conditioned by the "transhistorical," "universal" forces that shaped American political-discursive patterns and practices. She explains this in her later work on the blues by suggesting that "individual," contingent expressions of sexual love were unknown in the antebellum South, as they would have been violently suppressed by slave owners who viewed Black sexuality as a form of production they owned. Slave music is collective, articulating, however covertly, subjective yearnings for freedom, and not freedom itself. It is only post-emancipation that Black music, and specifically the blues, begins to reflect personal wants and needs in the public sphere, raising them to the level of universalist claims.

Davis sees Billie Holiday's music, then, as a collective enterprise that forms its aesthetic dimension not as the product of an individual's artistic expression but rather as the articulation of the collective's social situation as mediated by the singular talent. Drawing on Marcuse's theory of the aesthetic dimension's role in the struggle for liberation, Davis affirms that art offers a way of perceiving social reality that allows for an alternative vision to the dominant mode of ideological and instrumental comprehension imposed on society by hegemonic white male authority. However, Davis does not follow Marcuse in any but the most schematic understanding of the aesthetic dimension as he formulates it. For Marcuse, the aesthetic dimension of art is defined in opposition to repressive society, where "repression" maintains its psychoanalytic valence. Davis does not acknowledge social desire in this sense and therefore empties Marcuse's aesthetic dimension of its origin in the individual as a product of the artist's repression, reflective of society's. The result of her evaluation of psychoanalytic discourse is that Davis's presentation of aesthetic dimension appears closer to Adorno's concept aesthetic autonomy than to Marcuse's dialectic of art and liberation.

For Davis does not consider individual autonomy as a factor in the creation of the aesthetic dimension. Billie Holiday's art represents the community from which she originates and her racial disposition, considered as a biological fact. The content of Holiday's work, while appearing highly idiosyncratic, is in fact shared racially and communally, without approaching a universal sense of human being. In this sense, Davis's formulation of the aesthetic dimension, while following Adorno's theory of aesthetic autonomy and the avant-garde, most closely resembles his ideas on language. This formulation privileges the private sphere of African American experience over that of the wider American public sphere, while still positing the existence of a unique African American form of political resistance. The experience of freedom is articulated in African American expressive culture as a concrete, historically manifest phenomenon. That is to say that freedom is both an aesthetic experience and a political aspiration. As aesthetic experience, the cultural realization of freedom in art inspires the first act of liberation, as directed by the consciousness newly awakened to its own positive human being. In other words, Davis has not altered the basic critical-theoretical structure of her work in the intervening years between her lectures on liberation and her later work on jazz and blues singers. She has, however, attributed the liberation of the oppressed consciousness to the aesthetic dimension of a post-emancipation society grappling with slavery's legacy of violence, whereas the slave could only know liberation by committing, rather than commemorating, acts of violence.[1]

Within this context, Davis writes of the symbiosis of the individual talent and the history of a specific social and racial form of aesthetic production that generates the enduring work of art. Billie Holiday's music is both an entry in and a catalog of African American expressive culture. As such, it expresses what Davis refers to as Holiday's "aesthetic agency," which provides the form by which the individual identifies with the performance rather than the performer, as a mode of cultural and racial recognition. In the case of Holiday and in all cases, Davis insists, aesthetic agency is gendered, as the social experience of women is categorically different from that of men. This does not mean, however, that aesthetic agency fails to offer men, in the case of Holiday, insight into the African American experience considered as a totality. It creates instead a depth to Holiday's music that is discerned differently depending on gender. Part of this gendered experience will include erotic investment, yet not from the universalistic phenomenological perspective of genderless human being. Eros does not serve to characterize collective experience but rather to demarcate the limits of the individual.

Indeed, in *Women, Race & Class* (1981), Davis, writing in the context of sexual violence against female slaves, cites Frederick Douglass for examples of what she sees as widespread, violent resistance to assault:

> When Frederick Douglass reflected on his childhood introduction to the merciless violence of slavery, he recalled the floggings and torture of many rebellious women. His cousin, for example, was horribly beaten as she unsuccessfully resisted an overseer's sexual attack. A woman called Aunt Esther was viciously flogged for defying her master, who insisted that she break off relations with a man she loved. One of Frederick Douglass's most vivid descriptions of the ruthless punishments reserved for slaves involved a young woman named Nellie, who was whipped for the offense of "impudence".... Douglass adds that he doubts whether this overseer ever attempted to whip Nellie again. (1981, 15–16)

In particular, she allows Douglass to recount an overseer's torture of a slave who, it is strongly implied by both Douglass and Davis, has resisted his attempts to rape her. Tied to a tree kicking and screaming, the woman is whipped to within an inch of her life—and still curses the overseer who commits this atrocity. Douglass suggests that after this supreme display of defiance the overseer never again attacked her. In effect, Douglass provides the female version of his conflict with Covey, in which the ability to inflict physical harm on an overseer is replaced with the will and stamina to endure the overseer's violence.[2] For Davis, the slave's will to freedom is racial as well as historical.

Herein lies the fundamental difference between Davis's theory of liberation and human freedom and that of Marcuse and the Frankfurt School more generally. The universal character of human freedom demands a loss of the particular with regard to race, culture, and the history of a discrete collective or identity. Davis rejects this, positing instead the primacy of racial experience as determined by constituent cultural attributes and the material-social history of the political collective. The idea of Eros as Marcuse presents it—that is, as an affective force capable of inciting and advancing the struggle for liberation and human freedom by transgressing

ideological constraints and artificial yet naturalized social limitations—
forms no part of Davis's thought.

This is because, for Davis, the love presented in the blues originates in
the African American private sphere and is the basis for individual desire's
aesthetic representation as personal acts of freedom in the Black public
sphere. The "blues aesthetic" is not revolutionary but rather communicative action. Commenting on the introduction and proliferation of the critical phrase "blues aesthetic" in African American studies, Amiri Baraka
qualifies it by insisting that it possesses value only if it retains the constitutive revolutionary element of the blues. Positing that the blues is only "one
vector" of the greater continuum of African American aesthetics, Baraka
goes on to insist that no aspect of African American aesthetic production
can be considered free of its cultural-material origins, and that African
American expressivity is the result of historical forces and achieves no
formal independence from its embedded political character. Existing by
means of "a common psychological development," culture reflects the political consciousness of a people rigorously qualified by shared historical-
material pressures. In this respect, any discussion of the "blues aesthetic"
outside of its political function both as reflective expression and activist
intervention is no longer a consideration of either aesthetics or African
American culture. That is to say that, for Baraka, whereas the blues may
still encapsulate the dialectic of African American history and sociality in
terms of their form and function as mutually constitutive and functionally
identical, it is now also the embodied spirit of Blackness as manifest in African sexuality. This origin is experienced as sexual ecstasy: "The ecstasy
is the being, the is/life. So jazz is *jism*, come music, creating [*sic*] music.
Coming is the spiritual presence of the all-existent one focused, we can
see, inhaling" (1991, 104). This essence is that of love, or the bond the
provides coherence of spirit through the material history of a race. The
blues is the sonic expression of intraracial love, in both its erotic and its
filial senses. Because of this, love professes its own law, that of the consciousness of the race. Love is the cognitive apparatus and critical function of Blackness.

This realization comes from Baraka's reengagement with the African
basis of African American cultural expression, which he addresses directly
at the essay's end in a *"Blues People* Addenda." Here Baraka indicates that
his concentration in *Blues People* on the exclusivity of African America's
claim to African origins may have been incorrect. The actual case may be
that American culture generally owes its existence and essence to Africa's
emphasis on the socially cohesive force of sexuality. Putting aside the
question whether or not *Blues People* actually gave African culture pride of
place in its theoretical-historical framework of African American expres-

sivity, the claim that American culture as a whole is African-based brings Baraka's emphasis on love strongly in line with the perspective of the civil rights movement, insofar as love is the prime mover of a struggle for all of America, regardless of where this love came from. Had Baraka posited Christian instead of African love as the foundation of American culture, he would be in complete agreement with King. That said, his preference for African love is determined by an erotic aspect obviously absent from King's notion of love as filiation. The erotic nature of love calls for revolution rather than reconciliation. As Baraka writes in the poem "Revolutionary Love" (1978), "Black Revolutionary Woman / were you my woman, and even in the pit / of raging struggle, we need what we love, / we need what we desire to create, were you / my woman, I'd call you companion, comrade, / sister, Black lady, Afrikan faith, I'd call you / house, Black Revolutionary woman I'd call you wife" (2004, 325).

Baraka, then, feels that love is the expression of a people's spirit and the articulation of their historical being as a race, yet he disagrees with the civil rights icon on the nature of that love. In this sense, Baraka's conception of "revolutionary love" is paradigmatic for Black Power leaders and thinkers of the "Afrikan faith." Love is not a matter of "the brotherhood of all men"; it is the specific substance that binds the race to the "house" of the Black revolutionary woman. Love separates races as it defines the singular racial group in its iteration as a historical and political entity. In this respect, love is essential to any "revolutionary" program, in that it provides the basis for collective self-articulation in any historical respect. Revolutionary love is sexual, procreative, and therefore biological, as it seeks to guarantee the racial continuity and integrity of the race. It is, therefore, based on visual recognition, cultural familiarity, and political affiliation. In short, racially determined, sexual love defines all social relations. The dialectic of Black Enlightenment concludes in the realization that Blackness will not be theorized, at least not in Habermas's ontological and universalist sense of the term.[3]

The 1970s are often seen as the period of theory's "onset" in African American literary criticism.[4] This is undoubtably the case, yet, following Habermas, it is important to note that "theory" does not mean "philosophy," and need not signify "critical theory." The refusal to define "Blackness" outside of its genitive role as the origin of Black arts was a tacit rejection of the more academic philosophy shaping Amiri Baraka's early criticism. As LeRoi Jones, Baraka reshaped Adorno's philosophy of music and critique of the culture industry while adapting Heideggerian phenomenology to suit his conception of Blackness as the African essence productive of African American blues culture. Baraka's 1963 *Blues People* unabashedly presents a *theory* of Black music, yet it does so, also unabashedly, using philosophy. The choice is not without political stakes that become all too apparent in the latter half of the 1960s, when African American critics take up Baraka's challenge and that of the Black arts movement.

The "theory" of African American criticism's break in the early 1960s with the sociological and anthropological mode of critical discourse characterizing 1950s criticism looks to contemporary philosophy and the work of Gadamer, Adorno, Marcuse, Arendt, Habermas, and others. The works of these philosophers are not incidental to African American thought at this time: they help shape it. Yet, as popular as some of these philosophers were, their works were identified with academic philosophy that was seen as complicit with the "white critic" that LeRoi Jones condemned and the "white aesthetic" that Addison Gayle seeks to suppress.

The rise of "theory" in the 1970s is accompanied by that of Black studies in the academy.[5] The extent to which African American studies had to be distinguished as a discipline and a field from those with which it was inevitably enmeshed demanded a methodological and archival separation from some modes of interpretation that previously had been taken for granted. The data set and historical substance of its object made Black studies unique among its peers, and with this singularity came a degree of anxiety and consternation over institutional practices. The "theory" of the 1960s becomes the theory of the 1970s, whereby academic philosophy is jettisoned along with the ability to define Blackness in this way, in order to meet academe's demands of disciplinarity. The radicalism of 1971's Black aesthetic clears the field for disciplinary recognition and the eventual rise of African American studies, at the cost of philosophical universalism.

By the early 1970s, the dream of universalism in philosophy and in African American criticism had been deferred indefinitely. African American literary criticism instead became self-reflexive, contemplating an individual archive of texts and ideas that no longer required reference points beyond the scope of its immediate vision. Of course, African American criticism never stopped using philosophy; however, it remained contained within conceptions of Blackness that ultimately could not be defined universally, moving forever "towards" a universally situated theory of Black art without ever arriving there. The encounter with this openly Derridean aspect of theory is not surprising in the 1970s, as French Theory overtook literary study in the United States at that time.[6] In this respect, the difference between theory and philosophy in African American literary criticism both at this time and later was critical orientation. According to Habermas, philosophy questions the ontological foundation of epistemic assumptions, whereas theory provides the ontological foundations from which epistemic assumptions follow. LeRoi Jones's philosophy asserted the ontological separation of Black and white, which was revealed phenomenally in cultural production and articulated critically in hermeneutic interpretation. Amiri Baraka's work in theory asserts the impossibility to express, definitionally, Black and white difference. This shortcoming is revealed experientially in everyday life and expressed critically in a poetics of academic speculation. Where once literary criticism sought to define Black being-in-the-world hermeneutically in the Black work of literature, now Blackness is defined by the poetic sensibilities of the talented, individual critic. The end of theory in African American literary criticism has become the impossible reconciliation of LeRoi Jones's aesthetic universalism with blues particularism amid the ruins of ontology.

Acknowledgments

This book would not exist without the incredible intelligence and energy of Nan Z. Da, Anahid Nersessian, and Alan Thomas. I would also like to thank the University of Chicago Press's two anonymous readers for their careful reading and insightful suggestions. I owe a debt of gratitude to my amazing colleague Jeanne-Marie Jackson-Awotwi for her wonderful support. And I would like to thank my wife, Kerri, for everything.

Notes

Introduction

1. See Wright's 1937 "Blueprint for Negro Writing" for his most complete statement on literary production.

2. For primary texts in the now famous debate, see Howe's 1952 review of Ellison's *Invisible Man*, "Man Underground," and his 1963 essay, "Black Boys and Native Sons." Ellison's 1963 riposte, "The World and the Jug," and his 1964, "A Rejoinder," to Howe's, "A Reply to Ralph Ellison" (1964).

3. In addition to her anthropological works, see also Hurston's "Characteristics of Negro Expression" (1934) for an example of her anthropological literary criticism and the types of cultural categories through which it reads. See also Thompson 2007.

4. Baldwin was born in 1924, Baraka in 1934, and Ellison in 1914.

5. General accounts of Black Power on which this study relies are Slate 2012; Ongiri 2010; Rojas 2007; Joseph 2009, 2006; Conyers 2007; and Van Deburg 1992.

6. I am excluding here Black Marxism and Black thought associated with the Communist Party in the 1930s. This book's concern is with the Black appropriation of academic philosophy and speculation on racial being as political intervention, rather than with the conceptualization of radical political praxis from a Eurocentric point of view. See C. Robinson 1983.

7. See Lewis Gordon's *Existentia Africana* (2000) and his edited volume, *Existence in Black* (1997). For a reading of the Black intellectual with jazz and pragmatism, see Muyumba 2009.

8. On German émigré philosophy and intellectual thought, see Friedman 2014; Goebel and Weigel 2012; R. H. King 2004, 1992; Jay 1985.

9. On Heidegger's training and its appearance in the philosophy of his former famous students, see Wolin 2001.

10. A product of Black Power, Black liberation theology relies on this as well. See Cone and Wilmore 1993, 1979; Cone 1970, 1969.

11. On African American biblical interpretation and hermeneutics, see Powery and Sadler 2016; S. A. Johnson 2015; Marbury 2015; M. J. Brown 2004; West and Glaude Jr. 2003; Roberts 2001; Fulop and Raboteau 1996; Felder 1991.

12. This result, of course, is not synonymous with contemporary critical race theory or intersectionality as critical social theory.

Chapter One

1. For Gadamer's work in the United States in relation to "the new hermeneutic," see Braaten 2018.

2. On the Gadamer-Habermas debate, see Dallmayr 2000; How 1995.

3. See Kimmerle 1967. By 1966, Gadamer had already published an English translation of "The Universality of the Hermeneutical Problem" and other essays. His work was treated in Alonso Schökel 1963 and in Robinson and Cobb's 1964 edited volume, *The New Hermeneutic*. See also Ringma 1999.

4. For an early understanding of Gadamer on Schleiermacher, hermeneutics, and literature, see Geier 1968, 435–36.

5. By 1962, the book was widely discussed at the meeting of the Catholic Biblical Association. Indeed, already in 1965, some scholars and theologians were asking "How New Is the New Hermeneutic?"

6. Hirsch's 1967 book, *Validity in Interpretation*, continued the attack, albeit an uneven and at times flawed one. The vehemence of the critique was noted at the time. See Palmer 1969.

7. Hirsch manages this backhanded compliment: "Under the somewhat ironic title *Wahrheit und Methode* (Tübingen 1960) Professor Hans-Georg Gadamer has published the most substantial treatise on hermeneutic theory that has come from Germany in this century" (Hirsch 1965, 488).

8. On the methodological implications of Gadamer's distinction between statements and speculative language, see Walsh 2004.

9. Gadamer's work was seen at the time by many theologians as a watershed moment in hermeneutics. See Scharlemann 1968, 616.

10. Gadamer's hermeneutics began to achieve acclaim in the United States for its innovative interpretation of an established and important philosophical tradition. See Seebohm 1977, 186.

11. In Gadamer, the free play of words in poetic language escapes the instrumentality of those words' communicative context in ordinary language. This allows for the lifeworld of the subject to appear in the historicity of its own intentional sphere rather than in that of the situation of its use. Literature provides moral immediacy in the dialogic exchange between speaker and Other by revealing the objective factors involved in bringing the speaker to speech. While the literary context of the poetic language may still rely on instrumental subjective expression, its literary dimension communicates to the Other the objective historical conditions of the speaker in relation to her lifeworld. See Lawn 2001, 115.

12. Connolly writes: "Both because of and despite its privileged status in Gadamer's hermeneutics, there can be no complete understanding of a literary text" (Connolly 1986, 271). By extension, there can be no complete understanding of hermeneutic subjectivity's translation into objective cultural expression and communicative action.

13. On Gadamer, language, and intercultural exchange, see Roy and Starosta 2001.

14. On Gadamer, responsibility, and solidarity, see Warnke 2012.

15. The political dimension of Gadamer's presentation of "the Other" provides a linguistic basis for a hermeneutic of otherness that acknowledges informed solidarity without conceptual domination. See Walhof 2006, 569.

16. See Brooks 2003.

17. See Spillers 2013, 568.

18. For an account of religion and hermeneutics in Baldwin, see Evans 2017.

19. Another invitee, Hugh Foot, Lord Caradon, had little to say about Baldwin's fiery speech aside from: "Having stated my reasons for welcoming the invitation from the World Council and having told you how eager I was to come and why I am so glad that I did, I must at once say that I am alarmed by the magnitude of the subject of our discussion—and my alarm has not been diminished by listening to Mr. James Baldwin, whose passionate eloquence it was worth coming some thousands of miles to hear" (Foot 1968, 378).

20. The early development of Black liberation theology reciprocally coincides with that of Black Power writing in 1970. See Cone 1970, 1084.

21. For Cleaver, the embrace of any revolutionary position that does not extol the supremacy of Black male heteronormativity is a betrayal to the race and the racial class. See Mills 2012, 55.

22. Manditch-Prottas provocatively insists that "for Baldwin, Cleaver's logic is not altogether faulty; rather it is slightly miscalculated and consequently misdirected in its application" (Manditch-Prottas 2019, 180).

23. Baldwin's early essays are also political, despite their highly personal matter. See Tomlinson 1999, 135.

24. Aside from personal reflections, these essays are also and perhaps predominantly political. In them, the personal and the political are not merely presented alongside one another; they are utterly conflated.

25. The intersubjectivity of literary space mediates an understanding of what Fisher calls "futural politics" as "the conditions of possibility and necessity that structure human relationships in the social world" (Fisher 2017, 141).

26. Baldwin's emphasis on personal experience could be the focus of the derision and critical dismissal of his work by Black arts and Power Movement intellectuals, such as Baraka and Cruse. See Birmingham 2011, 605.

27. See Patell 2011, 359. Patell understands "literary force" in Baldwin as the means by which light is thrown on the intersection between diverse sociopolitical institutions, including mob violence and its unwritten yet legitimate relation to the law. In many ways, Baldwin's work demonstrates the destructive consequences of an understanding of law and right as social tradition beholden to the unmodified and unconstitutional exigencies of the private sphere.

28. As Tackach notes, "the King James Bible became his signal literary text during his Harlem childhood" (Tackach 2007, 109). The King James Bible was, then, more than the source of religious authority for Baldwin in his formative years. It was also his first and most powerful literary model.

29. For Baldwin's contemporaries misreading the political content of his aesthetics, see Birmingham 2011, 224. The misreading Birmingham describes of Baldwin's apparent aestheticism and Jamesian essayistic practice came to symbolize the political quietism of the racially compromised Black artist.

30. For Baldwin a "postsegregation vision" "can occur once whites move beyond being 'trapped in history.' To this point, whites escaping or being released from the trap of history, in the legal and moral sense, is the end of whiteness" (Freeburg 2013, 222).

Without first having a picture of being eccentric to history, no vision of an unsegregated society is possible. Autobiographical literature provides an alternative perspective on history or a view of it from the outside.

31. See Shulman 2011, 128.

32. Indeed, the "hermeneutic of the cross" that Baldwin learns in significant part through readings in the King James Bible is as much about beauty as it is about religious truth. See Evans 2017, 116.

33. In this respect, Baldwin's engagement with civil rights is oriented toward the recuperation of a usable past rather than legal interventions in the present. Personal reminiscence is tantamount to cultural example and the site for potential intersubjective intervention. For Baldwin, this—rather than changes in the law—leads to the destruction of those racist assumptions and biases that segregate bodies and mind. See Nabers 2005, 222.

34. Even more so than in Henry James's essays, after which Baldwin modeled his own work in the genre, Baldwin infuses his nonfiction with personal experience, particularly in the early essays. See Jackson 1978, 3.

35. Baldwin's understanding of the Black world, even when critically reconciled with it, still filters it epistemologically through his own formative American experience. See Waters 2013, 716.

36. Indeed, Baldwin's critical subjectivism, evident in his autobiographical essays, comes to bear the charge of "assimilationist" by the very merits of its aesthetic activism. See E. Miller 2004, 625.

37. Baldwin's ambivalent reaction to Black intellectuals outside of the United States working in other languages and cultural traditions "manifests itself in his occasional recourse to reflexive 'primitivist' constructions of Africa and a dichotomization of Black U. S. experience and that of the rest of the Black world" (Winks 2013, 606). This ambivalence eventually, if not resolves, then is reconfigured with a teleological belief that African America would in time find "a fraternal opening towards, and eventual active solidarity with, the colonized Black world" (Winks 2013, 607).

Chapter Two

1. For a general discussion of "conversation" in Gadamer, see Gill 2015.

2. Catherine Squires's definition remains the most comprehensive. She writes:

emergent Black collectives have generated social movements, new forms of publicity, and other responses to the realities of Black life in a world structured by race, class, ethnic, color, and gender hierarchies. To make this diversity more visible and to recognize that not all people who are classified as Black will participate in all or any Black publics, I propose we speak of multiple Black publics. Thus a Black public is an emergent collective composed of people who (a) engage in common discourses and negotiations of what it means to be Black, and (b) pursue particularly defined Black interests. This definition, although still wedded to the idea that there is a Black social group, does allow for heterogeneous Black publics to emerge, and also for people who do not identify as Black, but are concerned with similar issues, to be involved in a coalition with Black people. (2002, 454)

3. More recently, the Black Public Sphere Collective of the mid-1990s and Black Lives Matter today attempt to define the spaces of Black life institutionally, where predominately or even exclusively Black consumer clientele or other category-identified groups congregated to discuss informally issues of Black concern in forming a Black public opinion. In such spaces, direct aesthetic expression need not have factored at all into the formulation of public reason or as a socially contractual element of deliberative process. The legitimate counterpublic proposed by the Black Public Sphere Collective does not require and is not constructed by art forms, yet it can easily accommodate them where they are capable of building Black consensus of public reason. In other words, any Black aesthetic form has to provide a reasonable opinion on matters relevant to those participants identified in the spaces forming the structure and identity of the Black public sphere. Thus, even within this sphere, a racially defined space assumes a majority within a minority, as not all citizens of African descent frequent all-Black barbershops, schools, markets, etc. Hence, not all citizens racialized in this way conform to the majority-in-minority "social imaginary" necessary to conceptualize an ideal minority public.

4. The violence here alluded to would be that of complete dissociation with the legal foundation and basis of society in which the revolutionary subject rejects all that is considered "just" according to the law. See T. Benson 1970, 41.

5. As Manthia Diawara suggests, *The Autobiography* is also one of the clearest records of the "Black public sphere" in the twentieth century, locating the Black public sphere primarily in entertainment spaces and audience participation. That said, Diawara's assessment is as problematic as the concept of the Black public sphere more generally. Ignoring places of worship and relativizing modes of intervention used by figures as diverse as Diana Washington and Booker T. Washington, Diawara neglects to theorize the extent to which the Black public sphere relied on aestheticized modes of communication for its existence. See Diawara 1994, 36, 46–47.

6. Any sharp distinction between fiction and nonfiction in *The Autobiography* and other modes of literary self-fashioning Malcolm practiced would miss the rhetorical nature of his universalization of an ideal Black revolutionary subject. See Yousman 2001, 3.

7. LaMothe notices that the "various personae Malcolm adopts in *The Autobiography* are each employed in privileging an element of the interdependent personal, political, and religious aspects of the self. The coherency of this rhetorical project depends on the acceptance in advance of Black revolution as the teleological end of American society in its current social configuration" (2011, 524).

8. For Duerringer, "the representation of Malcolm X's agency, and particularly the elision of that agency, is a profoundly important element of the rhetoric of *The Autobiography of Malcolm X*, which enables the reader to forgive young Malcolm's vices, to imagine her- or himself as an activist, and to consider the possibility of racial progress" (2014, 157). Malcolm's rhetoric allows the reader to see him ideally and identify with him universally.

9. Rose has noted that the "goal of his lifelong quest for autonomy as a Black man was achieved when he became a participant in a community in which his race did not matter" (1987, 8). Installed after the revolution, Malcolm's ideal community would be that of literacy and participation accorded by the democratic truth of equality.

10. Malcolm exploits socially stereotypical, literarily identifiable, racialized images of animals in order to subvert their normative white supremacist significations. His underlying assumption is that the scene of race relations is a jungle or zoo in which all are animals, with the correction that the races have been traditionally ascribed to the wrong zoological type. See Flick and Powell 1988, 441–42.

11. Novak interestingly reads Malcolm as engaging in parrhesia, or "truth-telling," in the public sphere. See Novak 2006, 41.

12. Along with parrhesia, Malcolm also utilized the rhetoric of prophecy to great effect. Because of its universal, ideal character, Malcolm's parrhesiac mode of self-fashioning entails modes of resistance and prophecy. The truth of its ideality anticipates the arrival of the Black male revolutionary. Indeed, it is an arrival foreseen. See Terrill 2001, 34.

13. Painter identifies here "transubstantiations" that "simulate history by purveying autobiographical rather than biographical truths" (1993, 433).

14. See Condit and Lucaites 1993, 293.

15. In order to achieve this, Malcolm X, as Keith Miller writes, "developed counter-hegemonic literacy because he understood that the theory and praxis of assimilationist literacy had failed" (2004, 215).

16. On "Black communication," see Abramowitsch 2018, 306.

Chapter Three

1. Kenneth Warren writes, "In interpreting the Little Rock event, Arendt and Ellison accorded student agency a minor or nonexistent role. Instead, they described the young people as, respectively, victims of misplaced adult activism or cultural apprentices being trained into the discipline of the Negro's life world" (2003, 162). Of course, Arendt also fails to include in her story of Little Rock that the decision to send children to the school was taken by committee and spoke to all levels of social administration, political action, and judicial review. Indeed, it was not even the parents who chose this path: it was the school's superintendent. The events, including Will Counts's influential photographs, could be attributed to sheer chance.

2. For Ellison's theory of literature, see the following essays from *Shadow and Act* (1964): "Beating That Boy" (1945), 95–101; "The Art of Fiction: An Interview" (1955), 167–86; and "The World and the Jug" (1963), 107–43.

3. See Ellison, "Twentieth-Century Fiction and the Black Mask of Humanity" (1946), in *Shadow and Act* (1964), 22–44.

4. In this regard, and as Bradley believes, *Three Days* is a political novel expressed in aesthetic terms (Bradley 2012, 96).

5. Here, as in Baraka, even the culture industry has value for the realization of authentic Black humanity, if only in negation.

6. As Bland puts it, "Ellison's foundational ideas about the duties of Black artists and intellectuals in the public sphere became a kind of a through-line in how he crafted and maintained his own public role in the age of civil rights" (2015, 53). See also Bland 2015, 57; Kuryla 2013, 14.

7. In this respect, less nuanced readings of Black Power's criticisms of Ellison as apolitical and too aesthetic miss the visceral political polemics contained in the moral ambiguity of both Ellison's and the Black Power movement's positions. See Mills 2012, 148.

8. Kenneth Warren also elaborates on the coextensive properties between *Invisible Man* and Ellison's evolving political thought in the fifties (2003, 163). Warren points out, however, that Ellison accepts the Civil Rights Movement on a qualified basis, suspicious that, as certain social barriers fall with legislative gains, incommensurately high cultural losses may begin to accrue (Warren 2003, 174). Ellison formulates the matter similarly, in that historical continuity determines freedom of association and cultural expression. The sudden rupture with the past causes a confusion in the structures that orient identity toward the historicity of its racial understanding of human being. Forced association might have the effect of racial effacement through the elision of racial histories from the unification of racialized cultures.

9. That Ellison experienced anxiety over the continuum of Black historicity in America in the face of radical changes to the structural basis of its expression does not change the fact that he did act politically in support of the Civil Rights Movement. Ellison's reserve was aesthetic, and therefore political-theoretical. From a practical political point of view, Ellison could not criticize too harshly the gains of the Civil Rights Movement. See Harriss 2014, 247.

10. Smethurst relates that the conflict between Baraka and Ellison,... foreshadowed larger debates over the relationship (or non-relationship) of African Americans to the United States in the Black Power and Black Arts period. Baraka and Ellison's debate used models of Black music, particularly what Baraka termed a "blues continuum" rooted in the South and continually transformed in urban industrial centers while retaining a blues core (the "changing same" as Baraka would famously term it later), as guides for Black artists in other genres and media, whether to enmesh themselves further in the fabric of "America" or draw away to some other notion of polity or nation.

Furthermore, Smethurst writes that "Ellison's review of *Blues People* did not simply frame Baraka's book in a way that continues to resonate even now in cultural criticism, but also, along with the other essays in *Shadow and Act*, provided a way of reading, or rereading, Ellison's *Invisible Man* as embodying the possibilities of 'American' democracy and democratic culture in a manner that was not obvious when the novel first appeared in 1952. In fact, one might have seen Ellison's novel as close in spirit to *Blues People*—as did Baraka through much of his career" (Smethurst 2019, 41–42).

11. My reading of Baraka is informed by Benston 1976; Brown 1980; Watts 2001; Woodard 1999; Sollors 1978.

12. See Baker 1994.

13. A selection of the essays published in English between 1925 and 1965 would include "Transatlantic" (1930); "Berg and Webern—Schonberg's Heirs" (1931); "Husserl and the Problem of Idealism" (1940); "A Social Critique of Radio" (1945); "Theses upon Art and Religion Today" (1945); "The Authoritarian Personality" (1950); "How to Look at Television" (1954); "The Stars Down to Earth: The Los Angeles Times Astrology Column: A Study in Secondary Superstition" (1957); and "Modern Music Is Growing Old" (1958).

14. On Adorno's philosophy of language, Roger S. Foster writes informatively: "For Adorno, then, everything depends on allowing the inexpressible to find its way to language without turning it into a conceptual content, that is, something that might be integrated into the system of discursive relations that is constitutive of our conceptual activity. The key to this is allowing the inexpressible to appear in the movement" (2016, 70).

15. Baraka credits African Americans with the foundational genius of American culture. So while it is true, as Mary Ellison writes, that "Baraka has long ceased to see the world in terms of Black and white, but only in recent years has he acknowledged that in *Blues People*," he means that authentic American culture is Black (M. Ellison 124).

16. Ferguson suggests that in *Blues People* "Baraka (LeRoi Jones) ran directly against the inherently liberal formulations of Ellison and Murray by denying the essential Americanness of both Black Americans and the blues. For Baraka, Black Americans remained forever transplanted Africans, permanent aliens, or non-Americans, within the American cultural and political context, first for their Africanity and second for the special culture that they formed in adjusting to the harsh terms of American racial oppression. Thus, he regarded the blues as the outgrowth of a resilient African inheritance and as evidence of continuing cultural resistance" (2010, 701). This reading of Baraka and "Africanity" pertains more to the poet's self-revised stance than to the letter of the *Blues People* text.

17. In this respect, jazz is a type of normative measure for all other performative aspects of the race, including poetic expression and even racial identity itself. As Meta DuEwa Jones writes: "Baraka's additions to and alterations of verses, his shifts from speech into song, and his imitations of the sounds of instruments while performing his poems all suggest that, in a performance context, his work engages in a process of revision modeled upon the improvisatory ethos of jazz. The essence of Baraka's jazz-influenced poetry, like its counterpart, jazz music, is in the performance" (2003, 246).

18. Jazz, then, is also the aesthetic force shaping African American poetry and poetics. For jazz in Baraka's poetry, see M. Ellison 1994. See also Willey 2013. For general accounts of Baraka's poetics, see W. Harris 1985; M. Jones 2003.

19. See Millner-Larsen 2017, 88.

20. Picking up on Baraka's obvious debt to, and improvisation on, Adorno, Mushinski writes that Adorno shares an "affinity with Baraka's vilification of swing jazz ... one that helps to substantiate Adorno's racially insensitive association of the 'jazz band which abandons itself to the eight-bar rhythms of the hit composer' with a 'wild animal in a cage.' According to Adorno, if jazz is to fulfill its political promise, it must do so via a determined resistance rather than appeal to the caged sterility of mainstream cultural sensibilities" (2016, 149–50).

21. As Jeff Nealon points out, this fact led to "a painful paradox" (Nealon 1998, 89).

22. Lukács's *History and Class Consciousness* (1923) was translated into English in 1971.

Chapter Four

1. Cleaver's exit from prison sought to put into motion the ideology that *Soul on Ice* expounded, with few positive results. See Poinsett 1976, 85–86. See also Rout 1991.

2. On the "land question" and Black nationalist thought, see Rickford 2017.

3. See Turner 2010, 8. See also Schanche 1968.

4. Cleaver wrote his most influential book while in prison for rape, a crime for which he blamed the United States. His acts were criminal only as perceived by a criminal ideological state apparatus, and not in themselves. This idea is a perversion of Marcuse's ideas. For a contrary view, see Wellington 2006, 99.

5. The ambiguity surrounding violence and revolution colors the contemporary ac-

count of the Party and the Movement. An example is Mary Ellen Leary's 1968 take on Cleaver. See Leary 1968, 24.

6. See Bringhurst 2002, 87.

7. Cleaver's own acute awareness of the role played by the media in starting the revolution made a statement such as "the revolution will not be televised" both terrifying and laughable. His own carefully crafted persona was a priori televised, as the revolution could not be thought outside of the mediation of telecommunication and telecommunicative action. See Robé 2017, 126.

8. A generous reading of Cleaver's various poses and positions suggests that his was a spiritual quest that could not be contained by fidelity to a single, enduring belief. See LaVelle 2013, 56.

9. The notion that Cleaver was a "shrewd self-promoter" was widely circulated; and the patronage he received for speaking engagements after his release from jail speaks to this to some extent. See LaVelle 2013, 82. See also Foner's 1970 *The Black Panthers Speak*, which acts as both a support for, and necessary correction to, Cleaver's policy texts. See also Bobby Seale's 1970 account, *Seize the Time*.

10. Increasingly, Cleaver began to see the Cold War beyond an East-West axis and saw it instead as an anticolonial conflict against superpowers fighting to preserve the colonial order as they saw fit. See Malloy 2013, 541.

11. Already in 1969 Cleaver is considering the connections between domestic racism and the international oppression of the worker and the colonized. However, until his flight into exile he would continue to see African Americans as the revolutionary vanguard and to stress the need for a separate consideration of African America's problem. See Mislan 2014, 217.

12. Newton was not only conversant in Western philosophy, he also let it shape his ideas. See Hughey 2005, 652.

13. In 1969 Cleaver already articulates the need to move beyond the identification of the Black Panther Party with one man, largely because incarceration made it impossible to organize outside the penitentiary under the auspices of a single person if that person was imprisoned. At this time, he says that the Panthers "are continuously trying to develop new leadership in the party. We have some people ready to take over if the current leadership is put in jail, or something similar, but not enough. We want the Black Panther Party to be a self-perpetuating group, not a one-man organization" (Weinstein 1969, 74–75).

14. Henderson's suggestion that "the violence and criminality of followers in such organizations is often sanctioned by 'divine right'" or rationalized in the name of the revolution, as in the case of the Black Panther Party, is certainly provocative, if not overly speculative. Henderson continues: "These processes led to the assassination of Malcolm X by members of NOI [Nation of Islam] and the murders of James Carr, Fred Bennett, Sam Napier, Mark Baynam [Michael Baynham], and others by the BPP. Such conclusions provide an important critique of the Black Power movement" (1997, 191).

15. Understanding domestic American racism as internal colonialism inevitably led to the position that international unity among oppressed peoples was necessary. For Cleaver, however, this did not mean that all oppressed peoples were the same, an assumption he seems to have read in Marcuse. See Malloy 2013, 545.

16. Fanon's understanding of violence was crucial in establishing this view, along with the constructed image of Newton himself.

17. Part of the media persona cultivated by Cleaver as a leader of the Black Power movement was one of racial self-sufficiency and self-segregation for the purposes of empowerment. Yet this image is complicated by white patronage of Black radicals and the reliance on white media outlets to accrue cultural capital and political prowess. See C. Johnson 2016, 193.

18. In Cleaver's understanding of American internal colonialism, the police are the colonial army protecting American interests "abroad" and enforcing colonial rule. For African America, the rule of law is that of a police state. See Jensen and Hammerback 1986, 29.

19. The "Covey" episode in Douglass's autobiography was central to Cleaver's romanticization of Black manhood. See Nower 1970, 16.

Chapter Five

1. Davis portrays a Black Panther Party at odds with itself. See Dearey 2006, 223.

2. It is worthwhile to remember that, as Leslie writes, "students versed in critical theory were demanding that theoretical critique turn into practical political action. Theory was a brake on the movement, alleged some, as they denounced fellow students—mocked as Adornites and Habermice for promoting theory for theory's sake and disregarding their professors' function as a left alibi for bourgeois society" (1999, 119).

3. Davis's activism has overshadowed her significant contribution as a philosopher.

4. For more on Schmidt's reading of Marx and nature, see Foster and Burkett 2000; Swindal 2014; Moore 1967.

5. Adorno would offer a very different understanding of "freedom" than would Arendt. On their philosophical disputes, see Auer 2003.

6. According to Wellmer, "Adorno's metaphysics can be rescued from the constellation of his messianic materialism. The recovery of metaphysics in this context also means that it is rescued as the basis of possible critique. Rescue here entails that the ideas of truth, freedom, justice and democracy should be seen as transcending whatever is empirically given, while remaining immanently operative within society. These ideas can still be drawn on for a critique of the present, thus renewing the original project of critical theory" (2007, 135).

7. In this respect, Adorno's philosophy of history relies far more on contingency than does that of Marx. See also Heller 1991; Whyman 2016; Volpato Durta 2009.

8. For a good account of Adorno's negative dialectics of freedom, see Freyenhagen 2006.

9. As a cause célèbre, Davis's case signified the end of the inauguration of a different type of "high-profile" legal maneuvering in the service of Black liberation. Attorney Howard Dean Moore Jr. became the spokesperson of the Black Power legal defense and of a new form of celebrity legal intervention. See Camp 2019, 84.

10. In the 1970s, Angela Davis had an almost cult following in the German Democratic Republic (East Germany), where she represented the struggle for freedom against capitalist oppression common to Germans and African Americans. She was so famous in the GDR that children's books were written about her. See Bieber 2017, 96–97. See also D'Hippolito 2019; Hopkins 1997; Lorenz 2013; Schubert 2018; Slobodian 2015.

11. On Davis's arrest and trial, see Aptheker 1976. See also DeLeon 1972.

12. Davis's understanding of Kant on freedom is heavily influenced by Adorno's. See Jütten 2012.

13. For a reading of Marcuse's Hegel, see Gaskins 2018.

14. Davis's views on slavery are expanded in *Angela Davis—An Autobiography* to include the penitentiary system. See Gleich 2015.

15. This "intolerance" for philosophical nonsense was the ostensible reason Davis was fired from the UC system: "At the time of Angela Davis's difficulties, then, the U.C. campus had been subjected to the FBI's political involvement in misinformation and the undermining of the legitimate political rights of faculty and students. Ironically, just a few years later, Angela Davis was fired by campus authorities for being intolerant of other points of view and for not suitably respecting academic freedom" (Aby 2007, 297).

16. For Davis, the slave's experience would be continued in that of the penitentiary inmate. See Barnwell 2005; Mendieta 2006. See also Murty 2007; Simpson 2007; Sanders 1971.

17. For a general account of psychoanalysis and utopianism in the 1960s, see De-Koven 2003.

Conclusion

1. In *An Autobiography*, Davis creates an analogy between slavery and incarceration in which, "with Angela Davis as their guide and the prison as their space of transformation, the prison women move from slavery to freedom. This involves moving beyond their own struggles in order to join in the larger struggle for freedom, which Davis comes to represent to them" (Simpson 2007, 335). See also Mendieta 2006.

2. Although it is present in *An Autobiography* in the relationship between female prisoner and carceral system, this slavery analogy does not posit an individual, private erotic component. As Barnwell writes, "*An Autobiography* [can] be viewed as a political act of prison writing whereby Davis tells the story of her prison experience as that which involved collective resistance to deindividuating, dehumanizing routines of prison life" (2005, 312).

3. See Henderson 2019.

4. Winston Napier's still vital 2000 anthology of African American literary theory titles the section of selections from the 1970s "Onset of Theory and the Emergence of Black Feminist Critique."

5. I am here deeply indebted to Fabio Rojas's *From Black Power to Black Studies: How a Radical Social Movement Became an Academic Discipline* (2007).

6. See Cusset 2008.

References

Abramowitsch, Simon. 2018. "The Black Communications Movement." *African American Review* 51, no. 4: 305–27.

Aby, Stephen H. 2007. "Angela Davis and the Changing Paradigm of Academic Freedom in the 1960s." *American Educational History Journal* 34, no. 2: 289–301.

Adorno, Theodor W. 1947. "Wagner, Nietzsche, Hitler." *Kenyon Review* 9, no. 1: 155–62.

———. (1949) 2006. *Philosophy of New Music*. Translated by Robert Hullot-Kentor. Minneapolis: University of Minnesota Press.

———. (1963) 1994. *Hegel: Three Studies*. Cambridge, MA: MIT Press.

———. 2006. *History and Freedom: Lectures 1964–1965*. Edited by Rolf Tiedemann. Translated by Rodney Livingstone. Cambridge, UK: Polity Press.

Alonso Schökel, Luis. 1963. "Hermeneutics in the Light of Language and Literature." *Catholic Biblical Quarterly* 25, no. 3: 371–86.

Anderson, Paul Allen. 2005. "Ralph Ellison on Lyricism and Swing." *American Literary History* 17, no. 2: 280–306.

Ansermet, Ernest. 1919. "Sur un orchestre negro." *Revue romande* 3, October 15, 1919: 10–13.

Aptheker, Bettina. (1976) 2014. *The Morning Breaks: The Trial of Angela Davis*. Ithaca, NY: Cornell University Press.

Arendt, Hannah. 1958. *The Human Condition*. Garden City, NY: Doubleday.

———. (1959) 2003. "Reflections on Little Rock." In *Responsibility and Judgment*. Edited with an introduction by Jerome Kohn, 193–213. New York: Schocken Books.

———. (1962) 2006. "The Meaning of Love in Politics: A Letter by Hannah Arendt to James Baldwin." *Zeitschrift für politisches Denken* 2, no. 1: 1.

Auer, Dirk. 2003. "Einleitung: Affinitat und Aversion." In *Arendt und Adorno*, edited by Dirk Auer, Julia Schulze Wessel, and Lars Rensmann. Frankfurt: Suhrkamp.

Baker, Houston. 1987. *Blues, Ideology, and African-American Literature: A Vernacular Theory*. Chicago: University of Chicago Press.

———. 1994. "Critical Memory and the Black Public Sphere." *Public Culture* 7, no. 1: 3–33.

Baldwin, James. 1964. "Why I Stopped Hating Shakespeare." In Baldwin 2010, 65–69.

——. 1964. "The Uses of the Blues." In Baldwin 2010, 70–81.

——. 1968. "White Racism or World Community." *Ecumenical Review* 20, no. 4: 371–76.

——. 1970. "An Open Letter to My Sister Angela Y. Davis." *New York Review of Books*, January 7, 1971.

——. 1979. "On Language, Race, and the Black Writer." In Baldwin 2010, 140–44.

——. 1980. "Black English: A Dishonest Argument." In Baldwin 2010, 154–60.

——. 2010. *The Cross of Redemption: Uncollected Writings*. Edited with an introduction by Randall Kenan. New York: Pantheon Books.

Baldwin, James, and Shlomo Katz. 1971. "Of Angela Davis and 'the Jewish Housewife Headed for Dachau.'" *Midstream* 17, no. 6: 3–10.

Baraka, Amiri [LeRoi Jones, pseud.]. 1963. *Blues People: Negro Music in White America*. New York: William Morrow.

——. (1963) 2010. "Jazz and the White Critic." In *Black Music*, 15–24. New York: Akashic Books.

——. 1964. *Dutchman and the Slave*. New York: William Morrow.

——. (1966) 2010. "The Changing Same (R&B and New Black Music)." In *Black Music*, 175–204. New York: Akashic Books.

——. 1971. "Black (Art) Drama Is the Same as Black Life." *Ebony* 26, no. 4: 74.

——. 1980. "Afro-American Literature and Class Struggle." *Black American Literature Forum* 14, no. 1: 5–14.

——. 1991. "The 'Blues Aesthetic' and the 'Black Aesthetic': Aesthetics as the Continuing Political History of a Culture." *Black Music Research Journal* 11, no. 2: 101–9.

——. 1997. *The Autobiography of LeRoi Jones*. Chicago: Lawrence Hill Books.

——. 2004. "Revolutionary Love (Poem)." *Essence* 35, no. 6: 258.

Barnwell, Cherron A. 2005. "A Prison Abolitionist and Her Literature: Angela Davis." *CLA Journal* 48, no. 3: 308–35.

Benson, Thomas W. 1970. "Violence: Communication Breakdown? Focus on Recent Publications." *Today's Speech* 18, no. 1: 39–46.

Benston, Kimberly W. 1976. *Baraka: The Renegade and the Mask*. New Haven, CT: Yale University Press.

Bieber, Ada. 2017. "Who's Afraid of Angela Davis?: An American Icon and the Political Uses of Youth Literature in the GD." *Colloquia Germanica* 50, no. 1: 55–76.

Birmingham, Kevin. 2011. "No Name in the South: James Baldwin and the Monuments of Identity." *African American Review* 44, no. 1–2: 221–34.

Bland, Sterling Lecater. 2015. "Being Ralph Ellison: Remaking the Black Public Intellectual in the Age of Civil Rights." *American Studies* 54, no. 3: 51–62.

Bloom, Jack M. 1987. *Class, Race, and the Civil Rights Movement*. Bloomington: Indiana University Press.

Booth, W. James. 2008. "The Color of Memory: Reading Race with Ralph Ellison." *Political Theory* 36, no. 5: 683–707.

Braaten, Carl E. 1965. "How New Is the New Hermeneutic?" *Theology Today* 22, no. 2: 218–35.

Bradley, Adam. 2010. *Ralph Ellison in Progress: From "Invisible Man" to "Three Days before the Shooting."* New Haven, CT: Yale University Press.

Bringhurst, Newell G. 2002. "Eldridge Cleaver's Passage through Mormonism." *Journal of Mormon History* 28, no. 1: 80–110.

Brooks, Douglas A. 2003. "Gadamer and the Mechanics of Culture." *Poetics Today* 24, no. 4: 673–94.

Brown, Lloyd Wellesley. 1980. *Amiri Baraka*. Boston: Twayne.

Brown, Michael Joseph. 2004. *Blackening the Bible: The Aims of African American Biblical Scholarship*. New York: Trinity Press International.

Camp, Michael. 2019. "Resisting 'Law and Order' in California: Howard Moore Jr., Angela Davis, and the Politics of Prison Radicalism." *Journal of African American History* 104, no. 1: 84–106.

Cleaver, Eldridge. 1968a. "Introduction to Selections from the *Biography of Huey P. Newton*, with an Aside to Ronald Reagan." *Ramparts Magazine* 7, no. 6: 22.

———. 1968b. "Land Question." *Ramparts Magazine* 6, no. 9–10: 51–53.

———. 1968c. "Letter from Jail." *Ramparts Magazine* 6, no. 11: 17–21.

———. 1968d. "Requiem for Nonviolence." *Ramparts Magazine* 6, no. 9–10: 48–49.

———. 1968e. "Revolution in the White Mother Country and National Liberation in the Black Colony." *North American Review* 5: 13–15.

———. 1968f. *Soul on Ice*. New York: McGraw-Hill.

———. 1969. "Conversation with Cleaver." *The Nation* 208 (January 20): 74–77.

———. 1971. "Culture and Revolution: Their Synthesis in Africa." *Black Scholar* 3, no. 2: 33–39.

———. 1973." 'The Crisis of the Black Bourgeoisie.'" *Black Scholar* 4, no. 4: 2–11.

Condit, Celeste Michelle, and John Louis Lucaites. 1993. "Malcolm X and the Limits of the Rhetoric of Revolutionary Dissent." *Journal of Black Studies* 23, no. 3: 291–313.

Cone, James H. 1969. *Black Theology and Black Power*. San Francisco: Harper and Row.

———. 1970. *A Black Theology of Liberation*. Philadelphia: Lippincott.

Cone, James H., and Gayraud S. Wilmore. 1979. *Black Theology: A Documentary History, 1966–1979*. Vol. 1. Maryknoll, NY: Orbis.

———. 1993. *Black Theology: A Documentary History, 1980–1992*. Vol. 2. Maryknoll, NY: Orbis.

Connolly, John M. 1986. "Gadamer and the Author's Authority: A Language-Game Approach." *Journal of Aesthetics & Art Criticism* 44, no. 3: 271–78.

Conyers, James L. 2007. *Engines of the Black Power Movement: Essays on the Influence of Civil Rights Actions, Arts, and Islam*. Jefferson, NC: McFarland.

Cusset, François. 2008. *French Theory: How Foucault, Derrida, Deleuze, & Co. Transformed the Intellectual Life of the United States*. Translated by Jeff Fort. Minneapolis: University of Minnesota Press.

Dallmayr, Fred R. 2000. "Borders or Horizons? Gadamer and Habermas Revisited." *Chicago-Kent Law Review* 76, no. 2: 825–35.

Davis, Angela Y. 1971. *Lectures on Liberation*. With an introduction by Herbert Marcuse. New York: N.Y. Committee to Free Angela Davis.

———. 1974. *Angela Davis: An Autobiography*. New York: Random House.

———. 1981. *Women, Race & Class*. New York: Random House.

———. 1989. *Women, Culture & Politics*. New York: Random House.

———. 1998. *Blues Legacies and Black Feminism: Gertrude "Ma" Rainey, Bessie Smith, and Billie Holiday*. New York: Pantheon Books.

Davis, Jack E. 2001. *The Civil Rights Movement*. 3 vols. Malden, MA: Blackwell.

Dawson, Michael C. 1994. "A Black Counterpublic? Economic Earthquakes, Racial Agenda(s), and Black Politics." *Public Culture* 7, no. 1: 195–223.

Dearey, Melissa. 2006. "Soledad Sister: On the Absence of Angela Davis's *An Auto-biography* from Contemporary Historiographies of 1960s and 1970s Black Power Movement." *A/B: Auto/Biography Studies* 21, no. 2: 222–46.

DeKoven, Marianne. 2003. "Psychoanalysis and Sixties Utopianism." *Journal for the Psychoanalysis of Culture & Society* 8, no. 2: 263–72.

DeLeon, Robert A. 1972. "A New Look at Angela Davis." *Ebony* 27, no. 6: 53–60.

D'Hippolito, Joseph. 2019. "Angela Davis, East Germany and Fullerton," opinion. *Wall Street Journal*, June 27, 2019. https://www.wsj.com/articles/angela-davis-east-germany-and-fullerton-11561676857.

Diawara, Manthia. 1994. "Malcolm X and the Black Public Sphere: Conversionists versus Culturalists." *Public Culture* 7, no. 1: 35–48.

Djerassi, Carl. 2011. *Foreplay*. Madison: University of Wisconsin Press.

Du Bois, W. E. B. 1926. "Criteria of Negro Art." *The Crisis* 32: 290–97.

Duerringer, Christopher. 2014. "The Elision of Agency in the Autobiography of Malcolm X." *Howard Journal of Communications* 25, no. 2: 156–70.

Early, Gerald. 1986. "The Case of Leroi Jones/Amiri Baraka." *Salmagundi* 70/71 (Spring/Summer): 343–52.

Ellison, Mary. 1994. "Jazz in the Poetry of Amiri Baraka and Roy Fisher." *Yearbook of English Studies* 24: 117–45.

Ellison, Ralph. (1946) 1964. "Twentieth-Century Fiction and the Black Mask of Humanity." In Ellison 1964c, 261–317.

———. 1952. *Invisible Man*. New York: Random House.

———. (1963) 1964. "The World and the Jug." In Ellison 1964c, 107–43.

———. 1964a. "'The Blues.'" Review of *Blues People: Negro Music in White America*, by Amiri Baraka. *New York Review of Books* 1, no. 12.

———. 1964b. "A Rejoinder." *New Leader* 47 (February 3): 15–22.

———. 1964c. *Shadow and Act*. New York: Random House.

———. 2010. *Three Days before the Shooting*. Edited by John F. Callahan and Adam Bradley. New York: Random House.

English, Darby. 2011. "Ralph Ellison's Romare Bearden." *Studies in the History of Art* 71: 11–25.

Evans, James H. 2017. "A Hermeneutic of the Cross: Religion and Racialized Discourse in the Thought of James Baldwin." *Black Theology: An International Journal* 15, no. 2: 112–16.

Fanon, Frantz. (1961) 2004. *The Wretched of the Earth*. Translated by Richard Philcox. New York: Grove.

Felder, Cain Hope. 1991. *Stony the Road We Trod: African American Biblical Interpretation*. Minneapolis: Fortress.

Ferguson, Jeffrey B. 2010. "A Blue Note on Black American Literary Criticism and the Blues." *Amerikastudien/American Studies* 55, no. 4: 699–714.

Fisher, Laura R. 2017. "Possible Futures and Grammatical Politics in James Baldwin's *Another Country*." *Journal of Modern Literature* 41, no. 1: 137–55.

Flick, Hank, and Larry Powell. 1988. "Animal Imagery in the Rhetoric of Malcolm X." *Journal of Black Studies* 18, no. 4: 435–51.

Foley, Barbara. 2015. "Becoming 'More Human': From the Drafts of 'Invisible Man' to 'Three Days before the Shooting….'" *African American Review* 48, no. 1/2: 67–82.

Foner, Philip Sheldon. (1970) 2014. *The Black Panthers Speak*. Chicago: Haymarket Books.

Foot, Hugh (Lord Caradon). 1968. "White Racism or World Community." *Ecumenical Review* 20, no. 4: 377–84.

Foster, John Bellamy, and Paul Burkett. 2000. "The Dialectic of Organic/Inorganic Relations: Marx and the Hegelian Philosophy of Nature." *Organization & Environment* 13, no. 4: 403–25.

Foster, Roger S. 2016. *Adorno and Philosophical Modernism: The Inside of Things*. New York: Lexington Books.

Foucault, Michel. (1976) 1990. *The History of Sexuality*, vol. 1. Translated by Robert Hurley. New York: Vintage Books.

Fraser, Nancy. 1993. "Rethinking the Public Sphere: A Contribution to the Critique of Actually Existing Democracy." In *The Phantom Public Sphere*, edited by Bruce Robbins, 1–32. Minneapolis: University of Minnesota Press.

———. 2017. "The Theory of the Public Sphere: *The Structural Transformation of the Public Sphere* (1962)." In *The Habermas Handbook*, edited by Hauke Brunkhorst, Regina Kreide, and Cristina Lafont, 245–55. New York: Columbia University Press.

Freeburg, Christopher. 2013. "James Baldwin and the Unhistoric Life of Race." *South Atlantic Quarterly* 112, no. 2: 221–39.

Freyenhagen, Fabian. 2006. "Adorno's Negative Dialectics of Freedom." *Philosophy & Social Criticism* 32, no. 3: 429–40.

———. 2013. *Adorno's Practical Philosophy: Living Less Wrongly*. Cambridge, UK: Cambridge University Press.

Friedman, Max Paul. 2014. "Émigrés as Transmitters of American Protest Culture." *Journal of Modern Jewish Studies* 13, no. 1: 87–98.

Fuller, Hoyt. (1968) 1994. "Towards a Black Aesthetic." In *Within the Circle: An Anthology of African American Literary Criticism, from the Harlem Renaissance to the Present*, edited by Angelyn Mitchell, 199–207. Durham, NC: Duke University Press.

Fulop, Timothy E., and Albert J. Raboteau. 1996. *African American Religion: Interpretive Essays in History and Culture*. New York: Routledge.

Gadamer, Hans-Georg. (1960) 1993. *Truth and Method*. Translated by Joel Weinsheimer and Donald G. Marshall. New York: Continuum.

———. 1966. "Notes on Planning for the Future." *Dædalus* (Spring): 572–89.

———. (1970a) 2006. "Language and Understanding." *Theory, Culture & Society* 23, no. 1: 13–27.

———. 1970b. "On the Scope and Function of Hermeneutical Reflection." *Continuum* 8, no. 1–2: 77–95.

———. 1970c. "The Problem of Language in Schleiermacher's Hermeneutic." In *Schleiermacher as Contemporary*. Translated by D. E. Linge. Edited by Robert W. Funk. 68–95. New York, NY: Herder & Herder.

———. 1977. *Philosophical Hermeneutics*. Berkeley: University of California Press.

———. (1982) 1998. "Culture and Word." In *Praise of Theory: Speeches and Essays*, translated by Chris Dawson, 1–15. New Haven, CT: Yale University Press.

———. (1999) 2009. "Friendship and Solidarity." *Research in Phenomenology* 39, no. 1: 3–12.

———. 2001. "Education Is Self-Education." *Journal of Philosophy of Education* 35, no. 4: 529–38.

Gadamer, Hans-Georg, G. B. Hess, and R. E. Palmer. 1997. "Rhetoric, Hermeneutics, and Ideology-Critique." In *Rhetoric and Hermeneutics in Our Time: A Reader*, edited by Walter Jost and Michael J. Hyde, 313–34. New Haven, CT: Yale University Press.

Gadamer, Hans-Georg, and Richard E. Palmer. 2006. "Classical and Philosophical Hermeneutics." *Theory, Culture & Society* 23, no. 1: 29–56.

Gaskins, Richard. 2018. "Marcuse's Hegel: Hope and Despair in the Logic of Negation." *Society* 55, no. 4: 361–66.

Gates, Henry Louis, Jr. 1977. "Eldridge Cleaver on Ice." *Transition: An International Review* 7, no. 3–4: 294–311.

Gayle, Addison. (1971) 1994. "Cultural Strangulation: Black Literature and the White Aesthetic." In *Within the Circle: An Anthology of African American Literary Criticism from the Harlem Renaissance to the Present*, edited by Angelyn Mitchell, 207–12. Durham, NC: Duke University Press.

Geier, Woodrow A. 1968. "'Schleiermacher as Contemporary': A Consultation." *Christian Century* 85, no. 14: 434–38.

Gennari, John. 2003. "Baraka's Bohemian Blues." *African American Review* 37, no. 2/3: 253–60.

Gill, Scherto. 2015. "'Holding Oneself Open in a Conversation': Gadamer's Philosophical Hermeneutics and the Ethics of Dialogue." *Journal of Dialogue Studies* 3, no. 1: 9–28.

Gleich, Paula von. 2015. "African American Narratives of Captivity and Fugitivity: Developing Post-Slavery Questions for *Angela Davis: An Autobiography*." *COPAS: Current Objectives of Postgraduate American Studies* 16, no. 1: 1–18.

Goebel, Eckart, and Sigrid Weigel. 2012. *"Escape to Life": German Intellectuals in New York: A Compendium on Exile after 1933*. Berlin: De Gruyter.

Gordon, Lewis R., ed. 1997. *Existence in Black: An Anthology of Black Existentialist Philosophy*. New York: Routledge.

———. 2000. *Existentia Africana: Understanding Africana Existential Thought*. New York: Routledge.

Gussow, Adam. 2018. "W. C. Handy and the 'Birth' of the Blues." *Southern Cultures* 24, no. 4: 42–68.

Haag, Karl Heinz. 1963. "Das Unwiederholbare." In *Zeugnisse: Theodor W. Adorno zum sechzigsten Geburtstag*, edited by Max Horkheimer, 152–61. Frankfurt: Europäische Verlagsanstalt.

———. 1967. *Philosophischer Idealismus: Untersuchungen zur Hegelschen Dialektik mit Beispielen aus der Wissenschaft der Logik*. Frankfurt: Europäische Verlagsanstalt.

Habermas, Jürgen. (1968) 1971. *Knowledge and Human Interests*. Translated by Jeremy J. Shapiro. Boston: Beacon.

———. 1988. *The Logic of the Social Sciences*. Translated by Shierry Weber Nicholson. Cambridge, MA: MIT Press.

Hanchard, Michael. 1996. "Cultural Politics and Black Public Intellectuals." *Social Text* 48, no. 3: 95–108.

Harding, James Martin. 1997. *Adorno and "A Writing of the Ruins": Essays on Modern*

Aesthetics and Anglo-American Literature and Culture. Albany: State University of New York Press.

Harris, Roy Vincent, and Eldridge Cleaver. 1969. "Radicals: Are They Poles Apart?" *Look* 33, no. 1: 34.

Harris, William J. 1985. *The Poetry and Poetics of Amiri Baraka: The Jazz Aesthetic*. Columbia: University of Missouri Press.

Harriss, M. Cooper. 2014. "One Blues Invisible: Civil Rights and Civil Religion in Ralph Ellison's Second Novel." *African American Review* 47, no. 2/3: 247–66.

Harrisville, Roy. 1964. Review of *The New Hermeneutic*. *Journal of Biblical Literature* 83, no. 2: 197–98.

Harvey, Tyrone L. 1996. Review of *The Black Public Sphere: A Public Culture Book*. *Contemporary Sociology* 25, no. 6: 817–18.

Heller, Kevin Jon. 1991. "Adorno Against the Grain: Re-Reading Theodor Adorno's Philosophy of History." *Praxis International* 11, no. 3: 354–76.

Henderson, Errol A. 1997. "The Lumpenproletariat as Vanguard? The Black Panther Party, Social Transformation, and Pearson's Analysis of Huey Newton." *Journal of Black Studies* 28, no. 2: 171–99.

———. 2019. *The Revolution Will Not Be Theorized: Cultural Revolution in the Black Power Era*. Albany, NY: SUNY Press.

Hirsch, E. D. 1965. "Truth and Method in Interpretation." *Review of Metaphysics* 18, no. 3: 488–507.

———. 1967. *Validity in Interpretation*. New Haven, CT: Yale University Press.

Hopkins, Leroy. 1997. "'Black Prussians': Germany and African American Education from James W. C. Pennington to Angela Davis." In *Crosscurrents: African Americans, Africa, and Germany in the Modern World*, edited by David McBride, Leroy Hopkins, and C. Aisha Blackshire-Belay, 65–81. Columbia, SC: Camden House.

Horkheimer, Max, and Theodor W. Adorno. 1997. *Dialectic of Enlightenment*. Translated by John Cumming. London: Verso.

How, Alan. 1995. *The Habermas-Gadamer Debate and the Nature of the Social: Back to Bedrock*. Aldershot, UK, and Brookfield, VT: Avebury.

Howe, Irving. 1952. "Man Underground." Review of *Invisible Man*, by Ralph Ellison. *The Nation*, May 10, 1952. 454.

———. 1963. "Black Boys and Native Sons." *Dissent* 9: 353–68.

———. 1964. "A Reply to Ralph Ellison." *New Leader* 47: 12–14.

Hughey, Matthew W. 2005. "The Sociology, Pedagogy, and Theology of Huey P. Newton: Toward a Radical Democratic Utopia." *Western Journal of Black Studies* 29, no. 3: 639–55.

Hurston, Zora Neale. (1934) 1996. "Characteristics of Negro Expression." In *The Negro: An Anthology*, edited by Nancy Cunard, 124–31. New York: Continuum.

Jackson, Jocelyn W. 1978. "Problem of Identity in Selected Early Essays of James Baldwin." *Journal of the Interdenominational Theological Center* 6, no. 1: 1–15.

Jay, Martin. 1985. *Permanent Exiles: Essays on the Intellectual Migration from Germany to America*. New York: Columbia University Press.

Jensen, Richard J., and John C. Hammerback. 1986. "From Muslim to Mormon: Eldridge Cleaver's Rhetorical Crusade." *Communication Quarterly* 34, no. 1: 24–40.

Johnson, Cedric. 2016. "Between Revolution and the Racial Ghetto Harold Cruse and

Harry Haywood Debate Class Struggle and the 'Negro Question', 1962-68." *Historical Materialism* 24, no. 2: 165-204.

Johnson, Sylvester A. 2015. *African American Religions, 1500-2000*. New York: Cambridge University Press.

Jones, LeRoi. *See* Baraka, Amiri.

Jones, Meta DuEwa. 2003. "Politics, Process, & (Jazz) Performance: Amiri Baraka's 'It's Nation Time.'" *African American Review* 37, no. 2/3: 245-52.

Joseph, Peniel E. 2006. *The Black Power Movement: Rethinking the Civil Rights–Black Power Era*. New York: Routledge.

———. 2009. "The Black Power Movement, Democracy, and America in the King Years." *American Historical Review* 114, no. 4: 1001-16.

———. 2011. "Still Reinventing Malcolm." *Chronicle of Higher Education* 57, no. 35: B6-B9.

Jütten, Timo. 2012. "Adorno on Kant, Freedom and Determinism." *European Journal of Philosophy* 20, no. 4: 548-74.

Kimmerle, Heinz. 1967. "Hermeneutical Theory or Ontological Hermeneutics." *Journal for Theology and the Church* 4: 107-21.

King, Richard H. 1992. *Civil Rights and the Idea of Freedom*. New York: Oxford University Press.

———. 2004. *Race, Culture, and the Intellectuals, 1940-1970*. Washington, DC: Woodrow Wilson Center Press.

Kuryla, Peter. 2013. "Ralph Ellison, Irving Howe and the Imagined Civil Rights Movement." *Society* 50, no. 1: 10-15.

LaMothe, Ryan. 2011. "Malcolm X's Conversions: The Interplay of Political and Religious Subjectivities." *Pastoral Psychology* 60, no. 4: 523-36.

Lavelle, Ashley. 2013. "From Soul on Ice to Soul on Fire: The Religious Conversion of Eldridge Cleaver." *Politics, Religion & Ideology* 14, no. 1: 75-93.

Lawn, Christopher. 2001. "Gadamer on Poetic and Everyday Language." *Philosophy & Literature* 25, no. 1: 113-26.

Leary, Mary Ellen. 1968. "The Uproar over Cleaver." *New Republic* 159, no. 22: 21.

Lee, Don L. (1971) 1994. "Toward a Definition: Black Poetry of the Sixties." In *Within the Circle: An Anthology of African American Literary Criticism from the Harlem Renaissance to the Present*, edited by Angelyn Mitchell, 213-23. Durham, NC: Duke University Press.

Leslie, Esther. 1999. "Introduction to Adorno/Marcuse Correspondence on the German Student Movement." *New Left Review* 233, no. 1: 118-22.

Levy, Peter B. 1998. *The Civil Rights Movement*. Westport, CT: Greenwood.

Lewis, David L., and Charles W. Eagles. 1986. *The Civil Rights Movement in America: Essays*. Jackson: University Press of Mississippi.

Lorenz, Sophie. 2013. "'Heldin des anderen Amerikas': Die DDR-Solidaritätsbewegung für Angela Davis, 1970-1973." *Zeithistorische Forschungen* 10, no. 1: 38-60.

Lukács, György. (1923) 1971. *History and Class Consciousness: Studies in Marxist Dialectics*. Translated by Rodney Livingstone. Cambridge, MA: MIT Press.

Malloy, Sean L. 2013. "Uptight in Babylon: Eldridge Cleaver's Cold War." *Diplomatic History* 37, no. 3: 538-71.

Manditch-Prottas, Zachary. 2019. "Meeting at the Watchtower: Eldridge Cleaver,

James Baldwin's *No Name in the Street*, and Racializing Homophobic Vernacular." *African American Review* 52, no. 2: 179–95.

Marable, Manning. 1981. "Beyond the Race-Class Dilemma." *Nation* 232, no. 14: 417–33.

Marbury, Herbert Robinson. 2015. *Pillars of Cloud and Fire: The Politics of Exodus in African American Biblical Interpretation*. New York: New York University Press.

Marcuse, Herbert. 1955. *Eros and Civilization: A Philosophical Inquiry into Freud*. Boston: Beacon Press.

———. 1964. *One-Dimensional Man: Studies in the Ideology of Advanced Industrial Society*. Boston: Beacon Press.

———. 1971. "Angela Davis in Prison: A Letter." *Ramparts Magazine*. February 1971: 22–25.

———. (1977) 2003. *The Aesthetic Dimension: Toward a Critique of Marxist Aesthetics*. Boston: Beacon Press.

———. 2005. *The New Left and the 1960s*. Vol. 3 of *Collected Papers of Herbert Marcuse*. Edited by Douglas Kellner. London: Routledge.

Mendieta, Eduardo. 2006. "Prisons, Torture, Race: On Angela Y. Davis's Abolitionism." *Philosophy Today* 50, no. 5: 176–83.

Miller, Elise. 2004. "The 'Maw of Western Culture': James Baldwin and the Anxieties of Influence." *African American Review* 38, no. 4: 625–36.

Miller, Keith D. 2004. "Plymouth Rock Landed on Us: Malcolm X's Whiteness Theory as a Basis for Alternative Literacy." *College Composition and Communication* 56, no. 2: 199–222.

Millner-Larsen, Nadja. 2017. "The Subject of Black: Abstraction and the Politics of Race in the Expanded Cinema Environment." *Grey Room* 67, no. 2: 64–69.

Mills, Nathaniel. 2012. "Cleaver/Baldwin Revisited: Naturalism and the Gendering of Black Revolution." *Studies in American Naturalism* 7, no. 1: 50–79.

Mislan, Cristina. 2014. "From Latin America to Africa: Defining the 'World Revolution' in the Black Panther." *Howard Journal of Communications* 25, no. 2: 211–30.

Moore, Stanley. 1967. "Marx and the State of Nature." *Journal of the History of Philosophy* 5, no. 2: 133–48.

Murty, Madhavi. 2007. "Interpreting Angela Davis for the American Middle Class: Race, Radicalism, Passion, and News Magazines." *Conference Papers: International Communication Association* (2007): 1.

Mushinski, Matthias. 2016. "Jean-Louis Comolli's Secret Life as a Free Jazz Critic/Thinking Free Jazz as an Avant-Garde of the Masses." *Framework: The Journal of Cinema and Media* 57, no. 2: 138–60.

Muyumba, Walton M. 2009. *The Shadow and the Act: Black Intellectual Practice, Jazz Improvisation, and Philosophical Pragmatism*. Chicago: University of Chicago Press.

Nabers, Deak. 2005. "Past Using: James Baldwin and Civil Rights Law in the 1960s." *Yale Journal of Criticism: Interpretation in the Humanities* 18, no. 2: 221–42.

Napier, Winston. 2000. *African American Literary Theory: A Reader*. New York: New York University Press.

Neal, Larry. 1968. "The Black Arts Movement." *Drama Review* 12: 28–39.

Nealon, Jeffrey T. 1998. "Refraining, Becoming-Black: Repetition and Difference in Amiri Baraka's *Blues People*." *Symplokē: A Journal for the Intermingling of Literary, Cultural and Theoretical Scholarship* 6, no. 1/2: 83–95.

Negt, Oskar. 1964. *Strukturbeziehungen zwischen den Gesellschaftslehren Comtes und Hegels*. Frankfurt: Europäische Verlagsanstalt.

Newton, Huey P., and J. Herman Blake. (1973) 1995. *Revolutionary Suicide*. New York: Writers and Readers.

Novak, David R. 2006. "Engaging Parrhesia in a Democracy: Malcolm X as a Truth-Teller." *Southern Communication Journal* 71, no. 1: 25–43.

Nower, Joyce. 1970. "Cleaver's Vision of America and the New White Radical: A Legacy of Malcom X." *Negro American Literature Forum* 4, no. 1: 12–21.

O'Connell, Christian. 2013. "The Color of the Blues: Considering Revisionist Blues Scholarship." *Southern Cultures* 19, no. 1: 61–81.

Ongiri, Amy Abugo. 2010. *Spectacular Blackness: The Cultural Politics of the Black Power Movement and the Search for a Black Aesthetic*. Charlottesville: University of Virginia Press.

Painter, Nell Irvin. 1993. "Malcolm X across the Genres." *American Historical Review* 98, no. 2: 432–39.

Palmer, Richard E. 1969. "Hermeneutics and Methodology." *Continuum* 7, no. 1: 153–58.

Parent, Emmanuel. 2007. "Ralph Ellison, Critique De LeRoi Jones." *L'Homme* 181: 131–50.

Patell, Shireen R. K. 2011. "'We the People,' Who? James Baldwin and the Traumatic Constitution of these United States." *Comparative Literature Studies* 48, no. 3: 356–87.

Poinsett, Alex. 1970. "Black Takeover of U.S. Cities?" *Ebony* 26, no. 11: 76–86.

———. 1976. "Where Are the Revolutionaries?" *Ebony* 31, no. 4: 84–92.

Powery, Emerson B., and Rodney S. Sadler. 2016. *The Genesis of Liberation: Biblical Interpretation in the Antebellum Narratives of the Enslaved*. Louisville, KY: Westminster John Knox.

Rickford, Russell. 2017. "'We Can't Grow Food on All This Concrete': The Land Question, Agrarianism, and Black Nationalist Thought in the Late 1960s and 1970s." *Journal of American History* 103, no. 4: 956–80.

Ringma, Charles. 1999. *Gadamer's Dialogical Hermeneutic: The Hermeneutics of Bultmann, of the New Testament Sociologists and of the Social Theologians in Dialogue with Gadamer's Hermeneutic*. Heidelberg: C. Winter.

Robé, Chris. 2016. "Detroit Rising: The League of Revolutionary Black Workers, Newsreel, and the Making of Finally Got the News." *Film History: An International Journal* 28, no. 4: 125–58.

Roberts, Samuel K. 2001. *African American Christian Ethics*. Cleveland: Pilgrim.

Robinson, Cedric. 1983. *Black Marxism: The Making of the Black Radical Tradition*. Chapel Hill: North Carolina University Press.

Robinson, James M., and John B. Cobb. 1964. *The New Hermeneutic*. New York: Harper & Row.

Rojas, Fabio. 2007. *From Black Power to Black Studies: How a Radical Social Movement Became an Academic Discipline*. Baltimore: Johns Hopkins University Press.

Rose, Shirley K. 1987. "Metaphors and Myths of Cross-Cultural Literacy: Autobiographical Narratives by Maxine Hong Kingston, Richard Rodriguez, and Malcolm X." *MELUS: The Journal of the Society for the Study of the Multi-Ethnic Literature of the United States* 14, no. 1: 3–15.

Rout, Kathleen. 1991. *Eldridge Cleaver*. Boston: Twayne.

Roy, Abhik, and William J. Starosta. 2001. "Hans-Georg Gadamer, Language, and Intercultural Communication." *Language and Intercultural Communication* 1, no. 1: 6–20.

Sanders, Charles L. 1971. "The Radicalization of Angela Davis." *Ebony* 26, no. 9: 114, 120.

Schanche, Don A. 1968. "'Burn the Mother Down.'" *Saturday Evening Post* 241, no. 23: 30.

Scharlemann, Martin H. 1968. "Hermeneutic(s)." *Concordia Theological Monthly* 39, no. 9: 612–22.

Schmidt, Alfred. (1962) 2014. *The Concept of Nature in Marx*. Translated by Ben Fowkes. London: Verso.

Schökel, Luis Alonso. 1963. "Hermeneutics in the Light of Language and Literature." *Catholic Biblical Quarterly* 25, no. 3: 371–86.

Schubert, Maria. 2018. *"We Shall Overcome": Die DDR und die amerikanische Bürgerrechtsbewegung*. Paderborn: Ferdinand Schöningh.

Seale, Bobby. 1970. *Seize the Time: The Story of the Black Panther Party and Huey P. Newton*. New York: Random House.

Seebohm, Thomas M. 1977. "The Problem of Hermeneutics in Recent Anglo-American Literature: Part I." *Philosophy & Rhetoric* 10, no. 3: 180–98.

Shulman, George. 2011. "The Politics of Redemption." *Raritan* 3, no. 2: 128–42.

Simpson, LaJuan. 2007. "Transforming the Prison: Outrageous and Bodacious Behavior in *Angela Davis: An Autobiography*." *CLA Journal* 50, no. 3: 323–39.

Slate, Nico. 2012. *Black Power beyond Borders: The Global Dimensions of the Black Power Movement*. New York: Palgrave Macmillan.

Slobodian, Quinn. 2015. *Comrades of Color: East Germany in the Cold War World*. New York: Berghahn Books.

Smethurst, James. 2019. "'Formal Renditions.'" *Massachusetts Review* 60, no. 1: 41–59.

Sollors, Werner. 1978. *Amiri Baraka/LeRoi Jones: The Quest for a "Populist Modernism."* New York: Columbia University Press.

Spillers, Hortense, J. 2013. "Introduction." *African American Review* 46, no. 4: 563–72.

Squires, Catherine R. 2002. "Rethinking the Black Public Sphere: An Alternative Vocabulary for Multiple Public Spheres." *Communication Theory* 12, no. 4: 446–68.

Steele, Shelby. 1976. "Ralph Ellison's Blues." *Journal of Black Studies* 7, no. 2: 151–68.

Stevenson, W. T. 1971. "Here Today, Here Tomorrow: A Caveat Concerning Theological Change." *Christian Century* 88, no. 28: 856.

Sundquist, Eric J. 2011. "'We dreamed a dream': Ralph Ellison, Martin Luther King, Jr. & Barack Obama." *Dædalus: Race in the Age of Obama* 140, no. 1: 108–24.

Swindal, James. 2014. "Marx on Nature." *Frontiers of Philosophy in China* 9, no. 3: 358–69.

Tackach, James. 2007. "The Biblical Foundation of James Baldwin's 'Sonny's Blues.'" *Renascence* 59, no. 2: 109–33.

Teigas, Demetrius, Jürgen Habermas, and Hans-Georg Gadamer. 1995. *Knowledge and Hermeneutic Understanding: A Study of the Habermas-Gadamer Debate*. Lewisburg, PA: Bucknell University Press.

Terrill, Robert E. 2011. "Protest, Prophecy, and Prudence in the Rhetoric of Malcolm X." *Rhetoric and Public Affairs* 4, no. 1: 25–53.

Thompson, Mark Christian. 2007. *Black Fascisms: African American Literature and Culture between the Wars*. Charlottesville: University of Virginia Press.

Tomlinson, Robert. 1999. "'Payin' One's Dues': Expatriation as Personal Experience and Paradigm in the Works of James Baldwin." *African American Review* 33, no. 1: 135–48.

Tracy, Steven C. 1983. "The Blues in Future American Literary Histories and Anthologies." *MELUS* 10, no. 1: 15–28.

Turner, Lou. 2010. "Toward a Black Radical Critique of Political Economy." *Black Scholar* 40, no. 1: 7–19.

Van Deburg, William L. 1992. *New Day in Babylon: The Black Power Movement and American Culture, 1965–1975*. Chicago: University of Chicago Press.

Verhaar, John W. M. 1969. "Language and Theological Method." *Continuum* 7, no. 1: 3–29.

Volpato Dutra, Delamar José. "Marx et Adorno La Philosophie de l'Histoire." *Civitas: Revista de Ciências Sociais* 9, no. 3: 459–71.

Walhof, Darren R. 2006. "Friendship, Otherness, and Gadamer's Politics of Solidarity." *Political Theory* 34, no. 5: 569–93.

Walsh, Russell. 2004. "The Methodological Implications of Gadamer's Distinction between Statements and Speculative Language." *Humanistic Psychologist* 32, no. 2: 105–19.

Warnke, Georgia. 2012. "Solidarity and Tradition in Gadamer's Hermeneutics." *History & Theory* 51, no. 4: 6–22.

Warren, Kenneth W. 2003. "Ralph Ellison and the Problem of Cultural Authority." *boundary 2* 30, no. 2: 157–74.

Warren, Robert Penn. 1965. *Who Speaks for the Negro?* New York: Random House.

Waters, Rob. 2013. "'Britain Is No Longer White': James Baldwin as a Witness to Postcolonial Britain." *African American Review* 46, no. 4: 715–30.

Watts, Jerry Gafio. 2001. *Amiri Baraka: The Politics and Art of a Black Intellectual*. New York: New York University Press.

Weinstein, Henry E. 1969. "Conversation with Cleaver." *Nation* 208, no. 3: 74–77.

Wellington, Darryl Lorenzo. 2006. "Soul in a Maze." *Dissent* 53, no. 2: 99.

Wellmer, Albrecht. 2007. "Adorno and the Problems of a Critical Construction of the Historical Present." *Critical Horizons* 8, no. 2: 135–56.

West, Cornel, and Eddie S. Glaude Jr., eds. 2003. *African American Religious Thought: An Anthology*. Louisville, KY: Westminster John Knox Press.

Whyman, Tom. 2016. "Understanding Adorno on 'Natural-History.'" *International Journal of Philosophical Studies* 24, no. 4: 452–72.

Willey, Ann. 2013. "A Bridge over Troubled Waters: Jazz, Diaspora Discourse, and E. B. Dongala's 'Jazz and Palm Wine' as Response to Amiri Baraka's 'Answers in Progress.'" *Research in African Literatures* 44, no. 3: 138–51.

Winks, Christopher. 2013. "Into the Heart of the Great Wilderness: Understanding Baldwin's Quarrel with Négritude." *African American Review* 46, no. 4: 605–14.

Wolin, R. 2001. *Heidegger's Children: Hannah Arendt, Karl Löwith, Hans Jonas, and Herbert Marcuse*. Princeton, NJ: Princeton University Press.

Woodard, Komozi. 1999. *A Nation within a Nation: Amiri Baraka (LeRoi Jones) and Black Power Politics*. Chapel Hill: University of North Carolina Press.

Wright, Richard. 1937. "Blueprint for Negro Writing." *New Challenge* 2, no. 2: 53–65.

X, Malcolm. 1954. Malcolm X FBI File, Summary Report. Detroit Office, March 16, 1954, 3–12. In X 2013, 62–71.

———. 1964a. "The Ballot or the Bullet." In X 2013, 318–26.

———. 1964b. "It's Ballot or Bullet Answers Malcolm X." *Cleveland Plain Dealer*, April 4, 1964. In X 2013, 314–15.

———. 1964c. "Message to the Grass Roots." In X 2013, 265–73.

———. 1964d. MMI FBI File, Summary Report. Chicago Office, June 19, 1964, 3–6, 11–13. In X 2013, 334–39.

———. 1964e. "2,000 Hear Malcolm X in Cleveland." *The Militant*, June 13, 1964. In X 2013, 316–17.

———. 2013. *The Portable Malcolm X Reader*. Edited by Manning Marable and Garrett Felber. New York: Penguin Books.

X, Malcolm, and Alex Haley. (1965) 1992. *The Autobiography of Malcolm X*. New York: Ballantine Books.

Yaffe, David. 2006. *Fascinating Rhythm: Reading Jazz in American Writing*. Princeton, NJ: Princeton University Press.

Yousman, Bill. 2001. "Who Owns Identity? Malcolm X, Representation, and the Struggle over Meaning." *Communication Quarterly* 49, no. 1: 1–18.

Zangrando, Joanna S., and Robert L. Zangrando. 1970. "Black Protest: A Rejection of the American Dream." *Journal of Black Studies* 1, no. 2: 141–59.

Index

Adorno, Theodor, 3, 5; and Angela Davis, 7, 11, 123, 130; and dialectical relation of history and freedom, 126–29, 170n5; *Dialectic of Enlightenment* (with Horkheimer), 124; *Drei Studien zu Hegel*, 126; and Haag, 126; on jazz, 168n20; metaphysics, 170n6; "Music, Language, and Composition," 73; and nature as nonidentity, 127–28; philosophy of history, 170n7; philosophy of language, 167n14; philosophy of music, 73–75, 168n20; *Philosophy of New Music*, 9, 73; "Wagner, Nietzsche and Hitler," 81

African American cultural criticism. *See* Black aesthetic; Black cultural criticism; Black philosophy

Ansermet, Ernest, 79

anthropological theory, and mid-twentieth-century African American thought, 1–2, 4, 9, 70, 71–73

Appadurai, Arjun, 45

Arendt, Hannah, 3; *Human Condition*, 123, 133; letter criticizing Baldwin's "Letter from a Region in My Mind," 65–66; reading of Greek political thought on freedom and slavery, 136; "Reflections on Little Rock," 66, 166n1; view of civil rights legislation, 66–67

Aristotle, 15, 16, 18, 138

Axelrod, Beverley, 107

Baker, Houston, 47

Baldwin, James, 6; and aesthetic representation and power, 5; and African American speaker and public sphere, 29–30; and Bible's dissemination of racist ideological assumptions, 34; on Black English, 6, 26–31, 39; "Black English: A Dishonest Argument," 26; Black hermeneutic analysis, 6, 8; and Black intellectuals outside of US, 164n37; and Black liberation theology, 25; and Black public sphere, 39, 46, 64; and civil rights movement, 164n33; and Cleaver's attack upon, 25–26; conflation of personal with political, 27, 163nn23–24, 163n26, 164nn33–36; critical dismissal of work by Black arts and Black Power movements, 163n26; critique of the church, 24–25; and *Erziehung* and self-cultivation, 28–29; and "hermeneutic of the cross," 164n32; and historical authenticity of race through language, 33–34, 36–39; on learning to speak French, 32–33, 35–36; "Letter from a Region in My Mind," 65; misreadings of by contemporaries, 163n29; "On Language, Race, and the Black Writer," 27; open letter to Angela Davis in prison, 24; and persistence of "auction block," 26; and phenomenal Blackness, 2–3;